THE
REVOLUTION
OF NIHILISM

AMS PRESS

NEW YORK

THE
REVOLUTION
OF NIHILISM

WARNING
TO THE WEST

By

HERMANN RAUSCHNING

ALLIANCE BOOK CORPORATION
LONGMANS, GREEN & CO.
NEW YORK
1939

Library of Congress Cataloging in Publication Data

Rauschning, Hermann, 1887–
    The revolution of nihilism.

    (Studies in fascism)
    1. Nationalsozialistische Deutsche Arbeiter-Partei.
2. Germany—Politics and government—1933-1945.
I. Title.
DD253.R38 1973   320.9'43'086   72-180666
ISBN 0-404-56402-X

Reprinted by arrangement with A. S. Barnes & Company,
Cranbury, New Jersey.

From the edition of 1939, New York
First AMS edition published in 1973
Manufactured in the United States of America

AMS PRESS INC.
NEW YORK, N. Y.   10003

Contents

Preface

GERMANY, like the forbidden land of Tibet, has become the goal of explorers; and it has been the subject of marvelling and also of indignant reports. Many of these flatly contradict one another, and this makes the search for truth no easier. The obscurity that lies over Germany is spreading beyond her frontiers and darkening the world. The German riddle is not only growing sinister, it is threatening men's lives

Inadequate knowledge of what has actually been happening in Germany could not but result in mistakes in policy. But the foreigner has not been alone in his ignorance: even the German living in the Third Reich has had but the vaguest notion of what has been happening to him. Need it be added that the writer himself misunderstood the nature of a movement which passed for national, when he joined it—out of conviction and not out of opportunism?

It demands patience and rather a long-drawn-out process at the outset to separate the husk from the true kernel of events. A bare narration is not sufficient for an understanding of them. A psychological estimate of the men at the head of the new Germany, strange and in their way remarkable men, would be a tempting occupation, but would lead us away from the actual source of what has been an inevitable process. It would be simplifying much too much if we were to identify that source with the world economic depression, or with the loss of the world war, or with the unchanging character of Prussian imperialism. These things played their part, but the roots of the developments in Germany lie deeper. They lie in moral and intellectual processes, some of them of long duration. These must not be overlooked.

Perhaps too much attention has been given by students and observers to published doctrine and outward events in Germany —the trappings of a political movement. The functions of the "élite" and the "masses" in the new methods of political control have received less attention than the persecution of the Jews, the anti-Christian activities, and the racial doctrine. The synthesizing element in the political aims of the regime has not been revealed. The main purpose of this book is that revelation—the revelation of the process underlying the ostensibly national movement, a destructive process of revolution of a new and extreme type.

This book was planned originally for the German reader, who involuntarily and, as a rule, in perfect good faith has suffered a tragic entanglement in that process. Much of the book was of little interest to the non-German, and the book has accordingly been abridged. That its prognosis was well-founded is shown by the fact that, though it was written mainly in the winter of 1937-38, and published shortly after the annexation of the Sudeten territory, it has not been contradicted by subsequent events in a single point. The pogroms of the winter of 1938 took place as forecast; the developments in foreign policy up to the occupation of Prague are along the lines anticipated in these pages. (The only substantial addition in this English version is on pages 276 to 290.)

This applies above all to the interpretation of Hitler's actual political aims and to the emphasis laid on his inability to produce any constructive peace policy. Many non-Germans have insisted that the characterization of his policy as revolutionary imperialism is an exaggeration: that characterization has been justified before all the world in the past year. It is to be feared that the analysis in this book will be justified in other points by coming developments.

What is now going on in Germany is a transient disfigurement of the true and permanent character of the nation. I hope, too, that the recognition of the nature of National Socialism which this book aims at promoting may also contribute to the extension of sympathy to a future renascent Germany, which will have need of such sympathy in order to recover its place in a peaceful Europe.

HERMANN RAUSCHNING

Paris, May 1939.

Introduction

THE TEMPTATION of our day is to accept the intolerable, for fear
of still worse to come. But before considering what would convert
an intolerable situation into a better one, or possibly a worse, we
have to face another question—the crucial question of what must
inevitably be the end of a process if it is left to itself and its
logical outcome. This is the subject of the remarks that follow
on the present condition of the German nation. What will be the
end of all these exhausting efforts and upheavals, what must
inevitably come of them? That is the question that occupies the
thoughts of every thinking man to-day in Germany. What must
come of this revolution, in which the present leaders of the nation
continue staunchly to profess their faith? And there is a yet more
fundamental question: what *is* this revolution, what is its nature?
A national "awakening," with the unmistakable features of a radical, all-embracing revolution; surface discipline and order,
beneath which the destruction of all elements of order in the
nation is plainly visible; a vast display of energy and achievement, which cannot hide the wasteful and destructive exploitation
of irreplaceable resources, material, mental, and moral, accumulated through generations of fruitful labor; a boundless activity that can no longer conceal the ebbing of energies—what
is this Third Reich in reality, a new order in the making or a holo-
caust, a national re-birth through the historic energies of the
nation or a progressive, permanent revolution of sheer destruc-

tion, by means of which a dictatorship of brute force maintains itself in power? What in all this is make-believe and what is reality? What is deceit or delusion, and what is genuine in this movement? This is the vital question for the nation, a question not to be evaded with careful euphemisms or soothing self-deception.

There can no longer be any hesitation about the answer that must be given. And to anyone who looks beyond the present moment, in concern for the nation's destiny, the answer can only bring desperate anxiety. The phrase "despairing patriots" was used at an early date in connection with the revolutionary degeneration of the national awakening. It was in his speech at Marburg that one of them, no less a man than the former Vice-Chancellor, Franz von Papen, pointed to the deep rift in the German movement for national renewal, and it was his private secretary, the unforgettable Edgar J. Jung, one of the victims of June 30th, 1934, who revealed the abyss toward which the nation was being irresistibly driven. No one will be able to claim that the national criticism which had broken out in full force in 1933-34 cannot justifiably be revived because it was violently suppressed.

Those of us who played a responsible part in what is still busily celebrated as the "rebirth of the nation" are in duty bound to protest against the most tremendous betrayal that perhaps was ever committed in all history. I am entitled to make this denunciation of the revolutionary development in the Reich in the name of a growing number of those who shared my conviction of the nation's need for a fundamental change of policy. For the very reason that we acknowledge the eternal values of the nation and of a political order rooted in the nation, we are bound to turn against this revolution, whose subversive course involves the utter destruction of all traditional spiritual standards, utter nihilism. These values are the product of the intellectual and historical unity of Western civilization, of historic intellectual and moral forces. Without these, Nationalism is not a conservative principle, but the implement of a destructive revolution; and similarly Socialism ceases to be a regulative idea of justice and equity when it sheds the Western principles of legality and of the liberty of the person.

To-day in Germany any criticism, even from the noblest and most genuine of patriots, is accounted one of the worst of crimes, and placed in the same category as high treason. Twenty years ago we used to hear similar arguments about the necessity for a fixed resolve and unquestioning faith. Then as now the nation was kept in ignorance of the frightful gravity of its situation. We were told that there was no other way of maintaining the national will to resist—a bad psychology, a contemptuous belittlement of the moral forces of the nation. Other nations made good because they relied on the exact opposite of this psychological fallacy; the very fact of steadily facing the truth in all its desperate gravity lent them strength for the utmost endeavor. Is it a quality peculiar to the German that his readiness for sacrifice can only be maintained under illusions? Either our nation is not what it seems to think it is, and has not the grit of the others; or the political leaders have something to conceal.

But the nation that reveals this weakness of excessive capacity for illusion has a greater need than any other of criticism and plain speaking. "We have been lied to and duped"—such was the despairing exclamation, twenty years ago, of no demagogue but of the last leader of the old Conservative Party, von Heydebrand, when the truth about the terrible situation burst through the clouds of pseudo-patriotic propaganda. It seems to be our destiny to have to repeat the same mistakes with a berserker's infatuation.

The shortcomings of the present time cannot be made good by the muzzling of criticism; nor by patient waiting. "Let things take their course! In five years' time nobody will want to know about them"—so an important member of the Cabinet of the Reich, not a National Socialist, exclaimed to me in 1934, with Olympian short-sightedness, when I expressed my concern about the nature of the new German policy. No less out of place was the talk of "preservation of continuity." Only a fundamental change in Germany's course, only the restoration of equal justice for all and of personal freedom and security, can assure Germany's future. Yet there is no possibility of evolution in the direction of legality; those who harbor the idea are shutting their eyes to the essential feature of the "dynamic" revolution, that its course is in the very opposite direction of all legality, in the direction of the destruction of everything of value that the past held, a course of total nihilism. The hope of any purging of the movement from within is equally illusory, and so is that of the penetration of conservative elements among the personnel of the revolution. Behind such arguments lies to this day the same inability as in 1933-34 to realize the true character of National Socialism, and the irresolution that still cannot see that what is needed is a definite decision, not a mere tactical deal or bargain. It is precisely by their attitude of putting up with things as they are in the hope of effecting "appeasement" and a slowing down of the general course that all the leading personalities, the personalities on whom thinking people had rested their hope that something of value might after all come out of the deal of 1933, have thrown away the opportunities they once had of exerting influence.

Freedom of action can be preserved in face of a continuing process only up to a certain point. Beyond that point one inevitably becomes the slave of events. The logic of the process takes charge, upsetting all independent plans and calculations. All that is left to do is to submit to force, and it will be wise to submit with good grace. In Berlin in the autumn of 1934 I urged the need for a decision as to the general lines of the new policy at least for Danzig. I was anxious to resign, but was advised by influential personages not to do so, as the course of events could only be preserved from taking a dangerous turn if the leadership was not left to fall into the hands of the desperate elements of the Party. Subsequent events have shown the error of this "wait and see" policy. If such men as von Neurath and

xiv

Schacht, who shared responsibility under the new regime, had put up opposition in good time, in 1934-35, and had brought to bear the whole weight of their personal influence, they might have still been able to do a good deal. When they fell from power recently, their disappearance made no difference.

At the outset there were serious reasons against interrupting the continuity of the political movement started on January 30th, 1933. (It is impossible to say as much of the optimistic idea that National Socialism may purify itself.) It was felt that another revolutionary upheaval would inevitably have the gravest consequences, not only within the country but in its external relations. Thus most of the differences that existed at the time of the "*Kombination*," the deal that produced the Third Reich, have remained unreconciled; and the principal reason for this is undoubtedly that the new "realist" method produced amazing "successes" in foreign policy, and there was good reason to fear that if the slightest sign of internal weakness were allowed to appear there would be an immediate end of concessions from other countries. Many responsible members of the Party were strongly of the opinion in 1933-1934 that there must be a resolute break with the method of dictatorship and mass violence, but this view was overridden by the consideration that no visible breach in the progress of the movement must on any account be allowed to develop.

The general view now is that National Socialism can only be unseated after a sensational collapse, but this overlooks the urgent need for a change to be effected *before* that happens. The ideas at the back of this policy of waiting for a catastrophe are only intelligible when it is recalled that one of the objects of the bargain of 1933 was to give the dangerous National Socialist movement an opportunity to exhaust itself politically. Such was the tactical intention of the alliance of middle class nationalism and monarchist conservatism with revolutionary "dynamism"— the restless revolutionizing energy of the National Socialists. It has proved unsound, and equally unsound is the idea of ever being able to guide developments once the crash comes, from whatever side. If there were not this urgency for a change before it is too late (and that means an early change), while the present system still appears to be stable, it would be right to ask whether any criticism, however disinterested its motives, would not be likely to do more harm than good. It is a question which I have seriously put to myself and which has imposed definite limits and a definite character on my criticism.

Criticism of events in Germany has hitherto come mainly from those whose general outlook and political aims were opposed from the outset to the national effort to recast the political system and political life in Germany. I have no desire to enter into controversy with these critics, but it is in the nature of things that their minds should be occupied with other matters than our own anxieties. My purpose is one of practical politics—to show the conditions under which this revolution and its despotic dictatorship can be ended, and my political comments are confined to that practical purpose. I have no intention of compiling material for a historical work, or even of giving a final interpretation of events. My main concern is to point to possible centers of growth of forces which after this catharsis, this tragic upheaval, may be able, let us hope, to restore decency and legality, order and freedom.

One personal remark: I must emphasize that my resignation from the National Socialist Party and my hostility to the present system of government are due solely to the fact that I found myself for solid reasons increasingly in opposition to the German policy, and was bound to oppose it if I was not prepared to act in disregard of duty and conscience. I do not attempt to deny the outlook that once brought me into the ranks of National Socialism. I still hold to some of the essential considerations that determined my past political attitude. When the Party insisted that I should secure the *Gleichschaltung* of Danzig, should bring the Free City into line with the German system, arresting inconvenient Catholic priests, disfranchising the Jewish population, and suppressing all rival parties, I appealed to the decision of the supreme leader of the Party, giving at the same time the reasons for my own view, which was opposed to the National Socialist aims not only in these matters, but in foreign policy and in economic policy. The supreme leader of the Party declined to give a decision himself, and left the decision to my opponent in the matter, the local National Socialist leader. This made my resignation inevitable. That is the whole story: any other that may be told belongs to the sphere of defamation, distortion, and deliberate invention.

Anyone who at such times as these is not prepared to bear the burden of nation-wide vilification and political extinction had better leave politics alone. An objection that is harder to meet than the charge of holding treasonable opinions and of being a renegade is the question whether an ex-National Socialist can possibly have anything to say to the public. I must leave the answer to this to the reader. What follows may be taken, after all, as written to liberate the writer himself from error. Many who have gone astray as I did, from the best of motives, did so partly, at any rate, because they miscalculated the limits of the effectiveness of political "realism." This error seems to be one that is not confined to Germany.

Part One

"THE VICTORY OF THE REVOLUTIONARY
NEW ORDER"

POLITICAL MOTIVE FORCES AND TENDENCIES
IN THE THIRD REICH

"I have proved by my life that I am more competent than the dwarfs, my predecessors, who brought this country to destruction."
—ADOLF HITLER, in Vienna, 1938.

The Road to Nihilism

THE "ARRANGED" DICTATORSHIP

TWO YEARS before the German revolution of 1933 a book was published on the technique of the coup d'état. Its author, Curzio Malaparte, an Italian, developed the not unassailable but not unexciting theory that the modern coup d'état must be regarded as a problem of a technical order. In pursuit of his theory he analysed a number of coups d'état, successful or unsuccessful, most of them of recent date. His work was a warning. It showed how relatively easy, given a few favoring circumstances, it was to carry out a coup d'état. It was a work that could lead men into temptation. Here was displayed a means of crippling political opponents, without any great effort, from within their own stronghold. But—this is the first dogma of the theory—a coup d'état cannot succeed unless the political system and the social order are already shaken by revolutionary influences. Then, however, the coup will succeed with almost mathematical certainty, given a knowledge of the tactics of revolt. There are also, however, tactics of defence against coups d'état. Stalin first employed them against Trotsky's second attempted coup, in 1927. These tactics of prevention are based on the recognition that with squeamish police methods a revolutionary regime is not entirely safe from overthrow. But what is to be done if the political elements that are planning a coup find no widespread revolutionary feeling in existence? In that case there must be an arrangement for joint action with some substitute for revolutionism. The book is worth reading even apart from its theory; among other things it contains a quotation from Giolitti that is worth recalling to-day: "I owe to Mussolini the revelation that a state needs to defend itself not against the program but against the tactics of a revolution." People generally take a revolutionary program seriously, but pay too little attention to the tactics of the effective forces at its back.

It took three attempts in Germany to enable a coup d'état of nationalist forces to achieve such success that it could be given the character of an irresistible mass movement, a national revolution. All three attempts used the same tactics of "grafting revolutionary violence on constitutional legality." The first attempt, the Kapp "putsch," followed the revolutionary example of Napoleon, using parts of the armed forces for the direct attempt to change a government and to enforce a limitation of the powers of Parliament. Since Kapp's attempt the idea of using the army as the implement of a coup d'état with an appearance of legality has never been absent from the political ideas of the parties and groups of the Right. The Stahlhelm and the followers of Hugenberg did not discover in all their existence the fundamental error of this political idea. The Kapp putsch was an absolutely perfect model of the way not to organize a modern coup d'état. It revealed a complete absence of ideas of how the attack should be carried out, left entirely out of account the very things that Malaparte described as the technique of a coup d'état, and betrayed an exceedingly inadequate stock of ideas on the subject of the seizure of power. But even apart from Kapp's amateurishness as a putsch-maker, from his idea that the occupation of Ministries and the replacement of the police by the soldiery were all that was needed for the reorganization of the State, his failure shows the incurable weakness of any direct military action in a revolutionary enterprise. The army leaders may instigate a coup d'état, but in order to carry it to completion they need political machinery, and they must not allow the army to be dragged into direct, active participation. An undisguised military coup remains at all times a mere episode in the political struggle, and throws away the indispensable safeguard of the availability of the army for use in emergency in the day-to-day political struggles.

Accordingly, the Reichswehr took no part in the second attempt at a nationalist putsch, the first attempt made by the National Socialists; it remained deaf to all allurements. General Seeckt declared that only one man could carry out a putsch and that was he himself, and he was not going to do it. This was not out of loyalty but because he realized that, however favorable to success the conditions might seem, there had been inadequate political preparation for a coup d'état. This second attempt at a national revolution came to grief even more quickly than the Kapp putsch. It had been, if possible, even more amateurishly and sketchily improvised than the earlier one, in a whirl of romanticism; for the most part it was not the work of adults but of grown-up children.

Between the second and the third attempt lay years of political and military experience of the most varied sort in the field of coups d'état. It was learned that the modern coup is as far as could be from being a romantic undertaking; the main conditions for success, as Malaparte had shown, are a definite tactical plan and a special technique. It was also learned that a coup d'état can be carried out piecemeal, at intervals, and almost without a sound. It was learned that the grafting of revolutionary violence on constitutional legality can be facilitated by permitting constitutional governmental power to be taken over by a safe combination of Parliamentary forces, and then completing the seizure of power by actual revolutionary force.

The superiority of National Socialism over its nationalist competitors, such as the Stahlhelm and the Jungdeutscher Orden, lay in its steady preparation and training for seizing arbitrary power by a revolutionary coup after securing constitutional power by Parliamentary means, while its rivals continued to work out their plans in an atmosphere of romantic theorizing. Secretly, but with the utmost energy, the National Socialists concentrated on this two-stage plan. It was a plan that revealed a thorough grasp of the real conditions and the shedding of every vestige of puerile romanticism. The National Socialists refused to take advantage of what seemed to be favorable opportunities of participating in the government. Under their plan they were bound to refuse participation in any government, however much injury the refusal might do to the party, until their entry into the government brought them at least some of the requisites for securing legal power. They held to this course with remarkable resolution and discipline, even allowing their party to begin to disintegrate, because there was no other way of gaining an assured position from which to carry out the later revolutionary move. I think the unswerving pursuit of this one opportunity was one of the severest tests of the nerve and resolution of the National Socialist leaders.

On January 30th, 1933, National Socialism came into power, and there began the process of national "renewal" which was to lead to the recasting of all existing institutions and the appearance of the German nation in a new historic guise, that of the Third Realm. It was the third attempt at a coup d'état, using tactics which had manifestly been devised in the light of past experience; and on the surface, at all events, it had succeeded. The actual seizure of power was anything but an elemental revolutionary act proceeding from the heart of the nation. It was not even a homogeneous or an unambiguous event. It was nothing if not a "deal," an enterprise in which many elements combined from the most varied motives, elements differing radically in political outlook and character. The first question that arises from these facts is: were there no other political means than coup d'état and revolution of attaining the political ends in view? The next question is bound to be: were there any serious political ends at all that could justify such a combination of hostile political elements? And the crucial final question must be: was any agreement on aims of importance possible between the national elements that had collaborated; and, if it was, could the new governmental combination be a stable one, holding out the promise of a final recasting of the political life of the nation?

The inquiry as to the ends pursued by the national combination reveals at the outset of the earliest efforts to get to work a divergence of aims and ideas which has determined the whole course of subsequent events. There was certainly work to be done—definite tasks of general importance to the nation. But each participating group had its own special interests and its own particular aims, which it intended to promote on what it regarded as its own entry into power, and there seemed to be little prospect that these interests would be subordinated to the common national objectives. This applied most of all to the National Socialists themselves: they made no secret of the fact that they had their own plan for a new and comprehensive organization of the country, and that they regarded this as their main task. On two points the partners in the new regime were clearly in agreement—the need for remedying the national distress, and the inadequacy, in their view, of the past policy. They were agreed on the necessity for taking all possible steps to end the widespread existing destitution, and they agreed in not shrinking from the resort to extraordinary measures and even to compulsion.

I must refrain from entering into the question of the political course followed up to January 30th, 1933, or into that of the national distress as it was described and as it really was, important as the consideration of the past may be in judging the aims and methods of the "arranged" dictatorship. The situation in international politics, and the desperate economic outlook, were not the only subjects of deep and urgent concern; the more thoughtful realized also the spiritual crisis, in which the last moral and ethical standards and certainties were being whittled away; the tension of a deeply unsettled social order had produced an atmosphere of mistrust and a violence ready at any moment to pounce. Grave and urgent problems called insistently

7

for solution. "We are struggling," wrote Zehrer in *Die Tat*, "for three things—for freedom in world policy, for reconstruction of the State, and for a new economic constitution." More even than this was at issue: the nation was undergoing a transformation resulting not only from the crisis but from deep changes in its spiritual and social structure. Its needs could not be satisfied by the dogmas of party politics.

Nothing that had happened in Germany since the War was of more tragic consequence than the fact that Brüning was compelled to abandon his great work of reform by the monarchist agitation for a halt. Papen, who succeeded him, had no better policy than to try to mend matters by restoring the old system, by putting spokes in the wheel of destiny, and by evading decisions that brooked no evasion. Nationalists were gratified by his policy of making an end of party politics and of liberalism; the State began to be authoritarian, despotic. But this did nothing to solve any of the great problems outstanding. His Cabinet was deeply divided. All that united it was the negative purpose of breaking with the past system. Its two main sections, representing the industrialists and the big landowners, were directly opposed to one another on first principles: the industrialists were for freer trade and unrestricted capitalist competition; the landowners were for "autarchy," neo-mercantilism. "Enlightened capitalism" on one side, pre-capitalist patriarchalism or post-capitalist economic planning on the other. But the great new forces of Nationalism and Socialism remained unrepresented. The danger of Papen's solution degenerating in spite of him into black reaction seemed to threaten from one side, the danger of a revolutionary solution from the other. The responsible leaders of the Reichswehr, especially, felt unable to accept a regime that rejected and eliminated strong national elements instead of enlisting them.

The testing and searching for a practicable combination of forces that was in progress betrayed anything but a definite aim in view. In the midst of it all Papen's second idea, that of

8

an alliance with National Socialism, seemed the very thing that
was wanted. The new feature in Papen's plan, which remained
essentially monarchist, was the idea of securing the support of the
revolutionary mass movement of National Socialism, in the assumption that it would submit to control. Did Papen really see
nothing in National Socialism but its nationalism, could he have
overlooked its revolutionary "dynamism," its restless and boundless revolutionary energy? That is actually what happened;
sanguine in their superficial judgment, the monarchist elements
imagined that they would easily put those attractive young men
in their place. But there was another motive also, the fear of the
masses and of a revolution of the Left, the fear that the National
Socialist masses might go over to the extreme Left. It was decided to avert this by recourse to the device of a nationalist substitute, even at the risk of an unavoidable interregnum of National
Socialist disorder and experiment.

If ever there was an over-subtle, over-smart solution, it was this
second one of Papen's, the summons of National Socialism to
power at a time when it was at its last gasp; perhaps precisely
because it was. It betrays the utter superficiality of judgment
of the politicians of the last year before National Socialism came
into power. It would have been impossible to make a more wildly
mistaken estimate of the political forces in the country. The
peril of revolution was seen where there certainly was none, and
it was not seen where it had flaunted itself in speech and action.
Nothing was more remote from the future of the Reich in 1932-
1933 than a Bolshevist revolution or even a political revolt from
the Left! The very people who to-day spread the legend that a
Bolshevist revolution was on the point of breaking out know
perfectly well, and showed that they did by their own tactics at
the time, that in Germany a coup d'état was only possible for
those who could fall back on the possession of constitutional
power. Even if the old Republican parties had combined to carry
out a coup, making use of the constitutional power to cover a
coup by illegal parties of the Left, the Reichswehr would have

vetoed the move and so it would have been nipped in the bud. Only nationalist groups or elements co-opted by them, assured of the patronage of the Reichswehr, could attempt a coup with the slightest prospect of success.

We have to clear our minds of romantic ideas of revolution-making. The poetic glamour of the revolution of barricades and flying banners belongs to the past, and not even the recent past, as certainly as does the *frischfröhlicher Krieg*, the "brisk and jolly war." The power and resources of the modern State, with its executive organs, its police and army, make civil revolution virtually impossible. This will remain true of the future, and it disposes of all dreams of a mass revolt in the Third Reich. All that is possible is what happened on January 30th, 1933—coup and revolution by arrangement, from above, under the patronage of the constitutional powers. A civil war is possible only where the organs of constitutional power are in the hands of groups of divergent outlook, distributed among several parties, as in Spain.

It may be doubted whether it is to the advantage of a nation to suffer radical changes, affecting its whole future, by arrange-ment in this way, even though they involve little or no blood-shed, the nation itself playing no active part. The national revolution of January 30th was almost bloodless; but there was all the more bloodshed, from countless acts of terrorism, in the period that followed, and these acts of terrorism had not the excuse of revolutionary passion. Such terrorism produces cool, calculated cruelty, a horrifying cynicism, much more pronounced and harmful in its effects than such open revolutionary violence as took place after the rising of 1918.

I recall a remarkable statement made by Hitler to some visitors, of whom I was one, at Obersalzberg in 1932. The death sentence had just been pronounced on the murderers at Potempa, and the unforgotten declaration of solidarity with the murderers made by the leader of the Party had just become publicly known. A nation—so ran the declaration—may overlook and forget any-thing in so disturbed a time as the present, if it happens in an

open conflict between the holders of opposed views. If the Storm
Troopers were given a free hand, if it came to street fighting and
twenty to thirty thousand Germans lost their lives, the nation
would be able to recover from that. The wound would heal. It
would be like open fighting in the field. But a miscarriage of justice, a death sentence pronounced after cool reflection, and pronounced and carried out against the people's unerring sense of
justice, an execution of men who had acted in national passion,
like those who had been sentenced at Potempa as common murderers—that would set an ineradicable stain on the nation, that
would never be forgotten.

This attitude was certainly justifiable, though hardly in connection with the Potempa murders! It is true that acts of terrorism, sanguinary violence proceeding from the absolute dominance
of state or semi-state executive organs, as in the concentration
camps, during house searches, or in vengeance wreaked on de-
fenceless individuals "by virtue of revolutionary law," will never
be forgotten, and will remain an ineradicable stain on the nation
to the end of German history. And it is true that for many people,
if not for the whole nation, the spectacle of revolutionary destruction would be an inestimable relief from this heavy, pestilent atmosphere of insidious and ubiquitous terror. The incredible thing
is that a man who was quite able, as that declaration shows, to
judge matters for himself, should for five years, with his eyes
open, have permitted the very thing which he so emphatically
condemned on the occasion of the Potempa verdicts—should have
permitted and ordered it to be committed on a scale hundreds and
indeed thousands of times larger. It is appalling that he should
have permitted and ordered many sentences of death for acts
incomparably less grave than those at Potempa, or for simple
professions of faith.

Coups d'état following the tactics of inoculating legality with
the revolutionary impulse, of manipulating this legality until it
has passed through a stage of masked revolution and has re-
emerged as a new legality, are carried out in order to prevent a

11

period of anarchy, to keep control of developments, to prevent being placed at the mercy of incalculable "dæmonic" elements, and to attain the revolutionary end without setting the masses in motion. But if afterwards the revolutionary suspension of a state of law is instituted in cold blood, that action places the course of events at the mercy precisely of these dæmonic, incalculable elements. This method deals a much more crippling blow at justice and the sense of justice than when there comes a transient condition of open revolution, which all the elements of order will combine to bring quickly to an end. All retrospective acts of calculated reprisal dull the senses of the nation and reduce it to lethargy. The things that are happening in the German concentration camps and in the cells of the Gestapo, with the whole modern inquisitorial technique of spying and denunciation, the all-comprehending terrorism, are producing a nation that will be incapable for a long time to come of any really creative effort or of devotion to any great cause. A genuine revolution will release creative energies, as all true revolutions have done in the past. The revolution-by-arrangement ends in universal exhaustion. For in its artificial combination of forces it includes irreconcilable elements.

Irreconcilable opposites were harnessed together in the German revolution of 1933, with the result not of mutual stimulation but of mutual paralysis. In two respects the different outlooks coincide, in the nationalist jargon indulged in by both partners, and in their anti-Liberalism. But the anti-Liberalism is drawn from different sources. For the Conservative-nationalist-monarchist group Liberalism is the destroyer of all standards with its critical analysis; for the revolutionaries, the National Socialists, this Liberal disintegration was a mere half-measure; their anti-Liberalism extended to thorough-going nihilism; what they wanted, in the true spirit of Shigalev, was a *tabula rasa*, complete liberation from the past, on which to build a totalitarian despotism. The Conservative, national elements thought they had created a political machine; what they had really done was to

12

deliver themselves up to a revolutionary power whose creed was action for action's sake and whose tactics were the destruction and undermining of all that is of value in the existing order. A clique of leaders had made themselves masters of Germany's future, and they unscrupulously exhausted the nation's reserves as fuel for their own "dynamic" course.

"Of all the evils of defeat, of all the consequences of the Peace of Versailles, the most disastrous that could visit Germany would be the loss of her civic liberties." So wrote the Italian Malaparte in 1931. But his dictum does not give the full measure of the evil. Worse still than the loss of civic liberties is the destruction of the creative powers of a nation. The deepest defect of our time is the complete unproductivity and impotence of the conservative forces. Stahl, the Prussian Conservative, touched on this defect a hundred years ago; it is not peculiar to the German people: there is, he said, "only unproductive conservation and inventive destruction."

CATILINARIANS AND DESPAIRING PATRIOTS

As early as 1931 Malaparte had declared that the National Socialist dictatorship would only be achieved by a *"combinazione,"* by a deal with other elements. He based this prognosis on Hitler's irresolution. This is one of the current undervaluations. But he was right in so far as no one in Germany could attain dictatorial power and let loose revolutionary violence except by such a deal. But, continued Malaparte, "dictators who are the product of a *combinazione* are but semi-dictators. They have no staying-power." It remains to be seen whether this addition to his prognosis will be borne out as well as the first part.

Yet, whatever may have been the chance or fated combination of elements in the birth of the Third Reich, it remains an artificially produced birth, and the new Reich will bear for all time the marks of the forceps. The strong government of which men were in search proved neither strong nor reliable, as the most short-sighted were able later to see. It was just as artificial and

13

fabricated as everything else that was planned at this time. And in most men the conception of power had already turned into that of violence. The countenancing of violent methods, in which the Conservatives and Nationalists should have been the last to place their faith, entangled elements inspired by the best of intentions in a "realist" policy which was anything but nationalist or conservative.

What had the "combination" attained? A united national front, the basis of a new and vital national union? A new form of integration of a true State, a "realist union of wills"? Nothing of the sort; merely the juxtaposition of two partners with diametrically opposite aims, each making the secret reservation that he must quickly get rid of the other, or at least gain the upper hand over him. We need not enter into the question which element in the association that brought the Third Reich into the world had set out the more deliberately to make use of the partner in the deal, and virtually to impose upon him. Perhaps it was the army, which needed the civilians and their political machinery in order to be able to remain in the background during the coup d'état, in the necessity for which it agreed. Perhaps it was the tacticians of the reaction, proceeding from a totally mistaken idea of the nature of National Socialism and imagining that they could achieve two things by an intrigue with it, spare themselves and let their political rivals wear themselves out. Without any question the National Socialist leaders were perfectly clear as to their own aims and the means of carrying them out in the deal they had entered into. They were familiar with the tactics and the technique of a coup d'état not only of the Bonapartist type but of that of Trotsky and Lenin, and they knew exactly how they meant to proceed from a coalition government, an authoritarian regime, to their National Socialist revolution. Subsequently, that is to say, after their arrival in power on January 30th, 1933, they pursued every technical device of the Trotskyist recipe for coups d'état. By systematically occupying the key positions in the State and in industry, they placed themselves in effective possession of power. And by the method, their own invention, of *"Gleichschaltung"* or "co-ordination"* they achieved the indispensable aim of every revolution—the *tabula rasa*, the clear run for the revolutionary course. This system brought them several advantages. Not the least important of these was that few people realized the comprehensive scope of their activities. Here again the crucial steps were hidden from view. When the revolution was officially staged, on January 30th, 1933, it had in reality scarcely begun; when its successes were celebrated any sort of remonstrance had become useless: the seizure of impregnable power was an accomplished and unalterable fact.

What matters politically to-day is not the rise of National Socialism as a philosophy. Its roots lie certainly in the racial ideas of the pan-Germans of Austria and Germany, in their rabid anti-Semitism, their hatred of the Habsburgs and of the very principle of the Austrian State, in the movement away from Rome and the first beginnings of the enthusiasm for the myth of the pagan Teutons. All this, though not all of it is still actively pursued, may be effective to this day, it may still play an important part in securing emotional support of decisions, it may still be important for the platform and the show; but what is more important than the nature of the National Socialism of the past is what it has become. The crucial fact is that the revolution has progressed far beyond its racialist origins and is now using this doctrinal armory of its youth, in so far as it retains any of it, merely as a necessary element in propaganda. Racialism is its make-believe; the reality is the revolutionary extremism revealed not in its philosophy but in its tactics. It is impossible to understand the situation in Germany if this development is not realized. The development began long before the arrival in power. Behind it lay the unprincipled struggle for power, which for the time being was the one and only real objective. The osten-

---

* A euphemism for the subordination of every public activity in the country to National Socialist domination, usually by the simple process of placing National Socialists in charge.—Translator.

sible aims and objectives were simply the propaganda material employed for gaining a Parliamentary majority. Consequently the arsenal of political objectives was filled with the most contradictory and manifestly impracticable demands. And the main objective that began to stand out from the racialist nationalism and the moderated Socialism of the party propaganda was a revolutionary transformation of the whole political and social order. For the very reason that this objective was but vaguely outlined, it worked as a recruiting element. The movement attracted all those people who wanted a radical change in the existing conditions—the most primitive and the most obvious of revolutionary cravings.

The reasons for this development lay partly in the conditions of the time and partly in the character of the leaders. One thing must always be insisted on: the National Socialism that came to power in 1933 was no longer a nationalist but a revolutionary movement. The failure of the middle class to realize this was a fatal error. It was no longer possible to rid the movement of its revolutionary character; from its very nature it grew irresistibly in extremism. This was not apparent even to the members of the party. Even party members were startled when, in the spring of 1933, the practical steps taken by their leaders began to reveal the realities behind all the patriotic oratory— the unashamed pursuit of power and of key positions, and the cynical resort to a brutality hitherto inconceivable.

This apparent change in the character of National Socialism (in reality it was no change but simply a revelation of the true character of the movement) was so striking that the suspicion arose among members of the party that it was the work of enemies within the party who were out to compromise the movement. This "insidious plan" was even ascribed to a very influential member of the Cabinet of the Reich. The same feeling of disillusion and indignation was voiced among old and trusting members of the party as was expressed later in a leaflet issued in Vienna by old Austrian National Socialists: "Have we accepted persecution and poverty and deprivation, year after year, for this?" It was at this period also that the original preaching of Spartan economy, and of emulating the traditional Prussian "starvation to greatness," gave place to a grotesque extravagance throughout the party.

Catilinarians and despairing patriots! Many actors on the stage of the new Reich had something in them of each category. The despairing patriots of Left and Right alike saw the distress of a nation that was destroying itself, and longed to remedy it. Some delved into the treasuries of the past for guidance. Others placed their faith in a future that promised them an entirely new solution of human problems in a liberated nation with an assured existence. The Catilinarians of the Right demanded above all a strong State under their dominance; they confused order with subservience. They were for violence within limits—limits defined by a traditional civic morality which they were not prepared to abandon. The Catilinarians of the Left were out to absorb the whole State and to harness it to the service of their pursuit of power. They conquered the State and destroyed it. Their destructive, unsocial nature confined them to the abolition of the existing elements of order. They were possessed incurably of the devil of nihilism.

The tasks the associated elements had agreed on were the restoration of a strong authoritarian regime, the transformation of the State in the direction of absolutism, the reconstruction of an economic system that was falling to pieces, and the return to a united national, patriotic way of thinking as the first condition for rearmament and the renewal of Germany's power in the field of foreign policy. An ordered hierarchy, clear definitions of function, fixed and universally applicable valuations—such was the plan of the "national awakening." But behind it two tendencies were struggling with one another for mastery. They were represented by very unequal forces. On one side were the forces of reaction—retrogressive revision of the Constitution, the authoritarian State, the abrogation of the social legislation

or at least the introduction of important modifications by making
an end of the inviolability of wage scales and the freedom of association; an avowed return to patriarchalism, the restoration of
the old orders of nobility, and, finally, the restoration of the
monarchy. On the other side was the revolution of an "élite"
drawn from the masses, determined to conquer power and to
keep it.

THE AIMS OF NATIONAL SOCIALISM

"Our aims are perfectly clear. The world is only surprised at
our attitude because it does not know us." The German propaganda leader wrote this, with his characteristic pregnancy, on
the occasion of Lord Halifax's visit to Germany in 1937. "The
aims of National Socialism are being achieved, one after another. . . . It will come. It is coming, bit by bit. We have
time!" he continued. It is true enough that the world still does
not know National Socialism, but it is not correct to say that
the aims of the party were clear. We have to combat two views,
one that the course followed in the Reich was carefully planned
and thought out and directed toward definite objectives fixed
once for all, and the other that National Socialism is guided
on the whole by doctrinaire program points. There are many
who will contend that National Socialism reveals a broadly
conceived, dogmatically defined philosophy, possessing absolutely
definite doctrines in regard to all human relations which must
be unreservedly accepted by every loyal citizen. Nevertheless,
we must ask: is National Socialism doctrinaire? It is, of course,
beyond question that it is the product of doctrinaire ideas and
that doctrinaire personages play a part in it to this day. Of
much greater importance is the question of the connection of
what was regarded as National Socialist doctrine with the two
elements that characterize the movement, the irrational passions that undoubtedly play an important part, and its leading
personalities. A sharp distinction must be drawn in National
Socialism between this genuinely irrational revolutionary passion, affecting not only the mass of followers but the leaders

themselves, and the very deliberate, utterly cold and calculating pursuit of power and dominance by the controlling group. We may generalize: The doctrine is meant for the masses. It is *not* a part of the real motive forces of the revolution. It is an instrument for the control of the masses. The élite, the leaders, stand above the doctrine. They make use of it in furtherance of their purposes.

What, then, are the aims of National Socialism which are being achieved one after another? Certainly not the various points of its program; even if some of these are carried out, this is not the thing that matters. The aim of National Socialism is the complete revolutionizing of the technique of government, and complete dominance over the country by the leaders of the movement. The two things are inseparably connected: the revolution cannot be carried out without an élite ruling with absolute power, and this élite can maintain itself in power only through a process of continual intensification of the process of revolutionary disintegration. National Socialism is an unquestionably genuine revolutionary movement in the sense of a final achievement on a vaster scale of the "mass rising" dreamed of by Anarchists and Communists. But modern revolutions do not take place through fighting across improvised barricades, but in disciplined acts of destruction. They follow irrational impulses, but they remain under rational guidance and command. Their perilousness lies in their ordered destructiveness—it is a misuse on a vast scale of the human desire for order—and in the irrationality and incalculability of their pressure for the "victory of the revolutionary new order." This pressure is completely uncalculated, unconsidered, the pressure of men with no program but action, instinctive in the case of the best troops of the movement; but the part played in it by its controlling élite is most carefully and coolly considered down to the smallest detail. There was and is no aim that National Socialism has not been ready for the sake of the movement to abandon or to proclaim at any time.

The National Socialist revolution, at the outset a nationalist seizure of power, is viewed much too much in the light of historic precedents. There are no criteria and no precedents for the new revolutions of the twentieth century. The revolutionary dictatorship is a new type, in its cynical, unprincipled policy of violence. The outsider overlooks above all the essential distinction between the mass and the élite in the new revolutions. This distinction is vital in every field. That which is intended for the mass is not applicable to the élite. Program and official philosophy, allegiance and faith, are for the mass. Nothing commits the élite— no philosophy, no ethical standard. It has but one obligation, that of absolute loyalty to comrades, to fellow-members of the initiated élite. This fundamental distinction between élite and mass does not seem to have been sufficiently clearly realized, but it is just this that explains many inconsistencies, many things done, that leave the outsider dumbfounded.

There has scarcely been a single old National Socialist who attached any importance to the program and program-literature of the party. If any section of the party was in it for action and nothing else, and completely uninterested in programs and ideologies, and strong for that very reason as the real backbone of a brotherhood, it was the section of the party that was its vital element, the Storm Troops. Their repugnance to programs was well known, there was no success in training them in "theories." And the National Socialist "Bible," that remarkable book which is now accorded the sanctity of verbal inspiration, was far from playing its present part among old "Pg's" (*Parteigenossen*), old members of the party; they paid no particular attention to it. Nobody took it seriously; nobody could, for nobody could make head or tail of it. The mass understood and understands nothing and does not want to understand. Each individual holds to whatever he can comprehend in it, to any particular bit that concerns him personally. The things that stir most men and fire their enthusiasm are the rhythm, the new tempo, the activity, that take them out of the humdrum daily life: with these things much can be done, the masses can be inflamed. They are matters of emotion, with much the same appeal as the call of the first *Wandervogel* movement, which brought men away from the security of their homes and sent them on a roving life: an emotion compounded of romance and boredom. The initiated member, the old Pg, knew that the whole tableau of philosophical outlook and party doctrine was only of symbolic value, something to stir men's imagination, to divert their thoughts from other things, to discipline them. It was a cover for realities which must not be "given away" to the masses. He himself, the old Pg, was a Catilinarian, a mere *condottiere;* or, if he was an idealist, in his progressive liberation from the crude ikon-worship of the National Socialist masses he felt a pride of partnership in the reality behind it, the heroic nihilism of the party, inculcated in the young men as soon as they were old enough for the senior groups of the Hitler Youth. If we try to understand what it is that tempts Hitler again and again to dwell on Freemasonry, on the Jesuits, or on the Teutonic Order, we come close to the essential secret of the National Socialist élite, the "mystery," as the Teutonic Order called it, the esoteric doctrine confined to the brethren who were called to initiation. It was the piecemeal character of their initiation into secret aims, the aims and methods of a ruling class, by stages of discipline, enlightenment, liberation, that set the eyes of National Socialism in envious rivalry on such organizations as Freemasonry.

The movement has no fixed aims, either economic or political, either in home or foreign affairs. Hitler was out even in 1932 to liberate himself from all party doctrines in economic policy, and he did the same in all other fields; and this "realist" attitude was adopted, and still is, not only by the leader but by every member holding any official position in the party, or admitted at all into its confidence. The only objective was the victory of the party, and even favorite doctrines were abandoned for the sake of this. The rise of National Socialism compelled the élite of the movement to become realists, and when they came into power they made this acquired pragmatism the foundation of the fanatical activity of the movement in the new, national field. It is no doctrinaire commitment of the movement that drives National Socialism into lines of action which from a realist and rationalist standpoint are incomprehensible, but its revolutionary, irrational character, which continually prompts it to any possible revolutionary destruction of existing institutions.

The fight against Christianity is not a matter of doctrine or program; this is clear to any reader of *Mein Kampf* or of the party program; yet it has come, simply because it lies more than anything else precisely in that direction of the destruction of existing institutions. For all practical purposes it should suffice for the racial State and for independence from all alien, supernational, superstate powers, if a German National Church were started. But the revolutionary destruction of the Christian basis goes much farther than this. A schismatic separation of German Catholicism from Rome, inevitable as it seems to-day, has already been put out of date by the developments in Germany. It will be a brief episode on the way to the comprehensive aim of destroying the Christian faith as the most deep-seated root of Western civilization and of the social order. It will be a stage that will assist the revolutionizing of the soul of the masses, not the actual final aim. Similarly the fight against Judaism, while it is beyond question a central element not only in material considerations but in those of cultural policy, is part of the party doctrine; but, for all that, it is now an element in the revolutionary unsettling of the nation, a means of destruction of past categories of thinking and valuation, of destroying the liberalist economic system based on private initiative and enterprise; it is also a sop to the destructive revolutionism of the masses, a first lesson in cynicism.

This irrational element in National Socialism is the actual source of its strength. It is the reliance on it that accounts for its "sleepwalker's immunity" in face of one practical problem after another. It explains why it was possible for National Socialism to attain power almost without the slightest tangible ideas of what it was going to do. The movement was without even vague general ideas on the subject; all it had was boundless confidence: things would smooth themselves out one way or another. Give rein to the revolutionary impulse, and the problems would find their own solution. An open mind and no program at all—that is what enabled National Socialism to win through in its own way with its practical problems. Its strength lay in incessant activity and in embarking on anything so long as it kept things moving. Conversely, it abandoned anything that could hinder it, such as the construction of the Corporative State and the reform of the Reich. What it needed and intuitively took up were the opportunities of revolutionary dislocation.

Nothing is more idle than to engage in heated discussions of the capitalistic and monopolistic character of National Socialist economic policy, or of the question whether Socialism or Reaction has been the driving force in its schemes of social reconstruction. National Socialist "anti-capitalism" is similarly just a bargain-counter, like almost everything else. If there is one thing that does not and cannot exist among the National Socialist élite, it is a genuine sense of social solidarity with the propertyless classes of the nation. One may count on finding just the opposite, and it is easily discernible in Hitler himself—an unconcealed contempt of the crowd, the common people, the mob: they are there not to be served but to be used.

National Socialism is action pure and simple, dynamics *in vacuo,* revolution at a variable tempo, ready to be changed at any moment. One thing it is not—doctrine or philosophy. Yet it has a philosophy. It does not base its policy on a doctrine, but pursues it with the aid of a philosophy. It makes use of its philosophy as it makes use of all things men have, and all they want, as fuel for its energy. Its policy is exactly what a critic of the era of William II said of the policy of that time: it is "opportunist policy," though in quite a different, a much more "realist", sense. It is opportunist policy in the sense of making

23

use of every opportunity of doing anything to increase the movement's own power, and to add to the elements under its domination.

National Socialist policy is in the highest degree subtle and sly, aimed at keeping to the front a system of "inflammatory ideas," in order the more effectively and the more startlingly to seize each opportunity. People used to say that any policy of important scope always needs justification by a great idea. But that was intellectual, ideological generalizing. It assumed that there are still ideas in which men believe. To the conscious nihilist there are no ideas. But there are substitutes for ideas which can be foisted on the masses by suggestion, and he has little hesitation in imposing on them whatever they can swallow.

The National Socialist "philosophy" is not the outcome of any lofty intuition; it is deliberately and carefully manufactured. Originally it developed out of much the same doctrines as those which Sorel formulated in his gospel of violence: a myth must be created to give the masses the energy for action. Thus the ruling consideration in the production of the National Socialist philosophy is its power of influencing the masses by suggestion, of instilling into them the sense of the duty of obedience. The great paradox of this revolution is that its lack of principle is one of the main secrets of its effectiveness. It is its strength; it is precisely in this characteristic that the actual revolutionary power of the movement lies, and its character of a "permanent revolution," impossible to bring to a close. The naïve element among its mercenaries has largely been removed by the decimation of the Storm Troops, but the subtler and far more effectual element, the élite under the leader's protection, has remained. This élite keeps alive the revolutionary spirit, in spite of all announcements of the ending of the revolution. National Socialism cannot abandon this dynamic element; in doing so it would be abandoning itself. And the question becomes more and more insistent, how long can a State, a nation, a society, endure a governing élite devoid of all principle, without disintegrating?

ERROR AND DECEPTION

Error or deliberate deception? Which was it? Was the National Socialist party in doubt as to its own real character; did it genuinely regard itself as a movement of national rebirth, or did it cleverly and deliberately adopt that disguise in order to attain power? Undoubtedly both the one and the other. There was an honest belief among a great number of the members of the party, and among its followers, that they were laboring in the service of national recovery. Even among the élite the consciousness of the actual part they were to play came only with the first great successes. But there were some among them who knew how matters stood, probably long before the arrival in power. Hitler himself pursued carefully calculated tactics: he damped down the Socialist tendencies in the movement and brought the Nationalist ones into the foreground. He was out to gain powerful patrons and friends who could help the movement into power. The temporary veto on the anti-capitalist propaganda desired by Gregor Strasser was due to his insistence. And this was not because Hitler was himself a reactionary, but because at that moment the Socialist note would have interfered with the political developments envisaged. It was precisely at this point that Hitler showed his real superiority over his élite: at the right moment he took a course which was extremely awkward for him and an extremely unpopular one, but which alone led along the road to power—the camouflage of the "dynamic" revolution as a movement of national renewal. He put up with the dissatisfaction and disgust of his élite, and allowed them to abuse him for his "inadequacy" as an "advocate," and for his supposed idea that he could attain power by means of speeches and parades, threats and extortion, and secret deals with bankers and soldiers, industrialists and agrarians. Yet from the point of view of the

25

THE REVOLUTION OF NIHILISM

movement and of its aims his course was the only possible one. He was justified in the outcome, and encouraged to continue in that course. He brazenly joined forces with the monarchists; brazenly denied his own views and affected to be a reactionary. With a technique of camouflage unprecedented in Germany, he arranged the deal that associated his party with the national rising which ended in the National Socialist revolution. He succeeded in a concealment of the true facts on a scale never before known. The deception continues to this day—a presentation of the revolution as an innocent affair, middle class and moderate. Deliberately concealing the true nature of the National Socialist revolution, the new élite successfully occupied Germany. Under its disguise it succeeded in foisting on the country, in place of an authoritarian State, an instrument of dominance that serves simply and purely for the maintenance of its own absolute power. Under the mask of a movement of national liberation, it achieved the despotic repression of the nation, with the voluntary assistance of the middle classes and large sections of the working class.

Only these facts provide the standpoint for a judgment of what National Socialism regards as its creative achievements, its work in the field of constitutional, social, and economic affairs. The outstanding feature to-day in these fields is beyond question their universal subjection to despotic control. A machinery of absolute and universal dominion is being erected in an entirely disorganized State. Nothing is more mistaken than to talk of a "totalitarian State" or a "classless society" within the realm of a nihilist revolution. In the place of these there is the machinery of absolute dominion, recognizing independence in no sphere at all, not even in the private life of the individual; and the totalitarian collectivity of the *Volksgemeinschaft*, the "national community," a euphemism for an atomized, structureless nation.

The retrogression from the conception of the State to that of the party in what a German sociologist has defined as its primitive sense, that of an organization for rule by violent means, is paralleled by the retrogression from the sphere of legality and constitutionalism to the primeval conception of Leader and Followers and the principle of absolute power and blind obedience. Within this organization of dominance which has replaced the State, there has developed as the indispensable means of rule the segregation of a privileged élite from the totally unprotected and disfranchised mass. The control of the remnants of the State by a party ("the Party commands the State") may be regarded as a phase in the process of the dissolution of the old forces of order by the revolution. This process ends with the absorption of the State and its functions by the "organization for rule by violent means." To-day the State is nothing but an administrative machine. There is no true sphere of the State in the Third Reich.

THE DOCTRINE OF VIOLENCE

National Socialism does not mean the crushing of the "mass revolt" but the carrying of it to completion. The astonishing thing is not that this could have happened, but that it could be done under the mask of a movement in the opposite direction, without those affected realizing the reversal of the course. To-day, after six years, there are, to say the least, still many respectable people associated with German "dynamism" who have not yet realized that their imagined national and racial rebirth amounts to nothing more than the adoption of the revolutionary system of "direct action" as the fundamental principle of the carrying of the "mass revolt" to completion.

Direct action is defined as "direct integration by means of corporativism, militarism, and myth"; this is to replace democracy and parliamentarism. But the true significance of direct action lies in its assignment of the central place in its policy to violence, which it then surrounds with a special philosophical interpretation of reality. Briefly this philosophical system amounts to the belief that the use of violence in a supreme effort liberates creative moral forces in human society which lead to social and national renewal. "Civilization is the endeavor to reduce violence to the *ultima ratio*," writes Ortega y Gasset. "This is now becoming all too clear to us, for direct action reverses the order and proclaims violence as the *prima ratio*, or rather the *unica ratio*. It is the standard that dispenses with all others." Violence, says Sorel, is the basic force in life. When all other standards have been unmasked by scepticism of all doctrines, reason itself is robbed of all force. The anti-intellectual attitude of "dynamism" is not mere chance but the necessary outcome of an entire absence of standards. Man, it holds, is not a logical being, not a creature guided by reason or intelligence, but a creature following his instincts and impulses, like any other animal. Consequently reason cannot provide a basis for a social order or a political system. The barbaric element of violence, which reformist Socialism and moderate Marxism would place in safe custody under lock and key, is the one element that can change a social order. That is why revolutionary direct action has won the day against the responsible, non-revolutionary Socialism of the working class, just as it has violently eliminated the middle class itself as the ruling class. Hostility to the things of the spirit, indifference to truth, indifference to the ethical conceptions of morality, honor, and equity—all the things that arouse the indignation of the ordinary citizen in Germany and abroad against certain National Socialist measures—are not excrescences but the logical and inevitable outcome of the National Socialist philosophy, of the doctrine of violence. This hostility to the intellect, to individualism and personality, to pure science and art, is not the arbitrary invention of a particularly vicious system of racial philosophy, but the logical outcome of the political system of revolutionary direct action with violence as its one and only historic motor.

THE NEW ELITE

The Leader-and-Followers principle simply destroys the possibility of building up a State. When this principle is dominant, the State can no longer exist. Nor can a social order endure. While still permeated with the idea of the "idyllic state of the rule of responsible middle class people," the nationalists confused their desire for the restoration of a regime of this type with the essence of the doctrine of violence, the principle of personal conspiratorial pledges of élite to Leader, which could produce a dictatorship ruling by violence, but never a monarchical restoration. In bringing the National Socialist Party into the "combination" they imagined that they had placed the reins of government in the hands of the aged President Hindenburg, assigning to the party leader the function of whipping up the enthusiasm of the country by his oratory. But the outcome was not as innocent as these self-styled realists expected. The special feature of the German development is the segregation out of the masses of a special élite which shares the privileges of power, and the atomization of the organized nation, which is reduced to an amorphous mass held together in new official mass groupings. It is the élite that actually organizes the revolutionary process; at the same time it controls the machinery of government. It represents the actual "Following" of the "Leader." Only in that capacity is it privileged. This National Socialist élite is nothing but the class that, in Pareto's phrase, is "arriving," forming, independently of any doctrine, the real kernel of a revolution. Pareto holds that a revolution is possible only when a ruling class that has lost its strength of will and is physically decadent, and no longer able to defend its hold of power by forcible means, is faced by a new class that has set out to take its place. In any case, the National Socialist revolution resembles the process described by Pareto, the rise of a new class and the abdication of an old one.

On the problem of the political élite, of the "ruling element with a historic mission," the monarchists, proceeding from a different starting-point, had developed much the same ideas as those underlying the National Socialist enterprise of creating a new upper class as an instrument of dominance. Some of the monarchist groups expected themselves to become the new upper class of the National Socialist mass movement, and their anticipation helped in no small degree to bring into existence the "combination" of 1933.

National Socialism, with its sharp elbows, pushed all these lofty aspirations rudely aside. It had no need either of an intellectual or of a social élite. *L'élite, c'est moi*, was its attitude. The ponderous and self-conscious discussions among the nationalists of the problem of the élite and the political leadership were in strong contrast with the unscrupulousness of the National Socialists in the practical task of selecting their élite. To them the formation of an élite was not a problem in political theory but a practical process connected with their struggle for power. They did not dream of introducing fresh blood into their élite from outside their own ranks. They were not interested in the slightest in the qualities of outside candidates, their intelligence, their capacity, or their social standing. These outsiders were just "pigmies," in the Propaganda Minister's phrase. What the National Socialists did take over was the language of those rivals. By appropriating for lip-service the ideas and standards of genuine political and social élites, they have succeeded to this day in deceiving a naïve nation, and masking the true fact that National Socialism brought to the top a primitive, vulgar élite under the cover of national and social aims. The fiction that every element associated with National Socialism in the struggle for power proved itself by that fact to be by nature and character a part of the élite exposes the mechanism of this primitive but effective method of selection. But the secret of the union of the élite is their lack of doctrine. No allegiance to any sort of philosophy merited membership in the actual élite, but the simple fact of having fought for its power. The actual selection, said the National Socialists, is our affair. Neither by intelligence nor capacity nor noble birth nor special standing were men qualified for entry into the élite, but simply by denial of the traditional decent citizen's outlook. Ordinary life gives the true leader's nature no opportunity for success, only temptations, which end his respectability. To have come to grief in ordinary life is no disqualification for revolutionary leadership —on the contrary. With the full momentum of their demagogic resources, and with the readiness to gamble of the true desperado, who has nothing to lose and everything to gain, this gutter élite were able to carry the day with ease against the rather too cautious and anemic members of the aristocratic clubs.

Their success was facilitated by their adoption of their rivals' political language. The National Socialist leaders concealed their true objectives so well that many members of the élite only realized after a considerable time that they had been drawn into a double existence, with fictitious spiritual, national aims, and one very real one, the pursuit of power. The actual participants in power within the National Socialist Party are a ruling minority of super-careerists. This cream of the élite use the power they have seized to feather their nests. The most outstanding quality of the élite is "the accurately chosen and ruthless application of all the physical and material power at its disposal." Here again the National Socialist leaders carried into practice the new doctrine of violence, the doctrine that spiritual assets are of value for the legitimation of political power and for nothing else; such things have no intrinsic authority, no value in themselves: there is nothing that counts, except force; it is by force alone that an élite comes to the top. Force is applied at all times, for the one purpose of maintaining the élite in power—and applied ruthlessly, brutally, instantaneously. But it is discreet to provide a reasoned justification for this application of force, through a suitable ideology. The true élite is entirely without scruples and without humanitarian weaknesses. Where these appear, where the use of force is hampered by scruples, the élite becomes decadent and opens the way for the rise of a new élite. Thus it is virtually a duty for every member of the élite to undergo training in brutality. It prefers at all times the most violent means, the most violent solution. Only in this way does it retain its position. In this way, as Pareto points out, the simple biological struggle for existence is transferred, in the struggle between the élites, into the sphere of human society.

Such are the views of the National Socialists, not systematically taught in public, not collected into a system at all, but conveyed from member to member in the actual cadres of the élite, and made the basis of all action. This is the attitude which is plainly adopted by the élite in actual practice. This attitude gives them their ruthlessness in the use of their power and resources, their rapidity of action, their readiness to take risks, and through all this their notorious superiority to all earlier ruling classes, all political groups, capitalist or Socialist. There are those who praise the rapid and ruthless action of the National Socialist leaders in home and foreign politics; all this implies is that the new élite make use of their power and resources mainly in order to maintain themselves in power and to extend their power.

But these practical rules and maxims of political leadership, adopted consciously or unconsciously by National Socialism, are applicable only in the course of a revolution permanently in progress. The revolutionary élite can maintain itself in power in its permanently critical situation only by continually pushing on with the revolutionary process. In its effort to hold on to power it is compelled to destroy the old social and political institutions, since it is in these that the strength of the old ruling class lies. When the political structure of the country has been razed to the ground, the élite will march over the frontier, to upset the existing international order.

The right men in the right place—that is a typical rule in civil life in peaceful times. In revolutionary times, and then only, there is no need for the "right" man. Any man will do who will exercise power with ruthless brutality. Only in a revolutionary period can the difficult problem of selection of personnel be treated with the negligence, indeed the criminal negligence, shown by National Socialism. But this can continue only so long as there is little or no effort at genuinely constructive work, little being done beyond the using up of accumulated reserves, and revolutionary destruction. For such work, the less education the leaders have the better.

The new élite of National Socialism is an affront to all historic and traditional standards. It is a deliberate breach with the past and the seal of a new order. The "ruling element with a historic mission" is formed by the National Socialist élite, and by them alone. This is due to their determined struggle for power after the coup-by-arrangement of January 30th, while the élite of the capitalist parties rested content with the externals of leadership, with posts from which they were driven out one by one as opportunity offered.

After all this it will surprise nobody that the National Socialist revolutionary élite are entirely without moral inhibitions, and that individually they reveal so strange a mixture of extreme nihilism with an unashamed adoption of the ways of the half-educated lower middle class. The cool and calculating resolution that marks the political dealings of this élite has hitherto been associated in people's minds with outstanding intelligence or at least versatility—at all events, when not dealing simply with criminals. In these people we find, however, a mixture of qualities, a naïve mixture of qualities always regarded up to now as irreconcilable with one another. But the unusualness of the mixture must not blind us to the fact that the operative part in the duality of these natures is a hard, resolute, ruthless will, even if their German is ungrammatical and their intellectual equipment manifestly of the lowest. It is characteristic, too, of National Socialism that it is only in exceptional cases that its leaders are removed on account of incorrect dealings—to put it euphemistically—under the civil code. Lack of morals in civil life is not frowned on: it is no ground for suspicion of a member's National Socialist orthodoxy. National Socialism demands, indeed, of its sworn élite that all personal moral scruples shall

33

be overridden by the needs of the party. Anyone who reveals that he is allowing himself the luxury of guidance by his own conscience has no place in the élite and will be expelled. It is not surprising to find that absence of moral scruples in the private life of a member of the élite is dealt with very gently by the party authorities. It is impossible to demand scrupulous correctness in a member's private life when any crime may be required of him in the interest of the party. Demands have actually been made of individuals in order to have a future hold over them, or to test their readiness to obey. In Danzig the Senator for Public Health was required, against the clear medical evidence, to declare in the case of the death of a National Socialist "militant" that the man had been killed by a blow struck by a political opponent. The Senator refused to make an official declaration in conflict with the truth; he was deprived of his office and his senatorship. This is one instance of a method pursued deliberately in order to make the élite a following sworn to blind obedience, a company from which every member's escape is cut off, because he has been incriminated.

THE DIVINE INSPIRATION OF THE LEADER

In the center of the movement stands the figure of the Führer, the Leader. This central figure cannot be replaced by anything else, a group or committee or board. Any such suggestions overlook the essential "charismatic" element of the leader, the element of his "divine inspiration." This element in the mass leader, the great demagogue and revolutionary is a reality that cannot be dismissed even by those who personally are not under its influence. A great deal of the nimbus of the revolutionary leader seems manufactured and is in fact manufactured; but the root of his mesmeric influence lies, like that of the revolutionary "dynamic" urge in the movement itself, in an irrational element, in the medium-like gift of the revolutionary. Hitler is a revolutionary and mass leader with the medium's gift of thrall, a thrall in which he is himself caught. "Then came the great thrill of happiness," wrote the *Arbeitsmann* (organ of the National Socialist Labor Front) of the effect of the personality of the leader on the masses. Another impression: "I looked into his eyes and he into mine, and at that I had only one desire, to be at home and alone with that great, overwhelming experience." This extravagant outburst came not from an "intense" woman supporter but from a judge in a high position, talking to his colleagues. I can vouch for this case from my personal knowledge. "For I am among you, and ye are with me"—the leader must speak in a religious mood, in lapidary phrases that can be used with suggestive force. "Our divine service," wrote the newspapers of a party congress, "was a turning of the thoughts of each one of us to the root of all things, to the Great Mother. That was in truth divine service." In the eternal battle between light and darkness, acceptance and rejection of life (to quote Ley, the leader of the Labour Front), the German, with his new faith in the leader, is faced with the great decision. He is also faced with the lighting effects and the orders for applause, the special platform and all the other gadgets of a glamour-machine.

Hitler is deliberately and unceasingly held up to the masses as a deity. One of the principal devices for securing National Socialist dominance is this deification of the man, his raising to the altitude of the sole savior of the nation. "We all believe on this earth in Adolf Hitler, our leader"; "we acknowledge that National Socialism is the faith that alone can bring blessedness to our people." These are official pronouncements by the party élite. The Messiah-figure of the leader is the indispensable center of their propaganda, as carefully devised as the whole of the apparatus of power. Some time before the seizure of power a prominent National Socialist expressed to me his opinion that the figure of the leader must be withdrawn more and more into seclusion and surrounded with mystery. He must only come visibly into the presence of the nation by means of startling actions and rare speeches at critical moments in the national destiny. Except for that he must withdraw from view—just like the Creator behind creation—in order to heighten his effectiveness by his mysteriousness. The very rarity of his appearances would make them events. No great leader should wear out his greatness in the daily drudgery of administration. And, declared this old "Pg," he could conceive that at a critical turning-point in the national history the leader might be more deliriously effective if he were dead. He might even have to be sacrificed in order to complete his work. Sacrificed by his own Pg's, his own party comrades, and his faithful followers. Only when Hitler had really become a mythical figure would the whole depth of his magical influence reveal itself. All this I was told in perfect sincerity and conviction. It was spoken out of a genuine faith, which at that time still existed, in a spiritual mission entrusted to National Socialism.

Our age, said Burckhardt, readily indulges from time to time in the awe of adventurers and visionaries. We may add that it permits itself to be carried away by brutality in the guise of religious ecstasy, and by any storm over national and social affairs if it involves hatred of some third party. The effective principle in this is the "magic of extremism." In its presence, Burckhardt found, argument becomes completely impossible. Once more we may observe the degeneration that struck observers in the age of the decay of Hellenism—faces and figures grown ugly; nowhere any nobility, either of physical heritage or of intellect or of soul; no sign left of any inner struggle or any genuine repose; only eyes that flash for a moment and then are blind again; brutal expressions, sinister gestures, puffy or distorted features, the grimaces of the inane. The magic of leadership is magic primarily for such types as these. They reveal not only the "fury of partisanship" but the enviousness and the lust for domination of the lower middle class.

But this process of the mesmerizing of the masses is only made possible by the general revolutionary disintegration of all the genuine elements of national welfare and public order. Thus neither the devotion to the leader nor the faith in him is of purely artificial production. Their appearance is due less to the foisting of a "Messiah" on the masses than to the loss of validity of the old and genuine standards and allegiances. The question still remains how such immense dynamic power could proceed from petty and contemptible sources. It is characteristic of the present time that an appearance of gigantic achievements can be created with no basis in fact. The technical and organizing resources available enable any sort of phantasmagoria to be given for a time the semblance of reality. Politics are bound up to-day with the existence of a specialized "machinery."

THE MACHINERY

Darré, who stands out among the national leaders of National Socialism on account of his organizing ability, is head of the Reichsnährstand or National Food Estate. This agricultural organization was created relatively late by the party; Darré himself calls it the *"agrarpolitischer Apparat"* (political machinery for agricultural issues), or "aA" for short. In so doing he reveals the nature of all National Socialist organization. He had not the slightest intention in organizing the National Food Estate of creating anything resembling a true guild corporation, a real administrative body for the agricultural occupations. The Reichsnährstand is nothing but a machine for the complete control and direction of agricultural production and of the farming population itself by the party. Here, in the sector of agricultural policy, there was revealed at the outset the system which, thanks to Schacht, was extended much later, by means of currency control and the Four Year Plan, to the whole economic system of the country—the control and supervision of the whole field of trade and industry, as a means to the control of the population engaged in trade and industry. All the gigantic organizations created by the National Socialists, some during the "period of struggle," some after the revolution, are machines for the control of the whole life of the nation. These are not new self-governing bodies, not organs and links in the State or the social order: they are political machines, machines for control, for propaganda, for supervision, for terrorist dominance. They are machinery for the influencing of opinion, never organs of independent formation of opinion. They are machinery that conveys a drive always in one direction, from above downwards, from the central political control right down to the private household, right into the most intimate elements of family life. In this respect the National Socialist organizations differ from all other associations. They are mainly concerned with nothing else than the safeguarding of the resources of power with which the dominant élite exercises its dominion. They include also a number of checking systems which appear to the careless observer as a senseless duplication of the organization; in reality these are based on the principle of reciprocal supervision by rival parallel organizations. The "struggle for power" became a training of the harshest sort for the leaders of the party; not so much through the conflict between Socialist and anti-Socialist as through rivalry between groups in the élite. It has, perhaps, been the greatest feat of the National Socialist Party that it has preserved its organization intact and endured the load test of eight years of ostensible legality, while in its own ranks the rebellious revolutionists by temperament, the desperadoes and gangsters, the despairing patriots, the ambitious, and the idealogues carried on their personal intrigues and separate moves. In the competition for power within the party, for places and allies, in an absolutely nerve-wracking and soul-destroying struggle behind the scenes, the great tactical experience of the party has developed and the ideas for the building up of its organization have been clarified, becoming then, after the arrival in power, the principles of domination in public life.

It is unnecessary to give an elaborate description of the organization of the National Socialist Party, which to this day baffles even the German party member. A better idea of the nature of this truly gigantic effort may be obtained by a few reflections on the tasks the organizations have to fulfil as the machinery of domination, and on the way the ruling élite protects itself from the tendencies towards sectional independence within the party. Such tendencies are implicit in every organization, and might lead to dangerous splits, rivalries, cliques, and, in short, to a new party structure and so to the crippling of the whole machinery and the ending of unified control. I give here the essence of the instructions which are "hammered" again and again into the National Socialist officials of all grades all over the country. The need for them is frequently enough exemplified in the shortcomings of various prominent leaders, their weaknesses and kinks, which simply have to be put up with, and provided against by closer collaboration between all the organizations. The personal shortcomings of certain of the eminent members of the élite are discussed quite openly among the higher officials. They cynically admit the rivalries and mortal enmities between leaders; and they mention the tendency of leaders to form their own private armies as an entirely natural result of the existing system. But this admission of personal weaknesses is certainly itself no sign of weakness. What is of prime importance is the determination, in spite of these admitted weaknesses, under no circumstances to allow the unity of the party to be broken and the instrument of dominion to be thus destroyed.

Is National Socialism the "Salvation Army of German patriotism," as a cynical critic maintained? There is something in the idea. The movement has made the small traders and lower middle class its backbone, instead of the Storm Troopers. And the whole machinery of the party is built up out of lower middle class elements. But it would be a great mistake to overlook the essential feature of the organizations, their very practical and extremely effective character as instruments of dominion, as the machinery of continuous terrorism and repression. The tasks the machinery of domination has to fulfil are: the permanent revolutionizing of the mass of party followers, the keeping alive of their will to fight, and the maintenance of the dynamic character of the movement. The rank and file have to be kept continually on the move and continually under tension. They have to be controlled down to the smallest detail in their whole lives. They have to be kept entirely dependent and under supervision, and prevented from giving way to any undisciplined impulse of their own. Each member of the rank and file of the party must be made to associate his whole existence with the party, and to identify himself entirely with the party, by the continued fear that if he does not do so he will be robbed of his livelihood. The rank and file must be made to feel that they are continually under observation, and must be kept in continual restlessness and insecurity, in a permanent state of uneasy conscience and fear. These tasks yield certain principles of organization, which amount in the end to this: the machinery must be absolutely watertight, and it must embrace every side of life. There must be no zones of immunity.

A further principle, that of finding as far as possible some official duty for everybody, in order to keep everybody actively associated with the movement, and to create a universal sense of participation in direct action, is regarded as an "important link in the national community." Every part of men's lives is drawn into the field of party responsibilities, and in this way everyone's private existence is rooted in the party, his vital interests are bound up with the party for good or evil, and no one can do anything in independence of the party. It is the principle of the ubiquitousness of the party and the ending of individual private existence. In this way the instrument of power becomes also an eternally vigilant machinery of espionage.

A very important principle is that of twofold organization. For every group of duties parallel bodies are trained, to cover the same field of work from different sides, with the principal object of watching one another and holding one another in check by their rivalry. This principle is regarded as so important that it is carried through right up to the top. A further principle of organization is the delimitation and grading of the fields of work

of all party officials by the two regulative disciplines of leadership and blind obedience. The fact that every person in an official position in the party is harnessed to the disciplinary mechanism in several directions, participating both in the responsibility
of leadership and in the duty of absolute obedience, has developed
a very practical and tightly drawn system of supervision and
counter-supervision, from which no official can possibly escape.
Finally, this whole system is kept under observation by a secret
party tribunal and jurisdiction, completely independent of the
State, whose activities are supervised in turn by special inspectors. The whole gigantic apparatus is centered on the single
supreme individual; but his final decision is only needed in exceptional cases, the self-acting mechanism disposing of most matters
in lower stages of the hierarchy. Thus the whole machinery
remains free for all practical purposes for the transmission of
orders from above, and in critical matters from the supreme
leader, down to the extreme limits of the organized party. A
grandiose and certainly a unique instrument of the leader's
will.

Its gigantic scale and its absolute comprehensiveness are not
the products merely of an idle interest in organization, but of
a measure of necessity. Nothing in the whole machinery is
there for its own sake. With all its stages and ramifications, in
appearance a product of the German mania for organizing, the
system is really the result of no comprehensive scheme or idea;
it is simply the product of the needs of the years of struggle,
aimed at securing the personal power of the élite over their
own forces. It had the further aim of forming an all-comprehending instrument of dominion, of the maintenance of the power
of the dominant élite over the country, after the arrival in power.
These aims account also for the complete "co-ordination" with
the movement of all existing organizations, down to those of
the canary breeders and the stamp collectors. It would be an
altogether superficial view to regard all this as the mere outcome of personal ambition. In order to assure its power, National

Socialism could not afford to leave in freedom even the most insignificant zone, even an entirely unpolitical one. It was compelled for its own security to subject every sort of activity to its machinery of control, not because there was any need, for instance, for canaries to be trained on National Socialist lines, but because it was necessary that each individual should come up against the all-embracing party at every step, so as to be under direction and supervision and influence even in his hobbies.

This *Gleichschaltung* of old organs of a rich social and cultural life inevitably robbed them of all initiative and creative energy, and sooner or later they were bound to wilt in their captivity; but this did not disturb the new élite. Commercial and industrial associations may retain their usefulness even if they are organized less for the representation of the interests of their members than for the domination of those interests by a jealous party authority. Their practical tasks will still have to be determined on definite lines. But associations that owe their existence not to any necessity but to free choice, all the cultural, social, humanitarian associations which placed their wealth of creative effort in the service of the advance of civilization, can have no function as instruments of domination and are doomed from the moment when they are *gleichgeschaltet.**

This leads us at once to the question how any machinery of domination of this sort can continue indefinitely to function. A nation and society thus brought into bondage is bound with mathematical certainty to lose its creative capacity. It is bound to do so quite apart from the unendurability of the intense and continuous effort demanded of every person by the party organization. Even the élite will not keep it up, and most certainly not the mass of the population. Sooner or later after any revolution the time is bound to come when the newly arrived upper class it has created must modify and relax the totalitarian apparatus of power. The question will then arise whether it has so accustomed the country to its rule that it no longer needs

---

* Co-ordinated, or, to abandon euphemisms, made to "toe the line."—Translator.

the complete machinery. But the "dynamic" or continuing revolution seems in this respect again to have its own peculiar character. It is a permanent movement for the sake of continuing change, and it cannot abandon its revolutionary character. So long as the movement remains, it cannot dispense with its apparatus of power, cannot rely on reconciling the country to its dominion. All hopes of any gradual abandonment in the Third Reich of the system of compulsion, of any scrapping of the machinery of domination, are thus illusory.

The confidence of the National Socialists in their hierarchy is not justified. A critical situation will inevitably develop, with a further degeneration of the dictatorship. We may at once point to a weakness which will not be removed either by the National Socialist groups in the factories or by the counter-revolutionary cadres of the S.S. (the "Black Guards"), or even by the subtle safety device of the party judicature. The greatest weakness in this instrument of power lies exactly where the party sees strength—in its totalitarianism and centralization. The system might lose and replace subordinate elements, but it certainly cannot afford to lose its head. It is thus conceivable that the whole gigantic apparatus of power might collapse in a night in complete impotence through a single mishap, might fall into an amorphous heap of debris, without a trace of life left in any of its sections. The federative principle and the delegation of power to free and independent bodies in genuine self-government do not mean decadence; they are the indispensable condition of any high standard of state and social life. They are also the first condition of the permanence of any system of public order. Such domination as that of the parvenu groups of National Socialist leaders may be able to last for a few years with the aid of their apparatus of violence. But the day will come when National Socialism will reach its end, and then it will give place to a true system of public order; or else the nation will itself come to ruin under National Socialism. There is yet another circumstance that must not be overlooked. Sooner or later a rule of this sort must come to grief owing to the character of its officials.

THE TACTICS OF DOMINATION

Next after the hierarchy in the means of dominion come the methods of forcible disciplining and of destruction of the earlier elements of orderly government. In this connection it would be natural to consider all the methods of violence, old or newly elaborated, which are used by modern revolutions—concentration camps, political terrorism, the secret police system, the employment of special cadres of the party for purposes of intimidation; and also the more subtle methods of spreading fear and of breaking men's character and independence. I must refrain, however, from pursuing this subject in detail, since the modern methods reveal such subtlety and such inventiveness that it would be necessary to quote concrete cases in order to bring conviction to readers in general. The time will not fail to come when this part of the story becomes generally known. After the events of June 30th, 1934, a high official of the Gestapo (the secret police) horrified at what had happened, said to me in Berlin that he wished that a happy fate might preserve the German people from ever learning the truth. Perhaps it is not right to wish this. In any case, merely to mention these things is to bring oneself under the suspicion of carrying on atrocity propaganda and consequently to destroy the value of what one has to say. I must leave it to some experienced police official to write the necessary specialist work on modern methods of violence, on the comprehensive system of public cruelty which has been elaborated. I will devote only a few words to the National Socialist tactics of domination.

National Socialism pursues in general a fairly uniform plan in this field, but varies it in detail in relation to particular groups of persons. The art of carrying on an interrogation, the technique of tiring out an intellectual and upsetting his nervous balance, the adjustment to idealists or to the characteristics of persons of lower middle class extraction, are already a regular tactical system. There is no softness or urbanity or cautious leading up to the point; the method is always to pounce on the victim, to corner him, startle him, browbeat him, and in general to rely on roughness.

At the back of all National Socialist activities is a thoroughly marked preference for immoral methods. The immoral course is always more effective, because it is more violent. The immoral course also gives the illusion of strength and daring in persons who are merely underhand by choice. It is a fundamental principle of National Socialist tactics to strike fear by deliberate and pronounced incivility and violence, and by making a show of readiness to go to any length, where the same purpose could be achieved without difficulty by milder means. But National Socialism is never single-mindedly in pursuit of anything; it always has the additional aim of further shaking the existing order with every success it gains. Its robust methods are deliberately calculated. And most of the roughness of manners and habits and of the barbaric style of government aims at producing the illusion of an elemental strength which the system does not in reality possess, an illusion for which there is no need where a certain reserve of strength is always in hand.

This preference for violence as the typical revolutionary method is not inconsistent with the crafty and very successful appeal of National Socialism to the lower middle class self-righteousness. Its violent character is only superficially inconsistent with its practice of posing always as the champion of justice, denouncing wrongs that cry aloud to heaven. Everything it does is represented as done simply in the defence of a sacred right and a moral mission. It could beat its breast, for instance, over the detention camp in which National Socialists were placed in Austria, as though there were no atrocities in the German concentration camps, and could denounce the intention it alleged of falsifying the Austrian plebiscite with an assumption of supreme unconsciousness of its own terrorist methods. Every lie is adorned with a show of virtue. Always National Socialism is defending a right, always pursuing honor and faith. Moral indignation comes next after brutality in the National Socialist armory of effective propaganda. It takes the place of reasoned argument. The revolution is true to type in its eternal moralizing, in its defence of "virtue" like the great French Revolution, in its sentimentality and emotionality. Its "Leader" always has sobs and tears at his command, exciting wrathful derision in the old militants of the party. This assumption of virtue and morality falls short, it is true, of the primitive naïveté of a genuine revolution. In its insincerity it is entirely in character with the brutality and the cynical amorality revealed in the everyday activities of the National Socialists.

Should terrorism produce discontent, there is always a public enemy to be discovered. Public indignation is poured over him from time to time, so that collective outbursts of rage may provide a diversion for accumulating private resentment. To provide continual diversions, and never to leave the citizen to himself with nothing to do, is another tactical rule of general application. It is an effectual method of treatment not only for the masses but for all opponents, including opponents abroad of German foreign policy. Keep people busy, give them something to think about, startle them, never allow them time for reflection; always lie in wait, ready to pounce; always take the initiative and so maintain the lead.

Hitler's very realistic estimation of the masses was revealed in *Mein Kampf*. It may be said in general that at the back of the whole tactics and method of propaganda of National Socialism there is a complete contempt of humanity: the whole system is based on taking men as they are and pandering to their weakness and their bestiality. Such is its universal recipe. National Socialism banks on human sloth and timidity—just as much in the case of the intellectuals, the middle classes, and the old ruling classes, as with the masses. It does so especially with foreign countries. In Germany it yields a much more effective means of domination than would the exclusive dependence on terrorism. The exploitation of envy and ill-will, of the lowest human instincts, the sowing of dissension between opponents, and the appeal to their ignoble qualities and notorious weaknesses have thus far unfailingly helped National Socialism to success, incidentally destroying the basis of a general sense of morality which was weak enough to begin with.

The system owes its internal strength to the general voluntary co-operation in the work of the secret police, the general acceptance of denunciation as a patriotic duty. But the completely amoral regime of National Socialism steadily ignores the fact that this resort to the worst of human motives, and to the extreme of brutality and violence, to hatred, vengeance, envy, ill-will, to licentiousness, to robbery, to lying on principle, its resort to all these motives and methods has set in motion a ruin of the national character on a scale hitherto unimaginable, which must inevitably recoil in the end on the ruling élite themselves. The élite are clearly untroubled by the dangers of this whole course, because in spite of their bombastic declamations about the thousand years of their "Third Reich" they have a very strong subconscious sense that their furious, hysterical onward drive has not a very long course ahead of it. In any case, the greatest statesmanship could not set up a "revolutionary new order of this world" on a nihilistic moral foundation of this sort.

The Reichstag fire, organised for political purposes by party members on the instructions of German Ministers, is a thoroughly illuminating example of the method universally adopted by the party. It is the party's special device, applicable universally. Crimes are arranged and attributed to opponents. The people are kept in a state of fear, utterly intimidated. At the same time they are stirred up into a blaze of indignation, given the sense that they have been saved from destruction, and made to feel thankful to a strong regime that gives them security. Hundreds of times this plan is carried out on varying scales. National Socialism is always ready to make play with its Bolshevist propaganda-bogey on a vast scale. The nation is kept in a state of alarm, and meanwhile, in the same breath, the regime takes credit for the maintenance of peace and order. Few things are more characteristic of the regime than its unscrupulous, lying glorification of an existing law and order which it destroys or publicly insults by whatever it does.

One word, finally, on the simplest and most elementary, but perhaps most effective and most characteristic method of domination employed by National Socialism—the marching. At first this marching seemed to be a curious whim of the National Socialists. These eternal night marches, this keeping of the whole population on the march, seemed to be a senseless waste of time and energy. Only much later was there revealed in it a subtle intention based on a well-judged adjustment of ends and means. Marching diverts men's thoughts. Marching kills thought. Marching makes an end of individuality. Marching is the indispensable magic stroke performed in order to accustom the people to a mechanical, quasi-ritualistic activity until it becomes second nature. No less an authority than the pseudo-German Rosenberg, in his *Gestaltung der Idee*, has given the classic explanation of this occupation with marching: "The German nation is simply out to discover at last its own style of living, a style of living that is fundamentally distinguished from what is called British Liberalism. . . . It is the style of a marching column, no matter where or to what end this marching column may be directed." At the back of all these night marches, marches out, marches back, these mass demonstrations and parades, was the consideration that the sense of primitive community through functional integration is created and fostered by marching in columns, military drill, military evolutions, the rhythm of a host in step. Nothing could show more shockingly, more grimly and indeed spectrally, the utter emptiness of a political movement and its concentration on mere externals than this elevation of marching to be its motto and essential principle. We have it here admitted that the nation is marching aimlessly, just

for the sake of marching. It is a confession of the lack of any
sort of doctrine in this revolution for revolution's sake, this
hustling activity just to distract men's minds.

A PHILOSOPHY FOR SHOW

It is perhaps not generally known, at all events I do not remember any public mention of the feature, that Hitler has a deep
respect for the Catholic church and the Jesuit order; not because of their Christian doctrine, but because of the "machinery"
they have elaborated and controlled, their hierarchical system,
their extremely clever tactics, their knowledge of human nature,
and their wise use of human weaknesses in ruling over believers.
Hitler wants to see the points of the National Socialist program regarded as analogous to the Church's venerable *Credo*,
the confession of faith. He is aware that for fifteen hundred
years the Church has withstood all assaults from logical criticism on its ancient creed. He sees that anything can be done
with a creed of that sort, no matter how irrational or inconsistent. The flock of believers will accept anything, and will listen
to no reasoned opposition. But there is one thing that, he knows,
must never be done: no change must ever be made in a creed, even
if the creed no longer has any practical significance in men's lives,
if it is no more than an ancient monument. Any change would
only perplex and unsettle the faithful.

These considerations must be borne in mind in examining the
National Socialist philosophy. What the National Socialist
leaders require is just the opposite of what a non-revolutionary
leader needs: the more inconsistent and irrational is their doctrine, the better; the more sharply defined are its outlines. Only
the inconsistent has vitality. The National Socialist leaders know
that their followers can only take in details, that the masses can
never see the wood for the trees. Anyone capable of appreciat-
ing generalizations must either be brought into the élite or fought
as an intellectual, a Liberal. Thus, in the elaboration of the
National Socialist philosophy everything that might have gone

to the making up of a systematic, logically conceived doctrine is dismissed as a trifle, with sovereign contempt. And anything that seemed useful has been incorporated, whether or not it was logically consistent with what was already in the program.

But the much-discussed "philosophy" of National Socialism needs also to be considered in relation to historic tendencies in men's ideas if its actual revolutionary bases and its practical aim are to be understood. One effective element was considered to be a real belief in a new myth that can take the place of Christianity, to serve the needed rejuvenation of the nation. But it was considered no less important to bear in mind the practical indispensability of a philosophy for show. The present-day "philosophy" is certainly a very diluted substitute—the dilution was very necessary—for Hitler's first vague and tentative ideas for one of stupendous grandeur. Here again Hitler felt himself called upon to proclaim the true doctrine to the German nation of the future. But the essential element in the philosophy of to-day is that it is a very effective and an indispensable means of revolutionary destruction of the old order. Consequently it has long been no more than an instrument in the hands of the élite of the party. This élite has passed beyond all belief even in its own substitute for a logical system, and has fallen into complete nihilism. It has accordingly, in the main, turned away from its leader in his capacity of prophet. It may be that the leader is already no more than an isolated, antiquated requisite of the earlier period of the growth of the revolution, destined ultimately to be of no further use except as a stage property.

In any case, all these things are merely things for show, means of propaganda, doctrines foisted cynically on the nation by an élite who are themselves completely indifferent to them. The brilliant achievement which National Socialism managed to palm off as its philosophy developed was the grafting of all sorts of different fruits on the stem of the common crab-apple planted at the time of its first meetings in the vaults of a suburban beer-house in Munich. There were all the elements of the patriotic summons to the defence of the country, taken over from the last years of the world war. Clearly associated with these were the ideas of the pan-German, "racial" policy. These two conglomerates of ideas were among the earliest stock of the original nucleus of the party. Two further ideas had to be brought in with some difficulty, for they were diametrically opposed to one another. One was the Socialist re-ordering of society, and the other the return to monarchy and to the dominance of the old ruling classes. Traditionalist and nationalist ideas had to be brought in, such as the Prussian spirit, with which great play was made later on, at the Potsdam congress of the party. Middle class nationalism, with its keen interest in the traditions of the State, had to be worked in, and attention paid to the hereditary standards of the army officers. Finally, account had to be taken of the outlook of the Christian churches; room had to be found for the ideas and aspirations of the farmers, the artisans, and the small employers; and above all, attention had to be paid to the youth of the country.

All these considerations formed the framework of the National Socialist philosophy, which next had to be set out, as a matter of the first importance, in fiery phrases that would work on the masses and serve as the starting points for continual appeals to the emotions, in order to produce intoxication and ecstatic response. Everything had to be brought in that appealed to the indignation or aroused the enthusiasm of each person present at the meetings, each member or follower of the party, producing a fluid, anonymous crowd, open at all times to the force of suggestion. "Talk in generalities," was the continually repeated instruction from the National Socialist leaders in the "period of struggle," in every field of propaganda, big and little. Talk in generalities above all at times of threatening crisis, with signs of unrest. And never enter into discussions, never attempt to be informative, never appeal to good will or to sober reflection. Speak in terms of innuendo, of menace, whip up enthusiasm by showing it, storm, appeal, promise, talk of the great supermundane mission of National Socialism. No details, no concrete promises. Such were the instructions. And they were justified by results; they showed the National Socialist "philosophy" working successfully. Concrete promises divide, generalities unite. So effectively, so undiscriminatingly, in such elementary terms, intelligible to the most simple-minded of propaganda corporals, was the philosophical training imparted. Its supreme purpose was the collecting of the crowd, the emptying of its mind, the rousing of its feelings, the summons to a pretended higher existence, on a heroic scale; or to a happiness as one of a herd—Strength through Joy, Beauty of Labor, Enjoy Life. Simple but effective, for it is not meant for the despised intellectual, who is no more than an odd individual here and there, but for the masses, to place them under a spell and lead them by the nose.

There can be no denying the evidence of all these necessary ingredients in the so-called philosophy of National Socialism. It bears the scars of its past history in the totally contradictory ideas of its spiritual forefathers. In the words of Mephisto, it collects anything and everything for stuffing into the respectable citizen's cranium, and succeeds in "uniting great-heartedness with guile." It is not a whole, and it is absurd to treat it as a whole. It is of functional importance only, a means and nothing more. It is the main element in propaganda. The question to be asked of it is not its meaning but its purpose. It serves mainly for the propagation, in a form assimilable by the masses, of revolutionary aims which can be harbored at first hand only by a small élite. The function of the philosophy is to keep alive the fighting character of the movement. "Train them in the philosophy," "constantly impress on the men the fighting character of our movement," "when we have won, our real fight will be only beginning"—these were the instructions given over and over again to the National Socialist propagandists during the so-called *Kampfzeit*, the "period of struggle" (for power). "Dynamism" is kept alive in the masses only in the form of permanent pugnacity. The masses tend all the time to grow slack, and need constant stimulating. Nothing is of more importance to National Socialism than the possession of "enemies," objects on which this pugnacity can sharpen its claws. This is the root explanation of such senseless and horrible myths as that of the totally evil character of the Jews. If there is no other enemy available there is always the Jew, whose despised figure can always be made to serve as fuel for the fighting spirit, and at the same time to keep alive the happy feeling of belonging to the company of the elect. Whenever during the "period of struggle" the attention of the masses had to be turned away from existing problems, or simply when it was desirable to rouse the fighting spirit of the followers of the movement, the Jew-Freemason record was regularly set going.

All these elements, so primitive and threadbare in their psychology, are nevertheless thoroughly effective in practice. It would be a great mistake to suppose that so cunning an individual as the German Minister of Propaganda is not perfectly well aware that the atrocity propaganda against the Jews, including the "Protocols of the Elders of Zion," is preposterous nonsense, that he does not see through the racial swindle just as clearly as those compatriots of his whom it has driven out of their country. It would be simply foolish to imagine that any member of the élite truly and sincerely believes in the bases of the "philosophy." They have been deliberately concocted for their demagogic effectiveness and for the furtherance of the party's political aims. They have also been chosen with a cunning realization of the needs of the masses and particularly of the German masses. Other representations of good and evil, of hero and weakling, may "work" in other countries; the selection for Germany was already indicated by the experience of the pan-Germans and the anti-Semitic "racial" parties. They had proved already the effectiveness of anti-Semitism and of racial mystification with the masses.

The popular attractiveness of nationalist ideas of expansion by conquest had also been revealed even before the War. All that National Socialism did was to work up these ideas, already propagated among the middle classes under the past regime, into yet more demagogically effective shape.

In recent years there have been important and growing changes. Not only the leaders, but the masses, and the army of minor officials, have been brought face to face with realities. The elemental force of a revolution transforming the whole life and outlook of the country is breaking through the papier mâché world of make-believe and semi-romanticism, and revealing to every man, no matter how eager his desire for a secure existence, the impossibility of reversing the engine or even of stopping it. No one to-day can resist the impression—sincere supporters of the regime regretfully admit it in confidence—that this platform philosophy is betraying a staleness that prevents it from stirring up revolutionary enthusiasm any longer even in the best-drilled mass demonstration. The philosophy is beginning to reveal its insincerity. It is losing its propaganda value as a means of suggestion. It is becoming an actual stumbling block for the followers. It is revealing, in such persons as the Jew-baiter Julius Streicher, the lower middle class character of its origin. The question for the future will be whether the party can survive a gradual modification of its philosophy, whether, while retaining essential parts of the old philosophy, it can introduce harder, more masculine elements, closer to the kernel of the actual doctrine of dynamism, of direct action, of violence, and develop a new myth, perhaps of Social Revolutionary type. Beyond question, for the new recruits, the youthful elements, the old tune has lost its catchiness. Party members are beginning to laugh at the Leader's spiritual outpourings, his sermons on art, his mediocre German, his crude economics. Party leaders are getting apprehensive about his speeches: they are "dreadful." Only among the faithful laity are they still taken seriously as revelations of supreme wisdom.

THE ROAD TO NIHILISM

THE REVOLUTION WITHOUT A DOCTRINE

It is paradoxical, and must seem illogical, to describe a movement which comes before the world in the heavy armor of a comprehensive and absolutely binding philosophy as a revolution without a doctrine. Yet the recognition of this fact is the first and most fundamental condition for the ending of the present situation in Germany.

It is certainly difficult to liberate oneself from the popular conception and to realize that the philosophy of National Socialism has not the quality of doctrine, of a rational body of principles for the German revolution. But there will be still more objection to the view that not even the nationalist pan-German tendencies of the movement have any longer a foremost place in present-day German aims. It is, of course, possible to bring forward overwhelming evidence that nationalist objectives influence the internal politics of the existing regime, as well as its foreign policy. But the National Socialist revolution is not confined to these nationalist tendencies; they represent only the first, preparatory phase in the struggle for power. National Socialism has reaped the benefit of the justified national agitation for liberation from the Treaty of Versailles and its dictated provisions. It has also reaped the benefit of the militarist and pan-German ideas and aspirations in leading circles of the army and of the civil population. But these are not the whole of its aims. It makes use of them for their effect as elements in the spreading of revolutionary feeling, but its aims stretch far beyond them, and to-day it regards them as elements of minor importance. National Socialism is not a nationalist movement but a revolution, a process of destruction, making an end even of nationalist conceptions and achievements. The revolution owes its nationalist appearance to the facts that it began as a nationalist movement and that it achieved the first great steps in home and foreign policy under the banner of nationalism.

It is necessary to realize the completely new character of the modern doctrineless revolution. It is necessary to get away from the idea that what still attracts the principal attention both of opponents and of adherents of National Socialism represents the essential element in what is happening in Germany. It will have to be realized that what is more likely is that we are at the outset of a movement with incalculable possibilities of development. At present it is nothing but destruction, the dissolution and annihilation of the old elements of public order. It is destroying everything it lays its hands on. What positive qualities it has, what sort of a function it might have in the building up of a new order, nobody can yet say. What it calls its new order is nothing but a vast misuse of the human aspiration for ordered conditions. Those who still rest their hopes on the reactionary character of National Socialist dynamism will be just as deluded as the genuine Socialists who fail to realize its nihilistic and revolutionary character, and consequently are at cross-purposes in their fight against it.

National Socialism has not only destroyed the achievements and the past power of the working class, a fact that might justify its description as a counter-revolutionary movement; it has also destroyed the political and social power of the capitalist class and of the former ruling classes of society. It is also proceeding to the total and irrevocable destruction of the economic position of those classes. The National Socialist revolution is thus at least two things at once—social revolution and counter-revolution. This implies, however, that in the strict sense of the words it is neither.

In our day there are no longer any revolutions in the sense of liberation through a doctrine. In the realm of nihilism there can be none. Nihilism, as the total rejection of any sort of doctrine, must develop of necessity by its own logic into an absolute despotism. The development from Leninism, the backbone of which was, after all, an unshaken belief in human reason, to Stalinism, the expression of total nihilism, has been logically and historically inevitable. In the last two decades the destruction of the last of human political valuations has been complete. By many of the older generation, with their firm faith in rationalism, the process has not been realized. But in this period the tendency to complete moral scepticism has not only destroyed the last vestiges of human valuations in the element of theory, but has produced a complete rejection of every sort of doctrine in practical affairs. This fact is masked, it is true, by the fact that political nihilism has dressed itself up in the paradox of an absolutely binding, more or less rationally argued, "philosophy" or doctrine, which it has raised virtually to a religion. But the variety of the doctrines and philosophies of the revolutions that have broken out in various countries cannot conceal their essentially uniform character of totally despotic and totally destructive systems.

It might be tempting to demonstrate a close relationship between Fascism, Bolshevism, and National Socialism, to describe each of them as a special type of the dynamic movement, the doctrineless revolution, and to find distinctions between them only in the degrees and shades of their revolutionary impulse, or in the historical occasion of their initial phase. It is not long since the leader of Fascism himself arrived at the conclusion that Stalinism represents the development of Bolshevism into a sort of Fascism, the Fascism, it is true, of a Genghiz Khan. This assessment is justified in so far as Stalinism is nothing more than the jettisoning of the Communist doctrine of the Russian revolution and its development into something else. One thing is certain: the German movement is only at the outset of its revolutionary career, while Stalinism seems already to have come to the end of a career. There are, at all events, essential features common to all three of the European anti-democratic movements. But their anti-democratic political and social order does not necessarily imply a common revolutionary attitude.

There is, however, another bond of union between the three anti-democratic dictatorships, the constantly growing belief that a complete overthrow of all existing institutions is the indispensable prelude to a national renaissance. It is especially among the younger generation that the new ideas are widespread and vitally operative, the idea that all doctrines, nationalist and socialist alike, have become out-of-date and meaningless, and the idea that all that is necessary is devotion to the revolutionary movement for its own sake, a movement that is its own meaning and purpose, as the outlet to a new, unknown and dangerous life, but at all costs a life of strength and energy. These young people already see the one essential common element in the great revolutionary processes in their destructive character, and they no longer attach any importance to the doctrines that divide them. They have already got beyond the narrow limits of nationalism and imperialism, but they have also dismissed the dogmatic theories of a "just" social order as the source of earthly happiness. They see life's meaning in its perils, life's purpose as domination, the means as violence, and the goal as the world-wide totalitarian empire.

The Permanent Revolution

THE RENEWAL OF THE ELITE

WHAT is the élite? Who belong to it? From what sources is it kept up to strength? It is not surprising if the oligarchies of the new despotic systems are seated less firmly in their positions of power than those of the older and better balanced systems of government. Bolshevism is not alone in suffering the annihilation of the whole of its old guard, all of the old and tried revolutionaries. Hitler, in his speech of July 13th, 1934, called the élite of his revolutionary bands, who had been destroyed by his order on June 30th, "sons of chaos." In that speech he made the statement that there were bodies of paid revolutionary troops "whose character and purpose in life were illuminated by nothing more effectively than by the simply appalling lists of convictions of elements that had been admitted into them." In what respect do the present élite differ from the standard of those personal opponents of Hitler's? Hess, the Deputy to the Leader, thought fit, in a speech to a soldier audience, to appeal for sympathetic indulgence toward the weaknesses of certain of the older members of the National Socialist élite, working up to the argument that but for these excellent members, with all their defects, officers and army would not be there and Germany would not be where she then stood. Those who accepted the new Germany and National Socialism must accept the National Socialist élite.

They must be taken as they were: the German national revolution stood or fell with them.

Was this true? The youth of the nation does not think so. Nor does the working class, which still exists as a class. And the many members of the old upper class, who entered the cadres of the élite organizations, especially the S.S., in order to regain within the National Socialist movement, in the upper grades of its hierarchy, the positions they had lost as a social class—they, too, do not think so. Hess's apologia for the old élite before the corps of officers was in consonance with the attitude of the Party Leader, who had come very reluctantly to the decision to decimate his Storm Troop élite. It was not, in the main, any lack of resolution on Hitler's part, of determination to free himself by a drastic but necessary move from the dross that had collected along his upward path, that made him hesitate to remove the Sons of Chaos until it was almost too late; it was rather the clear recognition that only these elements, this collection of accomplices, would be loyal to him to the uttermost, in consequence of their dependence on him; that it was essentially these parvenus, bound to him for good or evil, who buttressed the foundations of his power, and that he might fall with them.

It is highly probable that in Germany, as in Russia, the time will come for the total elimination of the old élite by the inevitable liquidator of the first phase of the revolution, or, rather, of the second phase, if we regard the first as that in which the masses had faith in the party, the faith which was shattered by the events of June 30th, 1934. The party has tried to solve the problem of the recruitment of its élite by a revival of the idea of orders, on the lines of the old Teutonic Order. The practical outcome has been a system of selection of leaders that at most produces officials for the less exalted positions. That is not enough to provide for the maintenance and replenishment of the élite. A revolution can only continue in being through the replacement of its élite by revolutionary methods, and it is almost a law of revolutionary progression from one stage to the next that it takes place through the entire replacement of an old élite by a new one. No one knows that better than the youth of the party; but the old élite are not unaware of it. That is why the Leader tried to bring the revolution to an end. In place of revolutionary selection of the new élite he arranged for the training of young leaders in his *Ordensburgen*, fortresses of a sort of new Teutonic Order, and for a system of selection based on the old capitalist lines of patronage and nepotism.

The revolution cannot be ended, however, by decree, but only by the fulfilment of its purpose, by exhaustion, or by a return to the past—or, perhaps, only by all three combined. It is certain that the initiator and first representative of a revolution cannot be its liquidator. Meanwhile the forces that produced the revolution are still operative, but can operate only within the phase attained and in the new revolutionary environment. That is to say, new forces are determined to make their way ahead. No doctrine is needed to push on the process of radicalization. Personal motives also help to keep it up. The groups who begin the new struggle for power and for the key positions develop the theories that serve their ends. It may be said already that there are two sources from which factors of a revolutionary overthrow of the old élite are beginning to collect—the extremist youth and the working class. The old élite may succeed in holding on to power for a considerable time yet; they may do so by themselves appropriating the doctrine of their rivals and so robbing it of its polemical value. Then the Opposition will produce further slogans.

This development will be complicated or entirely interrupted if war should come. Certainly the prospect of checking by a war the process of radicalization within the revolution will be one of the main considerations that will make the idea of war attractive to the old élite. Quite different will be the situation of the younger members of the former ruling classes, who are entering the important cadres of the Storm Troops and by now have won an influence that is not to be despised, and at all events a basis of increasing power. This retrogressive movement within the machinery of the revolution may be of some importance to the future. It is producing a sort of restoration of the old ruling groups on the new revolutionary plane. These elements have a decided tendency to retard the radicalization of the revolution. They are conservative elements, tending to preserve and safeguard the existing situation in the party, to keep in power the élite actually in possession of power. This effect has manifestly been perceived by the more far-seeing of the National Socialist leaders. Otherwise it would be impossible to understand the active recruiting from among monarchist circles for the cadres of the élite that has been plainly evident, with the result that not a few younger sons have entered these cadres. The parvenu élite is trying to buttress its own position in power, won against a competition that remains very active, by giving the old ruling classes a personal interest in a share of the power. The essential condition imposed is lip-service to the National Socialist philosophy, which for the initiated covers a very unprincipled form of contemporary realism. It will, in any case, be important to watch this development closely. It is being steadily pushed on from both sides, by the National Socialist leaders and by the monarchists. It tends towards the idea of an evolution of National Socialism in the direction of monarchism, an idea that has not yet been abandoned.

In this way conflicts of opinion are being generated which might eventually split the movement, and might even lead to something like civil war. Here everything is in flux and any forecast is almost impossible. One thing is certain, that among the opposition groups that are competing for power, and among the members of the old ruling classes who are entering the élite at the price of a declaration of loyalty to the new regime, the pretended doctrine and philosophy of National Socialism go for nothing. What is going on is a struggle for power, an underground struggle, which one day may come into the open, between new parties, new "organizations for rule by violent means." And another thing is certain, that to all appearance the old élite is used up, helpless, absolutely incompetent and behind the times. Only in exceptional cases are leading members of the élite equal to their jobs. The majority are inefficient. The class of the population from which the great bulk of the first élite sprang, the small shopkeeper class, which is also the class from which the bulk of the faithful came, is unequal to the task of replacing the doomed élite.

THE YOUNG GENERATION

The young generation intend to live their own life, and not to spend it serving as understrappers to keep the present parvenus in power. Only the dull and spiritless ones among them are ready to accept things as they are. The active-minded youth are full of the sense of their opportunity and their mission; they consider that their part is to carry the revolution to the completion they envisage, to achieve world revolution. They are certainly anti-intellectual; they are even more rabid anti-rationalists than the present élite.

It is a long road but a direct one that leads from the pre-war youth movement through the war generation and successive post-war stages to the revolutionary youth of to-day. The "mission" of the young generation becomes more and more radical, revolutionary, and independent. Its most radical and powerful interpreter up to now has been Ernst Jünger; his revolutionary interpretation of the present time gives expression to the revolt of youth, but at the same time it reveals a total reversal of the outlook and purpose of the youth movement. That movement started with the aim of returning to primordial human nature, of living the simple life of the natural man, of preserving unfettered personality; it declared its essential purpose to be the bursting of all the bonds of a mechanized order of society; and it is ending in the total bondage of a revolutionary despotism in which all nature has been mechanized and every element is chained to a technical process. But every fulfilment of a revolutionary

63

instinct is blind to its final *volte-face;* every revolutionary instinct feels that it is achieving fulfilment when it attains its exact opposite.

The youth movement which we all know, the movement to which we all belonged in our time as senior schoolboys, was the first start of the revolutionary dynamism which to-day is culminating in the doctrineless revolution and turning into its own opposite. One is tempted to regard the years in which this movement started as marking a deep and radical cleavage in the general mental outlook. The generations which personally took part in the youth movement are able to understand and sympathize with many impulses with which the older generations, which had no personal experience of that first escape from the trammels of conventional existence, have no sympathy. Even the oldest ex-members of the youth movement, now in their fifties, are capable of a fellow-feeling for the youngest of the post-war generations. It is their common anti-Liberalism, their more or less radical rejection of the capitalist outlook on life, that unites all who have passed through adolescence since the turn of the century. The youthful restlessness of the original movement may have turned into a revolutionary restlessness of a very brutal sort, but there is no doubt that beneath the "hiking" for its own sake, or the urge to get on the move in order to still the inner revolutionary unrest, and to-day's random revolutionary dynamism with its rage for marching, there are deep common elements. I cannot pursue them, although in this very field there is sounder instruction to be had about what is actually going on among us than in the purely political field. Had this youth movement deceived itself as to its true nature when it thought that its urge to escape from conventionality could be satisfied by return to a pre-Liberal era? Was it really in search of the traditions of a class assumed to be close to nature, the peasantry, was it in search of the virtues of guild or corporative life, or the virtues of a genuine and national-minded Conservatism, or the concentration on all that was essentially German? Or was the new sense of life, the inner restlessness and desire for fulfilment, a continual readiness for change, growth, rejuvenation, a sense of life that was consciously anti-rational, producing the organization of a new sort of comradely association, an order based on leadership and vassalage? In these early preliminary stages of the "awakening" the division existed already between a pursuit of a genuine ordering of life out of the elements of our recent past, and a radical, revolutionary urge that threw State and society back to the primitive origins of a tribe with its headman and his followers.

After the world war, after the tremendous experience of life in the trenches, this movement turned to politics, finding renewal and growth through the *Bünde*, or brotherhoods. The change was confined to youths from middle class homes, and this fact set limits to its influence, but at the same time it had a disintegrating effect on the middle class which a proletarian movement would not have had. The revolutionary elements within the middle class came together in the youth movement and its *Bünde*, and began to destroy the middle class from within. But it was only through political association with the National Socialist Storm Troops, which had but a superficial resemblance to the *Bünde*, that elements of the youth movement made their contribution to the spirit of the new doctrineless dynamism. It is doubtful whether the anti-capitalist youth of middle class origin could have entered into a fruitful association with the proletarian youth. In any case no such association was attempted. But the revolutionary urge that came from the ruined middle class elements, a new social no-man's-land, from which the revolutionary élite of the National Socialist movement was largely recruited, had certainly something in common with the irrational urge of the youth associations. Both groups also talked the same nationalist language. These youths who once belonged to the middle class had passed through a sort of national revulsion of feeling in the war. They alone had been fighting for an ideal in the war. When they carried their principles into politics, they appeared to come to grief. They were uninterested in party concerns and party rivalries; these they regarded as typically capitalist matters. Thus the logic of events brought the youth movement into National Socialism, to which in turn it brought a few genuine impulses.

One thing the youth of the *Bünde* had never been—part and parcel of the State. The youth of to-day are also firmly in opposition to official National Socialism. They not only despise the methods of despotism and the crude doctrines of National Socialist philosophy, but feel that they are themselves destined to carry to completion the great revolutionary movement whose first phase they regard as ended and whose first élite they regard as out-of-date and incompetent. Whether this new generation has real qualities and special gifts that justify all this self-confidence is another question. The essential point is that National Socialism has not won over the youth, and that in its youth it is faced with its first important opponents, arguing not from the standards of the past but from the tasks of the future. The tendencies among the youth are, it is true, conflicting, and it is difficult for the outsider to assess the relative strength of the various shades of opinion. Youth speaks its own language. But this much may be taken for certain, that the youth are agreed that the stage thus far attained is at best to be regarded as a preparatory phase.

THE SECOND PHASE OF THE REVOLUTION

Perhaps there is a tendency in every revolution to a second phase, or to the final consummation of the revolutionary program. In the Third Reich this second phase owes its importance to the fact that it is quietly establishing itself by carrying out its practical tasks. As yet the army is preserving an open attitude toward this new movement. The army leaders are overburdened with professional duties; the older generation among them are undecided and divided in opinion. But the younger ones are filled with the utmost confidence and energy, and are equally critical of the past methods of the Third Reich and of the old traditions of the Prussian officers' corps. The army leaders will be compelled before long to make up their minds: the spirit of the new movement has much in common with their own traditions, but they find everything that is utterly repulsive to every soldier in the un-Prussian, unmilitary, hazy, rhetorical emotionalism and dilettantism of the present regime of the déclassés.

It would be satisfying to be able to see in the rejection of the National Socialist outlook a process of recovery. It would be a relief to feel that this stage-play with its inflated verbiage and its flapping banners was coming to an end. But the thought of what comes next is oppressive and alarming. As it developed, National Socialism bore the plain mark of transciency for all thinking persons. It always held the possibility of rational modification. What now threatens to come is the resort to the last assets of the nation, the last assets of humanity, drawing humanity into a colossal adventure from which there can be no return to normal life. If the threat of this new development of dynamism materializes, there will be a final collapse of the European society of nations and of the civilization of the West. Hitherto dynamism has fought against Christianity, against the sanctity of the home, against ethics and the intellect: for dynamism in its new form they do not even count as things to be fought. They are entirely irrelevant to a system concerned only with expediency. The things that were still inviolate in the National Socialist phase of the German revolution, amid all its brutalities, founder amid the new dynamism. Call it what you will—Bolshevization, State Socialism, a universal army-State: the theories hung round it are merely decoration; the dangerous element in it is the gnawing away of national elements of production to the length of total exhaustion. In no sphere of life will the new phase of the German revolution involve a relaxation of the pressure of the dictatorship or a return to any sort of constitutionalism. It holds fast to all the destructive work of National Socialism, down to its anti-Semitism. It takes over the technique and organization of National Socialism, and it takes over the revolutionary tendencies which have played a part in the movement up to now, and which National Socialism has partly subdued, partly distorted for its own purposes, and makes of them a ruthless, carefully thought out, rational system. Not a philosophy but a reality. Such is this consistent dynamism—the really dangerous form of the German revolution.

We may see the new order beginning already to establish itself in actual practice through the system of military preparedness and the requirements of the Four Year Plan. But in other fields also the contours of the new planning begin to stand out from the cloudy background of popular National Socialism.

Much of the new dynamism may have been the result of the great Soviet plan of reconstruction; but the essential point is that in the Third Reich the solution found, not by the free decision of the leaders but by the actual pressure of definite problems, resembles Bolshevism, a proof of the inevitability of the drift in that direction.

The rigidly consistent system of the new dynamism outgrows not only capitalism but every sort of romanticism and traditionalism. It puts even the "Blood and Soil" dogma out of date. That dogma, says Niekisch in his *Die Dritte Imperiale Figur,* published in 1935, is not a natural product "but a romantic fancy. Where natural attachment to blood and soil has come to an end, it cannot be restored by a free decision." The future of an "uprooted nation," and the German nation was one, like most of the nations of Europe for that matter, exists only in so far as it places "its own versatility in its service" in penetrating the whole world. There is no way back to its roots. The desire to find a way back is almost evidence in itself of a feeling of being too spent to be able to venture on the imperial flight into the wide world. This new versatility is dynamism.

We are at the outset of a fresh world-start. This "world technical trend," says Niekisch, is inevitable. The capitalist world has worked its own ruin, it has delivered itself up to the process of self-destruction, in complete unconsciousness up to the moment of its fall, just like the *ancien régime* at the time of the French Revolution. But if the capitalist world is lightheartedly living for the profit of the moment, blind to the coming disaster as was the French feudal aristocracy, the "*technica ratio*" is graver and more unemotional and more inexorable than any revolutionary tribunal. It establishes itself in indifference alike to opposition and to its own devoted advocates.

"Progress or dominion" is the alternative offered by the industrial system in the view of the theorists of the new dynamism. The capitalist misused industry in the service of progress. He is incapable of putting it to the use for which it really exists. It is the instrument not of progress but of dominion. It requires to be used as means of dominion; it waits for the strong hand that will reveal its true character as an instrument of power and will use it to that end. Such is their interpretation of the industrial system, given without any reference to traditional theory or practice, and without any heat or resentment.

It is in the nature of things that the planning and the methods of work of the Soviet State and the Fascist and National Socialist States should be growing more and more similar. They will become identical, completing, in so doing, a necessary and irresistible development, against which any sort of conscious political effort will be in vain. The "new world order resulting from world dominion" is rising "by means of the process of successive wars and civil wars." Thus this new interpretation of the German revolution ends on the note of concentration simply and purely on war.

These doctrines are not those of hectic outsiders: their importance lies in the fact that they are the anticipatory description of real processes which are more and more strongly setting in in the approaching second phase of the new revolution, and not in Germany alone. This new phase is not disposed of when we have labelled it and filed it away under "National Bolshevism." It *is* National Bolshevism! If it is anything at all it is a genuine and consistent National Bolshevism, while National Socialism is National Bolshevism *plus* noise and darkened counsel. It has beyond question a deep-seated affinity with the things that have developed in Russia out of quite different basic elements. And it is this fact that reveals so perilous a situation that it can no longer be justifiable to keep silence in face of German developments. It must not be overlooked that the bridge of doctrine exists here for an alliance with Soviet Russia, an alliance that still has important supporters in Germany, though for quite mistaken reasons.

This development does not proceed from the logic of economic considerations alone. It is necessarily pursued by an army command that wishes to have a truly loyal nation at its back. This, there can no longer be any doubt, will be possible only subject to the pursuit of genuine Socialism. The enforced step from Papen-monarchism to the Hitler revolution, enforced by the feeling that popular opinion must be respected, is leading on to a system that will steadily approach the "democracy of work" of the revolutionary theorists. Socialism in this "democracy" will certainly be no earthly paradise; it will be a harsh reality, the indispensable means of military preparedness. It will be of a widely different stamp from that of Marxism. Far from vetoing this solution, the army will have to seek it itself. It is pure legend that the army is reactionary. Its thinking is too realistic for that. It will not only tolerate a re-ordering of the social system but will make it its own task, just as with the present system of *Wehrwirtschaft* (the subordination of the whole economic system to the requirements of military preparedness), if it regards it as the necessary condition for preparedness. And universal mobilization is possible only under the system of State Socialism. The army leaders will not recoil from the logic of developments, however far it may lead from all that seemed to them at the outset to be desirable and possible.

The Socialism of National Socialism remained mere banal play-acting until the strain of the economic planning involved in the

Wehrwirtschaft that has become necessary made it an unavoidable element in the political system. This tendency will grow stronger. Not only in the social and economic spheres, but also in those of national discipline and of the moral safeguarding of military preparedness, there lie developmental forces that lead very close to complete State Socialism and to a new social order that will not permit the existence of private property, unearned income, or private enterprise. Men may refuse to contemplate this development, may shut their eyes to it and declare at each new point reached that that is enough; the inexorable pressure of the logic of events takes no notice of the private arguments and public manifestations of the will of the "leaders." It pushes on step by step, and will provide in doing so the ideological superstructure of its justification.

It is a grandiose, dismally gleaming picture of a rising world-empire, an empire really embracing the whole surface of the globe, that becomes discernible in Ernst Jünger's prophetic vision. Some of the younger active elements accept it with passionate enthusiasm. In this direction run the thoughts of the many members of the younger generation who are disappointed by the depravity of the National Socialist regime. It is the "mission of the young generation" as it is seen to-day. This vision has the actuality of an inescapable process and is supported by the passionate desire of the younger elements. Is there anything that can be put in its place? This is the vital question facing not only the German nation but the whole of Western civilization.

THE POSSIBILITY OF A PROLETARIAN REVOLUTION AND THE PROBLEM OF THE MASSES

Is there still any possibility of a Socialist revolution, aiming at the classless society under the dictatorship of the proletariat? The only possible answer is that the possibility is now beginning to exist. Here again the actual developments are moving in exactly the opposite direction to that which the official interpretation tries to indicate. The efforts to remove an alleged peril of revolution have made it acute. The present situation is certainly very likely to develop in the direction of the proletarian revolution. The regime is looking for signs of that revolution where there are certainly none, among the illegal movements. But they are to be found in the midst of the élite; the proletarian revolution has its future leaders, with their most fervent supporters, in the branches of the party. It is only within the cadres of the offic al party that that revolution has been provided with a revolutionary instrument of power which it has never before possessed in the Reich, either in the Communist cells or in the Social Democratic organization or in the trade unions. The party has trained the masses in revolutionism, a thing the Social Democracy never tolerated. In the National Socialist formations —the S.A. (Storm Troops) the S.S., the Hitler Youth—an "élite" has been continually under training in the principles of revolutionary tactics. We must not be deceived by the circumstance that the proletarian language of the present revolutionary élite differs from that to which we were accustomed before 1933. Marxism is dead in Germany, and with it its doctrine and language. The new élite is far too primitive and of far too crude a mentality to be able even to understand the Marxist language, much less to elaborate its principles and doctrines. Its ideas of the aims of the proletarian revolution are of the most elementary sort and have proceeded from a set of conceptions on which the class-conscious worker of the past would have looked down with contempt. This in no way alters the fact of the existence of a widespread revolutionary purpose, which would have the political instrument it needs ready to hand at any time if it should be decided to move. The former parties of the much-discussed "system," of Social Democracy and Communism, had an intelligent social doctrine and a theory of the class war and the Socialist revolution, but in Germany they were entirely without any real revolutionary purpose. In present-day Germany the new and unschooled leaders of the workers have thrown all social theories overboard; on the other hand there is a clear will to radical revolution. There has been a thorough radicalization, if not of the proletarian masses in the Reich, at all events of their National Socialist elements. Of this there can be no doubt. This has been the outstanding result of the National Socialist activities of the past five years. This radicalization has proceeded, however, on lines not hitherto usual. The active supporters of the new political ideas fall into new categories and have formed groupings unknown to the past. This has added to the difficulty of realizing what has actually been going on.

On the surface the German working class has been entirely excluded from politics. It no longer exists as a direct political factor. The Labor Front affects to be a quasi-classless association on the principle of the *Volksgemeinschaft,* the "united nation." The working class has been deprived of its past organs of political activity and economic self-help. The result has been that the working class, which, of course, still exists, has gone over to the pursuit of its political activities within the organizations of the National Socialist Party. There has been going on, or is now going on, a process of occupation of the party machinery by the old political elements. The working class has ceased as such to have a political will of its own, but it is exercising its political influence indirectly through and upon the party machinery, and in this way it is already exerting a stronger influence over the State and the economic system than did the class-war parties of the past. (I will not attempt to discuss the extent of the influence of the older men, the skilled workers, the foremen and leading men, who have considerable power in every factory or other place of work over the younger workers. The growth of this influence is certainly one of the few healthy developments under the existing regime. But this is another matter entirely.) The appointment of the new party officials for the representation of the interests of the workers is an important change which became inevitable in the internal functions of this section of the party organization. It represents an irresistible process of internal transformation of the party machinery by the natural social and economic forces. This occupation of the party machinery demands the abandonment of the old political language and the acceptance of the new "racial" language. The political will is camouflaged. At the same time, the influence of the new doctrines effects a substantial change in it. It becomes primitive, and, in so far as it deals with events outside the immediate local interests, it becomes definitely revolutionary, aiming at the achievement of the dictatorship of the proletariat by violent means. The exclusion of the workers as a class from politics has destroyed reformist Socialism, and this fact has simply given a monopoly of political activity to the most radical form of revolutionism. The political medium of this revolutionism is no longer the working class. The workers have delegated their political initiative to the party formations, holding themselves as a necessary reserve. But this has produced nothing more than a change in the organs of political activity. To-day the working class, though indirectly and not as a whole, has become the medium of a determined though not rationally defined revolutionary movement.

Concerning these things there are both deliberate deception and involuntary self-deception. The higher members of the party élite, who are gradually losing touch with the people, and to whom, as to all exalted potentates, it is no longer discreet for their subordinates to blurt out the whole truth, are no longer able to realize the full scope of the development. They interpret the revolutionary will as an active spirit of National Socialism, making the mistake of taking at its face value the language the masses now speak in substitution for the Marxist theories of the past. But there are also men high in the party who are deliberately encouraging the radicalization of opinion in the party formations and the idea of a Socialist dictatorship of the workers, and who in doing so are pursuing carefully thought-out aims of their own.

Many émigrés share the failure to realize that the situation in Germany is actually revolutionary. It must be difficult for an old party official to grasp what has happened in the Reich—the death of Marxism and, in spite of this, the existence of a revolutionary Socialist movement in full swing. He can see the difficulty of illegal work in support of the old doctrine, but he fails to see the much more radical political work that is being done in the new centers of political activity. Every shade of Marxism has disappeared in Germany—there is no doubt about that. But the release of the labor movement from the cast-iron doctrine of Marxism has given it its first chance to turn into a resolute and uninhibited movement for out-and-out revolution. The old Social Democratic party official, used to holding firmly to the doctrines of the revolution, overlooks the fact that this new revolutionary movement has dispensed with doctrine to gain what the old movement never possessed—revolutionary tactics. The Gestapo, the secret police, must themselves share the blame for the misreading of the present situation in Germany. The police are on the watch for evidence of the illegal movement; they are colorblind to the new shade of revolutionary opinion. Their whole organization is sailing in ballast. Their mechanism traps all the elements that are not really hostile to the State, elements that need not cause serious concern. The actual reservoirs of the revolution are beyond their reach. They squander money and energy on the suppression of men whose opinions are entitled to the highest respect, men who are defending a lost position, and they fail to see the vast ramparts of the new revolutionaries.

The perilousness of the new situation in the Reich lies in the fact that the proletarian revolution is being prepared in full view of the Government and with its help. Never before has a revolution been able to enter into the possession of the means of power by so direct a method as is happening to-day in the Reich. But yet another circumstance reveals the dangerous situation. The masses have not been effectively driven out of politics. Opponents of National Socialism especially are to be found talking of a "stupefying" of the masses that grows more and more manifest. This is too broad a generalization. There has been a steady loss of independence of thinking among the small shopkeepers, artisans, clerks in business houses, and the rest of the rank and file of the party. Among these the intellectual level has visibly fallen. With the loss of their independent existence they have lost the readiness to express independent judgments. The lower middle class, hitherto a political buffer between the independent middle class and capitalists and upper class on one side and the working class on the other, a class of political drifters, have to-day been depressed to lower class conditions and are vegetating in a mental and material state inferior to that of the working class. With no political will of their own, with no political leaders, with no adequate political representation in economic matters, this class has been split up into a thousand different interests. There was nothing to give it a political character of its own. It is this class that to-day is the basis of the social structure of the German nation. Here is material worth the attention of the regime at all times for the purpose of influencing national opinion. But here also is the material for a sudden outburst of violent revolutionary feeling. The constantly excited enthusiasm of this declassed element only masks its intense desperation.

The lower élite, the Storm Troops, S.S. men, Hitler Youth, and *Werkscharen* or National Socialist factory groups, have also passed through a process worth attention—the development of tactics of their own and of a new style of living. It is not surprising that the political methods and the style of living of the upper section of the élite have had an influence on the lower élite. The secret National Socialist doctrine of total nihilism, in the crudest of forms, has made unmistakable progress in the party formations. No one who has secured even a superficial insight into German conditions can have failed to realize the almost incredible deterioration of moral standards in the party formations. The unscrupulousness that has developed in the ranks of the S.A. and S.S. must sooner or later have the most fatal reactions on the general membership. Behind a few well-worn clichés about loyalty to the Leader and about the German nation there is concealed an outlook of undiluted materialism and a lust for every sort of violence, which will never be drilled out of the Storm Troops again. The simplicity and the crude conceit with which these men flaunt their brutality, as though it were something to be proud of, show the results of their education by example.

I will not offer instances. These processes cannot be illustrated by mentioning particular cases; to do so would be to invite the reply that these were chance excesses. But I had personal experience of the degree of unscrupulousness that has been reached among average members of the élite. While I was in office at Danzig a party member with the gold party badge, a university man, made proposals to me in all seriousness for the physical removal of the Senator responsible for finance. (This Senator's financial operations had aroused suspicion among the party, but there was not the slightest justification for it.) These proposals betrayed such familiarity with cunning methods of murder and its concealment, such unscrupulousness in the resort to extremes, that we must be prepared for anything if this élite should really embark on revolution on its own account. There can be no question that a revolutionary staff full of desperately dangerous ideas has been trained in the National Socialist machine. It was a complete mistake to imagine that there was any ground for relief after June 30th, 1934, any ground for supposing that the revolutionary character of the National Socialist machine had undergone the slightest modification. Its revolutionary character lies not in its open declarations and propaganda, but in the very existence of this élite and the character of its members, a totally anti-social body of men, likely to infect the whole of the youth of the nation with the miasma of their ideas and their unscrupulous readiness for anything. On June 30th public revolutionary talk was brought to an end. But the actual focus of a permanent revolutionary explosiveness remained. Far from restraining the revolutionary movement in the party, from getting rid of the alleged National Bolshevism of the Storm Troops, June 30th did a great deal to revolutionize the spirit of the whole party hierarchy.

No amount of psychological argumentation will upset that conclusion. The lynch justice performed on June 30th, 1934, left an indelible impression not only on the S.A. formations that suffered but on the S.S. lynchers. And the impression was the opposite of that which the leaders intended. Röhm's outspoken revolutionism, with which the Storm Troops had identified themselves, was suppressed, but in being driven underground it was made to fill men's minds. No one in the inner circles of the party has any doubt that another opportunity will come for carrying the revolution into its second phase; and no one treats seriously the official explanation of June 30th, that it was a mere expedition for the punishment of homo-sexuals. The brutal ruthlessness and the utter lawlessness of the execution of Röhm were carefully noted by the party for future guidance. I had personal experience of the helpless horror of some of the underlings in the party hierarchy who in entire innocence, and following their local leader in perfect faith, were craftily enticed into some sort of apparent illegality and found themselves in the hands of the political police. These men returned to their duties as party officials after their interrogation, in apparent acceptance of their position; in most cases they had no choice. But they reconciled themselves to what had happened only by abandoning all inhibitions of the past and devoting themselves to working as apostles of the new gospel of violence. Only innocent souls soothed their consciences with the explanation that Hitler was surrounded by a clique of bad advisers, that he had no knowledge of what was actually going on, that his intentions were of the best, that he was the prisoner of his entourage and must be got out of their hands.

The primitiveness of the revolutionism in the Storm Troops, the Hitler Youth, or the S.S. reveal the vagueness of their revolutionary ideas, but this very vagueness contains an element of danger and of the incalculable. This revolutionism stops at nothing. Its tactical principle is that all things are permitted, including disloyalty to superiors. Nobody will be so naïve as to imagine that consistent training in brutality and unscrupulousness could produce a spirit of decency, or that the systematic flouting and rejection of every principle of civilized law and order could produce a loyal citizen. A revolutionary type is being molded that differs radically from everything that went by the name of revolutionism in the cause of progress, but a type that for that very reason is the sort of henchman who alone, apparently, can help to carry out revolutions in our day.

Figure the type of the class-conscious German Social Democrat, upright in thought and action in all conceivable circumstances, dogmatic, narrow, small-minded, but decent through and through, law-abiding, liberty-loving, firmly insisting on respect for the individual, and detesting any sort of violence. He, too, was a revolutionary, or at all events he thought that he was. Alongside him stood the Communist, already accepting violence as a legal weapon; but there were limits beyond which nothing would induce him to go. Not fifteen years of Muscovite training had managed more than that. But National Socialism has managed it. In an astonishingly short time it has produced a revolutionary type which corresponds in every detail to the type of the unscrupulous Muscovite proletarian groups of that sanguinary revolution. There was a reason for this. Social Democracy and Communism alike came into existence as political parties of the organized workers. The militant formations of National Socialism grew out of the army of the déclassés, the unorganized, the desperadoes and the wreckage of humanity, the mercenary professional revolutionaries. To this day the Storm Troops have retained this hooligan character, although some of their worst members have been ejected. It is well known in the army how difficult it is to change the character once acquired by any unit. Down to 1933 the "National Socialist German Labor Party" was not a labor party in the ordinary sense. The "combination" of 1933, instead of enlisting the support of the organized working class, which was and is an element of order, employed the pseudo-working class of the National Socialist party troops as its foundation, and to-day we see the result of that false step. The character of permanent revolution ineradicably possessed by the Third Reich has its origin here. The foundation is revolutionary because it is unsocial. What an immense work of education of several generations of Social Democratic political activity was thus destroyed! It cannot be replaced by any externals of party organization, however pompous. The moral basis has been destroyed. The older generations who once belonged to the organized workers have sunk into scepticism and have lost courage, like the middle class. The younger generations are the militants of a new and robust Socialism of the most extreme type.

The question whether a proletarian revolution will come involves two others. One is that of the political significance of the unorganized masses that continue to exist under the present system. The other is whether a political situation will arise in which the party machinery could be brought to bear in a revolutionary direction.

The problem of the masses is still of central political importance. The entry of the masses into a share in the conduct of affairs has given its stamp to a whole period. No sphere of existence has remained unaffected. It may well be asked whether it will continue at present to have the same fundamental importance as in the past. The masses remain a political factor, but their place in direct action has entirely changed for so long as they remain no longer organized but simply used as a political instrument.

There is the familiar technique of the propagandist control of the masses, developed by working on the special mass mental processes which are psychologically recognizable. There is a subtly elaborated technique of employment of material means of terrorism and leadership through political formations in the face of which the unorganized masses are helpless. The prompt

80

success which both techniques have had and continue to have at present has strengthened many despots of to-day in the assumption that the masses have been rendered impotent, if not as a political force, at all events as an independent natural element of dangerous and incalculable power. As a natural element they can not only, it is assumed, be guided at any time, but also made use of as a politically valuable tool. Seen from the conductor's desk of the modern propagandists, the masses remain a political reality of the first importance, but only as a passive element, as an object of control, serving only the will of others and at all times in need of their domination.

The use of the masses as raw material is defeated by transforming them into an organized nation. Fascism sought to organize the mass of the people in the Corporative State, but the task has been beyond it, not through any external happening but for intrinsic reasons. In such Corporations as have so far taken shape, the formless masses have gained a mechanized form in collectivities in which they become dominant as they were not before. The immanent tendency of a collectivity to union with others in a comprehensive general collectivity enables the masses to gain a new form of domination. They return as organized masses to direct political activity. The way out is thus to atomize the masses in every field of life, to prevent the formation of associations capable of effective political action, and to assemble the masses only under conditions in which they can be kept passive and receptive. This is the tactical plan of National Socialism, which has carefully avoided moving in the direction of the Corporative State.

The attempt to maintain control of the unorganized masses by means of terrorism has revealed special dangers: the personnel of the regime changes in character. The question remains whether the control of the masses by propaganda through suggestion does not also lead indirectly to a modification of the political purpose, the will of the masses finding means of fulfilment in the course of a growing radicalization. The suggestive force of slogans

81

rapidly wears out. Up to now the attention of the élite has mainly been paid to the fact that the masses are strongly influenced by the continual repetition of things that have been made familiar to them. That is true. But it is a mistake to suppose that they can be influenced for years on end by the same sort of suggestive propaganda. Propaganda, to remain effective, must continually be heightened. Hence the search for effective slogans and, to ensure that they shall be effective, the investigation of the desires of the masses. In the course of time the leaders become more and more dependent on the masses, at least in a negative sense, throwing aside slogans which are found to have lost their attraction. The replacing of worn-out elements in the propaganda repertoire is an anxious matter for propagandists great and little. It is an elementary mistake to suppose that the masses can be got to do anything and everything, even by the wiliest of Goebbelsian propaganda. In any case, the time comes when it no longer works. Undoubtedly the masses can for some time be led even against their own instincts. But then the day may come, and with inexplicable suddenness, when the instincts will reassert themselves, in the reverse of the direction desired. There is also a process of overreaching in propaganda, a working of the soil to death, that leads to complete apathy. In both cases the masses begin to evolve slogans of their own. In this way the Socialist class-aim of the proletarian revolution, which had been conjured out of the minds of the masses by the racial myth and the whole philosophy of National Socialism, is inevitably brought back again as an indirect result of the increasing shrillness of slogans.

Thus the methods of propaganda and mass-suggestion come one day to the end of their effectiveness. The separate atoms of the nation continually fall back out of the mass into thinking independently for themselves. Suggestive slogans do not work for ever; they do not work when a man is alone, or when he is with his family or friends. Propaganda does not exercise continuous influence; it only delivers intermittent thrusts. Between these thrusts there come into play forces of another kind. The hypnosis does not last; at all events, the commands issued during hypnosis do not permanently retain their force. In the periods of consciousness a resistance grows against which the suggestive slogans ultimately prove impotent. Thus mass propaganda, working with the means of intoxication and suggestion on the mass mind, is an extremely dangerous instrument, very likely one day to turn against those who have used it.

The masses are at all times the fundamental element in the determination of the situation of a country, whether that of latent revolution or that of stable equilibrium. Action is taken exclusively by the ruling clique, but the masses give, if not the revolutionary impulse, at all events the indispensable guarantee of the permanent effect of the action.

The propagandist influencing of the masses is only too likely to produce a growing mass extremism, the tension of which can only be relaxed through the ecstasy of war or a Socialist revolution or a civil war. The two indispensable factors of a modern revolution, the masses and a party élite which is itself revolutionary in spirit, are coming into contact in Germany, with the resultant possibility of an explosion. It is impossible to see how, along the path pursued up to the present, the danger of a radical revolution could be avoided.

National Socialism makes use of the masses in its own highly individual and significant way. It makes use of them in connection with the special German situation in two directions. It enlarges upon the importance of the masses, provides them with a quasi-apotheosis in the conception of the *Volksgemeinschaft,* the "united nation," and emphasizes from time to time the power of this massed body, though it is a nation united only in its intoxication of spirit and is formless except on the march. In this way National Socialism provides itself with continued evidence of its indispensability for the purpose of mass leadership, which it alone understands and exercises with confidence. It clothes the technique of the handling of the masses in a philosophy. This technique, which is dependent on the maintenance of gigantic party machinery, is treated as a secret subject. It is the essential requisite for the maintenance of the power of the party. By its characteristic system of glorification of the masses, of raising them to the rank of the highest authority in life, of absolute authority, National Socialism expects to continue to hold them in its power. The myth of the nation is the trick by means of which the masses can be kept in a state of exaltation and open to influencing by suggestion at any time. The solemn rite in which at meetings the masses are celebrated as the united nation is the technical preparation for making them ready for influencing by inflammatory slogans. In this atmosphere speeches addressed never to the intelligence but only to the subconscious instincts have their success. This alone explains the character of these speeches, which call forth either ecstatic enthusiasm or ecstatic fury. In this the National Socialist propaganda follows recipes carefully thought out down to the smallest detail and many times tested. Anyone who has had experience of the way in which a special style of ecstatic oratory is cultivated, even by the pettiest officials of the party, will realize the deeper purpose of this style, with its calculated effect on the masses.

But National Socialism also operates on the masses in the direction of keeping alive the revolutionary tendency. Only so does it consider that the masses can be kept in the unstable condition in which they can be influenced at will. Only by posing as the counsel for the true Socialist revolution, in opposition to reactionaries, Jews, saboteurs, Marxists, and foreign democracies, does it create the emotional fluidity in which political slogans have effect.

National Socialism makes use of the masses as an instrument. It has not the slightest intention of organizing them and bringing them out of their amorphous condition. This explains its abolition of every sort of independent administration. It also explains the wrecking of every attempt to form a new society. Such is the pernicious character of the treatment of the masses elaborated by Goebbels. In his system propaganda is not a means of communication, with the purpose of adjusting leadership from above under the impact of criticism and of the public reception of proposals. It is simply and purely a means of domination, supported by the methods of terrorism and of brutal compulsion.

As yet this propaganda has not entirely lost its effectiveness in Germany. It has been carried on cleverly and with remarkable psychological subtlety. It might almost be said that it has succeeded in turning burdens which in the past aroused the utmost resentment into food for enthusiasm. The crisis of the system will come—it seems now to be coming—when this propaganda no longer works. The dictatorship cannot maintain itself by violence alone. This was realized even before the "combination" of 1933.

And the masses are waiting. They are undoubtedly hoping for some sort of socialization. This is the fruit of five years of National Socialist rule, with its radicalization of the masses, and its training of the cadres of the élite in total unscrupulousness. It is the reality behind the make-believe of the struggle against Bolshevism.

The Third Reich is actually bringing into operation a sort of Socialism. We may call it Prussian Socialism, or State Socialism, or the total mobilization of the nation, or the beginning of the grandiose "democracy of work." Undoubtedly the masses themselves continue to regard Socialism as something different from this—that bit of personal happiness, that security, that bit of fair treatment and personal dignity that a man needs in his life as an individual. National Socialism with its heroic ideal has clearly not ousted this eternal ideal of the masses. It would thus be folly to expect any long-continued relaxation of tension from the introduction of State Socialism. The revolution will proceed on its course. And it will do so through the initiative of a revolutionary élite in co-operation with masses excited into revolutionism. In view of the dangerous dependence of the "Leader" on the feeling and the purpose of these élite formations, which under the surface are growing more and more extremist, it is easy to foresee that at any time some trifling matter may suddenly turn the defenders of the new order into its most rabid opponents. Already National Socialism is entirely in the position of the Girondists who became incapable of withstanding the course of events. No one who has been able to gain an insight into the actual feeling of the members of the National Socialist formations will deny that, beneath the thin films of party proclamations, the revolutionary spirit is appallingly evident. When these men, left to themselves, come to discuss their superiors and the supreme leaders, their ideas run in one single direction—that of the incompleteness of the revolution. What these men believe in is action. That is the practical lesson they have learned. The danger of revolution exists; it will come when the almost inevitable revolutionary situation develops.

Ochlocracy, the dictatorship of the mob, is the goal toward which the development of the mass-democracy of Cæsarism is leading. Beyond any question there are members of the supreme leadership who would be ready to lead a proletarian revolution. In the years before the present regime came into power, there was published a popular novel dealing with Sulla. It was a favorite with Hitler's immediate entourage. These men, who drew their ideas of the past from literature of this sort, did not see how in their enthusiasm for that fair-haired, blue-eyed executioner of the noblest of the Romans they were laying bare their own character. Grants of land to legionaries and agrarian reform were not enough for the recreation of the greatness of Rome. In the struggle against the ruling classes, against the old families, in the extermination of the best of the nobility, in a dictatorship of the mob, even if the dictator bore all the marks of Nordic race, Rome destroyed herself. This enthusiasm for Sulla among the supreme party élite should be noted by those who are concerned. A revolution does not rest content with agrarian reform; nor with the restoration of military power. Nor will the "new nobility of blood and soil," the new form of proposed military colonization, provide a final goal for the new social order. At the end of this development there stands, unless it is checked in time, the dictatorship not of the workers of Germany but of the mob.

TABULA RASA

What is the actual revolutionary goal of National Socialist dynamism, whether disguised by the make-believe philosophy of the moment or by its immediate objectives? How do the present élite themselves envisage the victory of their movement? We may accept Hitler's reply: it is the victory of the revolutionary new order. But what is this new order? It is simply action, whether conceived as a German social and economic revolution or as a world revolution or, finally, as the "eternal war" which many men in high places in the movement consider to be the future condition of human society.

That war, however, is not the father but the destroyer of all things, the destroyer of all order and all the things of the mind. There is nothing that this destruction would spare. And nothing will be taken over from the old order into the new, neither army nor church, neither the institutions of property nor the elements of culture. Up to now, with a few exceptions, the German revolution has spared the persons of the leaders of the old order; it has not set them up against a wall, though in the occupation of Austria there was a notable increase of brutality in the treatment of the old leaders of society. But the loss of influence of these leaders of the old order is not less than if they had been removed by execution.

It is the essential task of every revolution to produce a *tabula rasa*, to make a clean sweep of the past political forces; but the nihilist revolution of National Socialism sets out to destroy everything that it cannot itself take over and convert to its own pattern. This explains its *Gleichschaltung* or forcing into conformity of all elements of society and of every independent activity, or else their total suppression. It explains why the revolution ignores the very conceptions of a private sphere in life and of legality. Even national customs and traditions, which National Socialism affects to have under its special care, contain anti-revolutionary principles and are accordingly docked or lopped or, if that is not considered enough, proscribed. But the National Socialist work of revolutionary demolition goes, of necessity, yet further. It embraces the whole economic field. The expropriation of property will inevitably follow, as well as the complete abolition of private enterprise, and the reduction of the workers to a serfdom which will not be lightened either by motor cars for the masses or by "Strength through Joy." The new social order will consist of universal and equal servitude, a general mobilization not only for the purpose of military preparedness but as a permanent revolutionary system—a servitude which will remove human labor from the sphere of economic and social considerations and subject it to the principle of blind obedience to an absolute despotism. The necessary concentration of the means of production, and of capital, in the hands of the State, leading to "nationalization" or "socialization," a progressive economic destruction of the middle class, and the all-pervading atmosphere of barracks and prison will be felt to be elements in keeping with the idea the middle class have long had of the Socialist revolution—desolation, impoverishment, regimentation, and the collapse of civilized existence.

Thus National Socialism is at issue with every independent activity or ordering of life. It is bound to make an end of freedom of initiative, of all that in the past has made for creative activity and progress: these things make its dominion incomplete. Nothing is more intolerable to it in its revolutionary course than originality, individuality, character, or true public spirit. Whatever it cannot dominate it must destroy, whatever it cannot absorb and master must go. Such is the truly barbaric maxim of National Socialism. It is the process of an enemy occupation of all the vital elements in the nation, ending in their destruction.

This destruction is not brought to a halt before the things of the mind. The fight against the intellectuals and against the freedom of science is not in the slightest degree the outcome of any inferiority complex; it arises from the clear recognition that in the field of the intellect the indissoluble unity of Western civilization remains active. In this field independence of thought and resistance to the revolution are bound to show themselves sooner or later.

For the rest, we must not suppose that the revolutionary practice of *Gleichschaltung* proceeds from a clear course thought out in detail in advance. The course of National Socialism has been much more of a hand-to-mouth affair than might have been expected from its early history and from the deal that preceded its accession to power. Behind all its "creative achievements," which are essentially nothing more than a squandering of existing reserves and a parasitic consumption of the organized resources and achievements of generations of labor, was a stupendous wave of wild mass emotion—envy, hatred, vengefulness, and the hot rivalry of small men in the pursuit of posts and power and success. All this only became clear to the middle classes and even to sections of the organized workers when the process was virtually completed. The absence of resistance to it shows that its true nature was not realized, or else that the middle classes no longer had the strength to resist. But it must be said in defence of the middle classes, and of all of us, that few were aware of the cynicism with which the demagogic means of swindling the nation were being brought to bear. Hitler, in a sentence which has been deleted from later editions of *Mein Kampf*, wrote this: "The German has not the faintest notion of the way the nation has to be swindled if one wants mass support."

Deliberate revolutionary advances of National Socialism have always begun in the directions most favored by circumstances— the National Socialist leaders have revealed remarkable skill in taking due advantage of their opportunities. They showed almost a genius for directing, inciting, or suspending the wild course of the *Gleichschaltung* movement, born of envy and hostility— always with the aim of pushing ahead the indispensable revolutionary process of clearing out of the way all existing organized elements. In exactly the same way the leaders are taking advantage of the process now necessary of concentrating the means of production and distribution under their own control, to take a further step in the elimination of the controlling elements of the past in trade and industry. What must be the end of all this is a question they leave to the future; the urgent task of the moment is the *tabula rasa*. This again is not the outcome of any doctrinaire policy, but of the necessity of keeping in the saddle and keeping things moving.

National Socialism succeeds everywhere as an element of dissolution, or of disturbance of the existing order, or where it finds fresh material to consume. It fails wherever it attempts any genuine constructive work. Naturally there must be deep-seated causes of so destructive a movement. The causes are social, moral, and politico-economic. Similarly complex is the reason for the disintegration in process among the middle classes and the ruling class of society long before the arrival of National Socialism. One is confined to the bandying of clichés about National Socialism and the Third Reich so long as one leaves these deeper factors out of consideration. The first thing to realize is that the purpose of National Socialism is actually the deliberate and systematic destruction of the social classes that have made history, together with the last vestiges of their established order.

The nihilist revolution evades every spiritual impulse, and sees in reason and the things of the spirit its mortal enemies. It robs science of freedom and compels it to serve the progress of the revolution. The purpose of the National Socialist fight against Christianity is the same: the total destruction of the last and most deep-rooted support of the forces of conservation.

The destruction of the spirit of Christianity in Germany is certainly more far-reaching than appears on the surface. The churches are still open. Men still have God's name in their mouths —they did, for instance, at the Nuremberg congress: "In serving our nation we serve God." But this Christianity is losing more and more of its past character. Such vestiges of any living Christianity as remain are steadily degenerating in the direction of a superficial and unthinking deism, and are thus becoming more and more fitted for the co-option of articles of faith drawn from "racialist" sources and the like. Not through any open controversy, but in the course of inner evolution, the Christianity which to this day is officially professed will gradually but inevitably be reinterpreted in the terms required not only for the *"seelische Geschlossenheit"* of totalitarian war but for the revolutionary abolition of the old forces of order.

One element of the destruction of Christianity must not be passed over—the disfranchising and destruction of German Jewry. We may leave out of account the conception of race and the forgeries with which National Socialist propaganda carries on its demagogic campaign of anti-Semitism, although it will be difficult to free the German body from this poison. But the question has not only its economic, social, and ethical sides but also its political side. The practical politician will be as little able as anyone else to overlook the destruction of conceptions of right, the training in revolutionary violence, that have been achieved by the satisfaction of the instincts of envy and greed through the removal of Jewish competition in trade and industry, the expropriation of a part of the nation without compensation, and its brutal deprivation of all rights. The appetite of the masses is in any case stimulated. They are given a demonstration of the fact that legal guarantees and conceptions of property and order are helpless in the face of violence. The anti-Semitic acts of the Third Reich are almost a formal introduction to a coming revolutionary upheaval. We may take it for granted that certain members of the élite have systematically made use of anti-Semitism in this way, as a training for the coming social upheaval, which will be the more inescapable the longer it is delayed. In any case it is the duty of every practical politician to think out the problem of anti-Semitism, if not from the ethical or any other side, at least from the side of its practical consequences. It will be especially the duty of a conservative politician to go into the question whether Jewry really is an agent of disintegration, as is the mistaken popular idea, and not in at least an equal degree an element of conservation and order. Beyond all question there does exist an agent of national disintegration in the vulgar type of National Socialism itself—no other than this brutal revolutionary anti-Semitism. Such a method of treating a section of the population, flouting all ideas of legality and the deep-rooted conceptions of personal dignity, freedom, and security, simply means opening the door to revolution and anarchy. What has been done cannot, however, be undone, and its destructive effects on the whole nation cannot be escaped. But a satisfactory restoration of the conceptions of legality could probably bar the way to further disintegration. From an ethical standpoint there is no Jewish problem. No believing Christian and no humane-minded person can be an anti-Semite.

Rosenberg and Ludendorff are right, if in nothing else, in their claim that the New Testament is inseparably connected with the Old, and we Christians with our Jewish heritage. But we cannot expect the practical politician to take these facts into consideration, any more than we can expect him to take humane ideals in general into consideration. No doubt the Jewish question, especially that of the parasitic elements in the Jewish lower class, represents a grave and difficult problem for the practical politician. But these questions are capable of solution within the framework of European civilization. Even apart from ethical considerations, common sense should rule out the idea of increasing national prosperity by appropriating the means of livelihood of the Jewish citizens. This is another "great illusion" of the same sort as the idea that a conquering nation can add to its wealth by annexing that of the conquered nation. Germany is not enriched but impoverished by destroying the wealth of the Jews. But the recognition of this truth will come too late, just as did that of the truth about loss and gain in the world war.

To-day there is one fact that stands out above all else. The parasitism which National Socialism and the "racialists" ascribe to the Jews is one of the main characteristics of National Socialism itself. National Socialism is living by the parasitic draining of the life-blood of its host, the nation on which it has fastened.

TOTAL DEVALUATION

Even the devotee of unprincipled realism does not usually deny that what Bismarck called the imponderabilia, the non-material considerations in political and social affairs, are of material importance. This is a banal truism, and it would not be worth mentioning were it not that in the modern form of political realism it seems to be held that these non-material considerations are easily accessible to manipulation. Is this actually so? Modern realist policy endeavors not only to influence the pull of the non-material considerations and to pick and choose among them, but systematically to find substitutes for them, confidently assuming that the substitution will not be noticed. The result is plainly visible to-day—the total devaluation of all principles and standards. Among the imponderabilia are the ethical considerations. These are not exchangeable and cannot be replaced by substitutes. It used to be regarded as a sign of lower middle class conventionalism to carry moral principles into political life. I think the time has come for correcting this view. It is precisely the lower middle class element in National Socialism that has thrown over all moral inhibitions as conventional and contemptible. This element has, in fact, returned to the entirely outworn and out-of-date idea that moral conceptions have no place in politics. It seems to me that the principle for thinking people in the generations to come is exactly the opposite one, that the most realist of policies cannot dispense with an iron ration of genuine ethical principles. When even the lower middle classes have become cynics, it is high time for people of intelligence to admit the reality of a spiritual and ethical cosmos.

The destruction of character is the great achievement of

National Socialism. The cynicism with which everybody has been ready to justify his capitulation before the terrorist regime bears eloquent witness to the moral disintegration beneath the surface of the "united nation." Obviously an increasingly unscrupulous cynicism is not the best soil for the growth of a "loyalty to the leader" (that supreme virtue for the National Socialist) that will stand firm in the time of real testing.

But there has been another unmistakable development in the party: these political gamblers are dismissing any fears in this respect with the optimistic supposition that some way out will be discoverable by which the allegiance of their following may be retained. It is a mistaken idea. Five years of the present course have so entirely and so universally depreciated every standard, have so destroyed the authority of every political principle, that nothing remains with which to build up any better system. The loss of principle does not apply merely to relations with National Socialism, or merely within the realm of National Socialist dominion; it is universal. The principles of nationalism, patriotism, social duty, justice and equity, fraternity and liberty, have not only been deposed in practice, but have been so undermined by false use and demagogic lip-service that they have been robbed of all effective appeal. If things are allowed to take their course there will remain nothing but an utterly wearied, sceptical, atomized nation, incapable for many years to come of any united effort. The youth of the movement may desire to convert this degenerate revolution into a genuine social revolution with concrete aims; but they will remain caught in the vicious circle of progressive destruction, and incapable of any sort of creative achievement, not only because all its slogans have been worked to death already by National Socialism, but because even the most resolute of these young men, with all their contempt of the brainless élite of National Socialism, are unable to acquire what they themselves lack, a genuine faith in the practical importance of the things of the spirit.

The idea of the awakening of the nation from scepticism and

94

indiscipline by training in the military spirit undoubtedly has an element of the heroic and a sort of greatness. But in Germany it is utopian, taking no account of realities. A nation like the German, with its ideal of *Gemütlichkeit*, of solid comfort, and its enormous ballast of unmilitary souls, cannot be so trained. Not the most subtle psychological technique will convert these peace-loving "fellaheen" into warriors. The born soldier can acquire the military virtues and can be the better for them; in the unwarlike masses they breed only brutality. The universal concentration on military preparedness, the interpretation of all life in terms of war, has brought the German nation near to exhaustion both materially and morally.

National Socialism has misused nationalist feeling to suppress Socialist ideas. It is approaching the time when nationalism is losing its appeal and the Socialist ideals must be revived. From these it will pass on to others, adulterating and debasing all that it touches. Nowhere is its destructiveness more impressive than in family life. It is loud in the praise of prolific procreation, but its whole system is destructive of family life. It is completing in this sphere the disintegrating tendencies of the nineteenth century, just as it is completing the proletarization and disorganization of the nation. The sowing of dissension within the family, the alienation of the young from the old, the breaking up of family life through excessive claims on the young "in the service of the idea," is surrendering the youth of the nation to elements which on a continually growing scale are trampling on the last vestiges of traditional moral training. As in its policy with the churches, National Socialism ostensibly upholds and even glorifies existing institutions, but in practice it is destroying them from within even more thoroughly than did Bolshevism, which at least acted openly and from conviction.

Those who know Germany know that the nation no longer credits itself with a will of its own. So deep has it sunk in five years of bondage. If war comes the nation will fight, and at the outset, perhaps, even magnificently. It will yield to every appeal to its passions. But of one thing, in its degradation, it seems to be no longer capable—action on its own initiative. This is the result which the National Socialist leaders, in their wisdom, wanted to achieve; and they have succeeded beyond all expectation. But the day will come when they will need the creative and regenerative energies of the nation and its spontaneous response, and in a nation dulled by drilling they will find none. They will find none even among the youth, on whose loyalty they have supposed that they would always be able to count.

It is conceivable that some of the shrewder among the foreign politicians have long foreseen this process and have built upon it. Their submission to the political aggressiveness of National Socialism may have been dictated partly by the consideration that National Socialism is a process of setting Germans to enslave Germans, and that, left to itself, it will depress them to a level of apathy at which in the long run they will cease to be dangerous. In the first year of the National Socialist regime I was twice visited by an English politician, a genuine friend of Germany. He spoke his mind unreservedly—

> "till I set you up a glass
> Where you may see the inmost part of you."

Like Hamlet with his mother, he urged Germany to "throw away the worser part." Germany was making it difficult, he said, for her friends among her ex-enemies to help her. At that time no one imagined that anti-Semitism, concentration camps, lawlessness and terrorism could ever secure a permanent footing in Europe. This friend of Germany considered that a man like Göring stood in the way of Germany's future. Could he not be induced to retire? For, said my visitor, so long as such men held responsible positions in Germany England could place no trust in the new Reich. I do not know whether this English politician remembers this conversation as well as I do. He went on to see Hitler, as did other Englishmen whom he advised me to meet. All of them changed their opinion: they lost their moral indignation, and they found Göring an imposing personality. What was it that produced the change? Was their friendship for Germany genuine? How can anyone be friendly to the German nation and also ready to accept this regime? And how can a German love his country and yet permit her to wear the livery of a regime of violence?

3

The Suicide of the Old Order

THE WEAKNESS OF THE CONSERVATIVE PARTNERS

THERE exists, or at all events existed, among certain circles of no small political and economic importance, in Germany and abroad, a conception of events in Germany which cannot be too strongly repudiated. This is that a number of great capitalists, thoroughly aware of what they are about; coolly calculating and entirely realist, are deliberately guiding the course of events from behind the scenes, or at least keeping a close watch on events, ready to come forward at any moment if necessary and to declare and carry into effect the actual aims underlying the whole of the developments in Germany. Supported abroad both economically and politically, these people, it is or was supposed, are allowing the National Socialist wave to spend itself. They have deliberately allowed National Socialism to come into the foreground, convinced that without some sort of revolutionary mass movement, in which the accumulated tension can find an outlet, the German nation cannot be shepherded into a genuine and lasting restoration of the old order. These people, it is or was supposed, had the means at any time of compelling a restoration of stability in German public affairs, but their deliberate purpose was to allow the National Socialist revolution to reach its climax, taking advantage of all the confusion it might produce in the relations between foreign powers, and only then to come forward with their own plan of a

German proposal for a far-reaching peace settlement and at the same time to end the revolution.

No such group exists or ever existed. What we find is a tendency in the opposite direction. The very groups which have been credited with the intention to end the revolution are preparing to legitimize the present regime. The efforts they have been making to secure wide support for the establishment of existing conditions on a firm footing reveal anxiety lest developments should enter a new phase. The monarchist and reactionary groups of the past are now devoting all their energies to two ends—to preventing new revolutionary developments and to preventing counter-revolutionary action from any quarter, whether monarchist or Liberal and democratic, lest everything that they consider to have been achieved should be thrown once more into the melting-pot. To-day, and it seems to me to be a fact worthy of note, certain capitalist and reactionary circles seem to be far from desiring, still less supporting, any attempt to challenge the legitimacy of the Third Reich. Whether the corps of officers supports this attitude remains to be seen. But the hopes of those who have come to terms with the new parvenu ruling class, and who imagine that their collaboration with it implies that the new order has the quality of permanence, are certainly mistaken. The new legitimacy will founder beneath a new wave of revolutionism, and the co-opted members of the old upper class will discover that they have merely been brought in for service as temporary understrappers.

It is difficult to understand the self-deception of large numbers of the former ruling class that still exists to-day, after five years of continually growing radicalization of the revolutionary activities of the regime. Behind this problem stands a question which might well drive the most patient and well-balanced to despair: how can the whole course that led to the "deal" of January 30th, 1933, be explained? It was the work of these very classes of society, and how could that be conceivable? How was it possible for them to accept, and to assume the responsibility for, such a

mutilation of their enterprise, which, in spite of its concern for
the protection of certain interests, was one of patriotism, aimed at
a national order of stability and justice and moderation? There
are various things that may be said, and much more will yet be
said, in reply; for it is here alone that a deeper understanding of
what has happened may be gained, and that the means of overcoming the revolution may be found.

To begin with, it must be recalled that the world of ideas of
the nationalist, conservative, and liberal middle class and aristocracy, and of the intellectuals, had long been invaded by
scepticism. The whole of these "ruling" classes, no less than the
mass of the proletariat of the great towns, had been moving towards nihilism. They had even been moving faster in that direction than the working class. Faith in traditions had been fading,
faith in machinery and devices and materialism had been growing, among the traditional ruling classes, and had turned them
from opponents into allies of National Socialism. The absence
of doctrine is perhaps the strength of the dynamic revolution:
the absence of tradition in the monarchist and conservative elements is certainly their weakness.

In these circles, whose scepticism did not enable them to see
through a "realism" that subsequently showed its true face as
simple unscrupulousness, all sincere attempts to find a genuine
solution were foredoomed to perversion. It should in fairness be
added that any genuine solution was impossible because of the
omissions or mistakes of past generations. German Conservatism
had been decaying and degenerating since the middle of the nineteenth century, and this is the chief explanation of the plunge
into a nihilist revolution. In the absence of the regulative element of a genuine Conservatism, the path was taken under the
guidance of National Socialism and of the revived anti-Semitism
to a despotic system, and through that to a directionless revolution, under the illusory idea that the nation was thus being rejuvenated.

Two weaknesses stand out as the main causes of the capitulation of the Nationalist and Conservative elements—a superficiality little removed from frivolity, and the development of a political outlook that went a good part of the way in the direction of National Socialism. The superficial view was taken that, in Bismarck's phrase, if the nationalist German could be got into the saddle he would ride; the principles and methods of the right national policy would reveal themselves in the course of actual administration. The nationalists had too high an opinion of their own qualities and too low an opinion of those of their lower middle class partner, with the result that they entered the deal for a coup totally unprepared, while the National Socialists were armed and equipped down to the last detail. The extent to which the Conservatives had themselves become revolutionary and nihilistic in their views of State, social order, and legality is instanced by the case of Carl Schmitt, a lawyer who later went over to National Socialism. Schmitt's view appears to be that what we call human society no longer exists in an era of control of the masses. There remains only an upper class of ruling officials at the head of masses usefully organized down to the smallest detail. A revolution will thus amount simply to a change in the personnel of the ruling upper class; any accompanying disorders will be immaterial. In the first steps taken by the National Socialists after coming into power, the Nationalists and Conservatives saw only the establishment of the officials and the ruling class in power and an organization and control of the masses which was proceeding in an extremely chaotic way but was at least clearly destined to last.

Justizrat Class, a leader of the pan-Germans and another of the gravediggers of German conservative patriotism, saw only a transient ill-fortune in a lost war, the possibility of which cannot deter the brave from "longing to bring about" a war. "If we win," he declared, "there will be an exaltation of souls, and a national Reichstag will be elected. That moment must be utilized for abolishing the franchise." If we were beaten, it would still, he said, be well. A lost war would lead of necessity to fundamental reforms under a dictatorship which might give a defeat of the nation the aspect, from a higher historical standpoint, almost of a thing to be welcomed. He saw "the discords of to-day growing into a chaos which can only be restored to order by the powerful will of a dictator. The dictatorship, supported by the army and by the assent of all who are loyal to the State, will carry out the necessary constitutional reforms." Was not this pan-German recipe followed to the letter by the coup of January 30th? It certainly looks like it. From this point of view the capitulation of the nationalist and capitalist Right wing before National Socialism is intelligible. They saw in National Socialism the executor of the pan-German mission, even at a time when the true revolutionary character of National Socialism had long been patent. The Conservative partners in the deal regarded the camouflaged dictatorship as no more than a transient phase, permitting the creation of an authoritarian State and the revision of Germany's frontiers and restoration of her power.

But even among Conservatives and Nationalists political ideas had developed, long before 1933, which yielded much more concrete conceptions of the necessary dictatorship than the simple bourgeois ones of Class's book *Wenn ich der Kaiser wäre.* Carl Schmitt goes beyond the retrogressive revision of the Constitution and the abolition of the franchise to the rejection of the whole "chimera" of a State based on the laws. The revolutionary democratic legislator who builds up the State on the basis of an ideology gives place in his conception to the man of violence, who by the force of his own will gives the State the stamp of a dictatorship. He gives place, in fact, to Fichte's "constraining lord installed by God, only formally a tyrant and usurper," a "lord constraining to Germandom," who "constrains" the German nation and all humanity "as recalcitrants by nature beneath the dominion of the higher insight." Here are plain links with National Socialism, the popular National Socialism of the first phase, with its nationalist doctrine. Along these lines the middle class man and the pan-German of the old style come to approval of the methods of tyranny, of the character of the new dictator, tyrant, and usurper. In this conception his methods are only despotic on the surface, but in reality salutary and necessary. Terrorism included, they are necessary to constrain the nation to unity and higher insight and Germandom.

That is how it was possible for the National Socialist dictatorship to develop, under the eyes of its capitalist partners, into a plain and unmistakable despotism, maintained by all the means of terrorism and violence. The first outstanding element in the revolutionary development in Germany was the artificial and arranged coup, which brought into being the confused and unanticipated conditions that made it possible for the "national rising" to turn into the National Socialist revolution. The second element, equally important, was the growth of a dictatorship, which was envisaged as only transitory, into the permanent institution of a despotism on the new principle of Leader and Following.

THE REACTION

We must go back a little further in considering this development, in order to see the full force of the fatal influences at work. What had happened was the fading out of a spiritual tradition among the "historic" ruling classes, among those elements of the nation which are mainly concerned for the preservation of historic continuity in State and society, and the replacement of this tradition by ideas connected with power and the protection of interests. The classes which to this day are generally described in the Reich as reactionary might contend with perfect justice that in protecting their own interests they were protecting those of the community. In the maintenance or restoration of the old elements with which State and nation have been bound up in the course of past history there is always a strong admixture of the motive of the preservation of national order and security, especially at times of such revolutionary tension as the years since the War. The dividing lines between genuine Conservatism,

THE REVOLUTION OF NIHILISM

which is an indispensable element in the life of every State, and a reactionary policy in the service of vested interests, are not always discernible with perfect clearness. They begin to become clear, however, as political methods diverge, and become unmistakable in the differences of political purpose. No one will any longer deny that it is mainly to the monarchist elements that Germany owes her present condition. There is no reason to doubt that the overwhelming majority of these elements brought about what has happened in the best of good faith and in the firm conviction that in protecting their own existence they were also protecting that of the whole nation, saving it from an upheaval of incalculable moment. It is not their political purpose that will be condemned, but the political means they chose. These means were not only discreditable but thoroughly ill-advised. Unscrupulousness in the choice and the use made of political means has frequently been characteristic of the reactionaries of the Right wing. They have found followers in this unscrupulousness, and they need not be surprised that in National Socialism they found that they had to deal with a master of it.

It is still difficult at first sight to comprehend the action of the monarchists in their final plunge into a policy the outcome of which is almost systematic self-destruction. Over-confidence and lack of insight are but an inadequate explanation. The deeper reasons must be sought at the point where the real weakness of German monarchism lies, the point that clearly distinguishes it from genuine conservatism, its complete scepticism as to the relevance of spiritual and moral forces to practical politics. Those who regard their own policy as one of the pursuit of concrete power in rivalry with other elements in pursuit of power, and political life as nothing but the violent conflict, using any and every means, between these power-seeking groups, fall necessarily into an unscrupulous power-policy, which blinds them to the only safe platform from which the struggle for lasting power can be successfully carried on to-day. No doubt the total nihilism which has been the motive force of the continuing revolution of the

National Socialists took shape among the old ruling groups as the unscrupulous "realism" of the systematic reactionaries. Reaction and "dynamism" are daughters of one mother, however much they may differ in appearance. This intimate relationship helps to explain an association which at first sight seems incomprehensible.

The economic interests represented by the "Reaction" are much the same in all Western countries, and have brought the big capitalists and financiers almost everywhere into more or less close association with political tendencies of the Fascist order. It is not the revolutionary dynamism of Fascism that attracts them, but the methods and political expedients of the system of dictatorship, which are common to Fascism and National Socialism. And nothing is more astonishing than the blindness of Conservative economic and social leaders, not only in Germany but everywhere, to the fact that dynamism, whether Fascist or National Socialist or any other, is revolutionary, and that its constructive elements are only in appearance conservative, and in reality work on the strict lines of State Socialism, leading of necessity to the expropriation of the leaders of industry and the deposition of the past ruling classes. To the outside observer it is simply inexplicable how captains of industry and financiers, used to careful and unemotional consideration and calculation, allow themselves to be deceived as to the true nature of the dynamic revolution, and still see in "Fascism" a patron of order and security, which will restore the ability of trade and industry to show profits. The restoration of "order," the disciplining of the workers, the ending of politically fixed wages and profit-destroying social services, the abolition of the workers' freedom of association, and the replacing of the continual alteration of short-lived parliamentary governments by a stable political system that permits long-range calculation—all these things tempt leaders of industry and finance and of society to shut their eyes to the fundamental difference between the true motives with which the dynamic dictatorships are set up and the motives which lead the conservative elements to support them. Reaction and dynamism were at one in Germany, and apparently in other countries, in regard to methods and means, but not in motives and aims. On this disastrous distinction the old leaders of industry in Germany and the old ruling classes are coming to grief through their union with the dynamism which was expected to save them.

It may be contended that the situation in Germany in 1930-1932 had become so disastrous that the most desperate means seemed acceptable if only they provided a respite. The economic situation was indeed disastrous. But the remedies offered were not so manifestly dangerous as they can now, after the event, be seen to have been. This is shown among other things by Schacht's plans, which amounted almost to genius, and which, had they only been kept within the limits their designer intended, might have had unquestioned success. The opportunities of developing the internal market at a time when the foreign market was becoming more and more inaccessible; of using the necessity of rearmament to produce a new trade boom; of taking advantage of a universal spirit of national enthusiasm to impose a sharper discipline on the masses and to induce the workers to accept a new labor statute made palatable by the phraseology of a new Socialism, a statute that would bring them virtually under military discipline, ending or restricting the inviolability of wage rates, the liberty to change from one job to another, and the freedom of association —all these seemed to their initiators to be plausible elements of a policy that could be carried out without an uproar. What they overlooked was the risk involved in carrying reaction to the length of depriving larger classes of the nation of their rights, and of letting these aims be pursued by revolutionary means. The gospel of violence placed by revolutionaries and reactionaries alike in the forefront of their policy masked the fatal contradiction between the group that desired settled order and security and the group whose methods meant the destruction of all settled order. The shortcomings of the leaders of the reactionary parties go far to explain their astonishing capitulation to the revolutionaries. But the true explanation is to be sought at the point where conflict of views came over practical tasks, tasks which were purely revolutionary in character, and, above all, the task of totalitarian mobilization: here someone had to give way, and the reactionaries were the weaker partner.

The social structure of the German nation has been shaken to its foundations. There was no necessity for fatalist acceptance of the inevitability of a plunge into social revolution. The plunge became inevitable only when the forces of conservatism totally misconceived their task and their choice of political means, as they did in the deal with National Socialism. It is true that, failing the return of the reactionaries to Conservatism, Germany is fated to fall into the chaos of a proletarian revolution. As yet the choice of what shall come after National Socialism is still open. But the time is short. And the opportunities of a political turn in the right direction, avoiding the self-immolation of all that remains of past traditions, are exceedingly meagre. There can be no denying that the process of the proletarian, nihilist revolution has already set in. It has set in involuntarily, and against the will of the leaders. It is very possible that the leaders will nevertheless turn to the deliberate furtherance of the process. This development cannot be countered by the mere restoration of the old order, nor by a revolution of the Right. It can only be stopped by a constructive process on traditional principles, but on new foundations.

THE DEGENERATION OF CONSERVATISM

A Conservative leadership of really outstanding quality, not merely one of tactical shrewdness, might have discovered the lines of a bold constructive policy. Men capable of such leadership were available. But they were viciously attacked and driven off as ideologists and dreamers by the old crib-biters of the party. From the earliest days of the Weimar Republic the actual leadership of the German National Party had abandoned true constructive conservatism for a reactionary determination to carry out a coup d'état, as the only radically effective resource. The Conservative leaders lacked the one thing that should characterize all conservative policy—patience. Thus they fell into the temptation of the period to resort to conspiracy. That substitute for a constructive policy was readily available in the existing turbulent conditions of permanent petty revolution. Their impatience led them from the outset into the pursuit of short cuts. The Kapp putsch, it is true, found little support from the political leaders of the German Nationalists, but the much more dangerous tendencies to enter into secret intrigues, concealed or open terrorism, and finally a policy of naked violence, established themselves as a new style of political realism. Advantage was soon taken of the many adventurers, anti-social or declassed elements, who are left stranded at the end of every war; they were entered as assets in the books of the new reactionary nationalism. There began with the lynching "Feme" and the putsch organizations of the type of "Consul" the unhappy course which found its logical development in the terrorist regime of National Socialism, and which had produced in almost all ranks of the German Right wing an assumption that the resort to violence was a natural political expedient and that political gangsterdom was essential to success.

These ideas were especially to the taste of influential elements among the military officers, who were almost driven into conspiratorial tactics by the narrow limits of the new army and the humiliating Allied army inspection—tactics which came to be used not only against the Allies but against the German Government itself. Thus the principle of camouflaged activity became almost second nature to the whole of the professional army, from the High Command down to the rank and file, with a distortion of moral ideas that profoundly influenced the whole army. Its members remained in a world of ideas resembling that of wartime, in which whatever served the practical purposes in mind was considered permissible and even a national duty. The carrying of these war-time ideas into political life in time of peace destroyed the distinction between legitimate and illegitimate means and the whole basis of political morality. Here lay the roots not only of National Socialist violence and lawlessness but of the widespread idea of the legitimacy of violence. The personal connections between the corps of officers and the Conservative leaders spread the infection of lawlessness through the Conservative and reactionary parties. Thus there spread throughout the whole field of politics a militancy which, it is true, was likely in any case to be produced by the necessity of rearming in secret and its effect on internal politics. The Weimar parties, however, must bear some of the responsibility for this, since their political passivity was wholly beyond the comprehension of the reactionaries. All the old revolutionary fire had died down amid the desire of the Social Democrats in power for peace and comfort. In proportion as the phalanx of the pseudo-revolutionary working classes showed itself to be the best of buttresses of law and order within the capitalist system, the will to revolt against the revolution of 1918 grew among the parties of the Right.

All these factors contributed to divert the conservative elements in the direction of reactionism. The great industrial and agrarian organizations were already working in the same direction. From their justifiable self-defence against destructive economic experiments and political tendencies, these associations soon went over to aggressiveness, advocating the reversal of the policy of social reforms. Meanwhile, under cover of the inflation, certain propertied elements succeeded in increasing not only their financial but their political power. It was amid these developments that Hugenberg, an entirely un-Conservative politician, permeated with the ideas of the pan-Germans, came to the head of the reactionary parties, and gave them the character that made the deal of 1933 inevitable. He inspired in the Conservatives the belief in the ability of a suitable political machine to achieve any and every political task—the crude and unthinking materialism, in other words, that underlay political "realism." But in their very realism the reactionaries remained unrealistic. A policy of national renewal and reconstruction cannot grow to fruition in the absence of the only soil in which it can thrive, loyalty and justice and freedom.

In our day there is a sort of international understanding between reactionaries. All are proceeding along the same fatal course of self-destruction. By their abandonment of the principles on which their whole existence depends, they are destroying the basis of their existence more thoroughly and more rapidly than the extremest of their political opponents could have done. None of them is ready to learn from his neighbor's mistakes. The great financiers, in their support of political dynamism, overlook the fact that they can continue to live at the expense of that movement only so long as there still remain free democracies to be reduced to dictatorships, and that they are assisting the very authorities that are restricting the field of independent enterprise. And in the same way all the groups that profess Conservatism are training and nurturing the very element that intends to overthrow them.

Perhaps the hour has now come for a broadly planned policy of genuine Conservatism. In Germany this was realized at the time of the nation's worst trials, but the opportunity was missed. Now the realization has unquestionably come again among the Conservatives, called forth once more by the desperate situation of the Reich. The vital question is whether the conservative, possessing classes, the elements that have been the traditional wielders of power, can do anything effective in the future, whether they still have a national task. And surely they have. But the time left is short. The foundations of national stability have been damaged by the Four Year Plan; if they are wrecked there will be nothing left but the pursuit of the revolutionary course to the bitter end, to chaos and the dictatorship of the mob. And the old conservative elements can only render fruitful service now if they are ready to risk their own existence. The struggle is one of life and death. Matters can no longer be ad-- justed by deals and tactical moves.

THE RENEWAL OF CONSERVATISM

Radowitz, the Conservative thinker and friend of Frederick William IV, once recalled a dictum of Metternich's. Metternich, in conversation with him, drew a distinction between principles and doctrines. Political principles were indispensable, he said, for every true statesman, but doctrines were the greatest of hindrances. We need to bear this distinction in mind in relation to a new "realism" in order to understand the decay of Conservatism in Germany. Many things can be done, given a total lack of principle, under the banner of realism, but the one thing that cannot be done is to pursue a Conservative policy. The repugnance to doctrine is understandable; the dismissal of political principles, in order to rely, in the name of realism, on violence, is itself a political principle of the first importance, that of dynamism.

In the last years of the era of William II there was scarcely any room left in practical politics for a German of Conservative outlook. Such alleged Conservatism as existed under the Weimar Republic was a caricature of true Conservatism. Such Conservative elements as existed in the post-war years, and there were plenty, wore themselves out in brotherhoods and conventicles, in the true German fashion, with problems which led them far from the political issues of the day into a maze of esoteric ideologies and doctrines. No political leader appeared with the energy and constructive ability to gather and lead these elements to the defence of Conservative principles against a pseudo-Conservative power policy. The result was that as the crisis grew more acute some of these elements remained in the twilight and political dogmatism of their literary clubs, others isolated themselves from politics in military brotherhoods, and the politically active section went over to National Socialism, imagining it to be an intellectually unformed movement which they could shape in accord-

111

THE REVOLUTION OF NIHILISM

ance with their own ideas. In spite of its manifest defects, National Socialism offered opportunities of pursuing initiatives in which the Young Conservatives were interested. The very name of its general objective, "The Third Reich," was a slogan of the Young Conservatives, the title of a book published in 1922 by Moeller van den Bruck.

Many Conservatives who had become spiritually homeless found their way into the ranks of National Socialism, from the very best of motives and in perfect good faith. They certainly did not do so for the sake of its program, which was all too plainly a mixture of inconsistencies and simple nonsense. They joined it for its resoluteness and its "moral energy." They put up with its revolutionary desperadoes, thinking that the movement would rid itself of its dross, and they put up with its demagogic propaganda. In joining the party they felt that they were gaining the one thing that was lacking in their own more intellectual political position, the approach they wanted to the practical politics of the day and to the controlling elements in politics. The lack of tangible instruments of power, the inadequacy of "brotherhoods" and the like, those groups of army-less leaders, was revealed at the moment when the gravity of the general situation made action essential. They felt more or less clearly that their ideas needed correction by touch with political realities, and they were eager to get down to practical service. In one respect they were profoundly in error in joining National Socialism, in the idea that demagogy can be overthrown by demagogic means, revolutionary disintegration ended by a revolutionary act. Our toleration, even temporarily, even with suspended judgment, of invasions of right and humanity and of the inviolability of the person, was a mistake arising from fundamentally wrong conceptions of the nature of National Socialist realism, and created the atmosphere in which persons of the highest character succumbed to the temptations of the system and sank to the level of Catilinarians. It is just at this point that the temptation exists into which the older Conservatives fell—the temptation to capitulate to an

112

unscrupulous use of power which was proving effective. And the Young Conservatives, before they could get their own political ideas clear, slipped into a political association destructive of every political virtue, an association in which, instead of being serviceable recruits, they became spiritual victims.

Conservatism has beyond question a stock of ideas which are of service in all sorts of spheres and under all sorts of conditions. But it lacks, in Germany, the realization of its own value. It has not definite enough political principles of its own, and above all not the resolute will needed for tearing itself away from its alien associations. The Young Conservatives, a product of the War and the shock of defeat, had never attained an effective existence. They were enthusiasts without practical experience, and capitulated before the fascinating potentialities of power. The older Conservatism had degenerated into a nationalism ready for violence within what it regarded as respectable limits.

Both old and new Conservatism had fallen victims to the error of identifying their own principles with the slogans of an out-and-out chauvinism. Conservatism cannot be chauvinistic. Chauvinism is a form of Jacobinism, a product of revolution. Conservatism, in our Western civilization, is bound up with federalism, not with the idea of a European imperium or hegemony. The ending of the revolution and the creation of a State are essentially tasks of an ethical and intellectual rather than a purely political order. The continuing civil war between social groups can only be ended by an absolutely binding agreement on a moral code. The Conservative conceptions of order presuppose an absolutely stable world order from which they can emanate.

But how can a Conservative philosophy be possible in a period in which the traditional institutions of law and order, with all the virtues which have become an organic part of them, and especially with the whole Christian teaching, have been destroyed from within? The catastrophe which has fallen upon us has shown us that the past conceptions of Conservatism were too narrow and backward-looking, and lacked fresh invigoration from the tasks of the future. The sacrifice of morality and natural justice in the terrorist system of the dictatorship has now revealed vividly to us the primary importance of things with which the new "realism" imagined that it could dispense in its political system. The old formulas and standards of Conservatism have been swept away by voluntary capitulation and compulsory *Gleichschaltung,* brutal destruction or terror-stricken flight. But the need for the self-preservation of our civilization is producing a new and modernized Conservatism. It has been suggested that the Christian standards are gone beyond revival. The confessional struggles in the Reich, and the individual revival and strengthening they have produced, seem evidence that that is the very opposite of the truth.

There is no room any longer for a nationalist Conservatism, only a European one. One of the fundamental changes in Conservatism is this release from narrow nationalist patriotism, since the civilization that has to be rescued and conserved is the common possession of the West. In this sense the idea of the Third Reich, before the National Socialist usurpation, was a Conservative idea. In Moeller van den Bruck's original conception it was not a German idea, it had no nationalist limitation; it was a political idea of European scope. It was a German idea of peace, contrasted with the dictated peace of Versailles. And certainly there was room for a great German realist policy, with a new standard of justice, aiming at a political order that would save from the Versailles Treaty the germs of the new and fruitful principles which it contained, and set them against the false as a free and just solution.

No one can doubt that in the midst of the National Socialist regime, and in sharp opposition to its young revolutionaries, there lives a great Christian, Western, German nation, deeply suffering, desperately biding its time. This Germany embraces all classes in every part of the country. The old links and associations have been broken, but a truly invisible church, a great community, is growing in their place. No concrete political aim has yet shown itself, and we are as yet only at the outset of the great, decisive struggle, the issue of which is not only a political but an ethical one. In this struggle German Conservatism finds its summons to renewed activity.

Radowitz, a much more profound Conservative thinker than the Conservative practical politician Bismarck, saw ninety years ago the approach of the same dangers as those amid which we live to-day. He saw the danger of the revolutionism that challenges the legitimacy of property, and that of the destructive power policy which ignores the place of ethics in statecraft. The moment the Conservatives virtually renounced ethics as an element in policy, the resort to the only refuge from chaos, to the material forces of army and masses, became inevitable. "Who knows," wrote Radowitz, "whether the Socialist despotism that will result from an accommodation between the two (army and masses) may be destined to provide the transition stage through which the modern State must pass, amid great sufferings and great experiences, before it reaches a form corresponding to the Creator's ordering of the world? Here, too, men will shut their eyes to the coming perils until they have become inevitable, dislocating the thousand-year-old social order of European humanity."

DOCTRINELESS RECOVERY

National Socialism must continue on its way to the end, or until a stronger will meets it. All else is illusion or deceit. There will be no abatement of its revolutionary fire; but it will throw overboard all the ideological camouflage of which it makes use at present. It will do so with such brutal openness that even the most benevolent nationalist critic will note the fact.

The consciousness of the loss of liberty poisons and destroys the character. A nation that falls into bondage and into the clutches of terrorism loses all strength of character. It also loses its productive and regenerative powers. No one can foresee what a nation will passively accept in such conditions. We do not know

115

what surprises the future may have in store for us in this respect. The spiritual and moral forces in a nation are crippled. Everyone knows the simple but amazing trick of fettering a fowl to a spot by drawing a chalk line round it. A similar enchanter's circle keeps the German nation in bondage. It is chained by autosuggestion, not by the power of its new rulers or the vast armory of terrorist means in their possession. One day the German nation will beyond doubt be startled out of the ban by some shock. Meanwhile the poison of thraldom goes on working. It not only destroys the character; the nation rots inwardly—a tree that will long stand in majesty, deceiving the inexpert, but rotten within. This age, with its frantic tempo, knows nothing of century-long processes like the decay of Hellenism or the decline of Rome. A few years have sufficed to produce the signs of relaxing energies and failing initiative.

And the system reveals an insuperable weakness—its artificiality, which could not withstand any serious test. Not one of the tasks of national renewal has found a genuine solution capable of enduring. In every field substitutes for genuine solutions have been made to serve. In some of the most elementary tasks the leaders have clearly not even realized the flimsy character of their work. The easy victories of National Socialism, which has never had to face any powerful opposition, have not only given it a feeling of irresistible strength but prevented its strength from being effectively tested.

The weaknesses of the whole German system, which no one capable of judgment can deny, render the future entirely uncertain. The nation itself bears the plainest marks of its injuries. This nation, driven, hunted, hopeless, obeying only impulses from without, continually shaken out of its composure, robbed of its self-reliance, in constant anxiety, losing spirit, losing elasticity, but excited into hysterical outbreaks, has become a sick nation, mentally unbalanced and neurotic. Such a nation is not in a condition to face a new war. Its features betray panic and a dangerous readiness for hatred. National Socialist propaganda has aroused and excited its destructive natural forces. The political rôle of the masses may have been reduced to insignificance, but as a natural force they remain formidable and untamed. National Socialism has destroyed the inhibitions that lay between their desires and destructive outbreaks. The diminishing suggestive influence of propaganda must lead one day to violent mass action, to slave revolts directed against all social order.

Above all, National Socialism has not welded State and nation into a new social order. It is precisely in this omission that it betrays the absence of doctrine in its revolution, its nihilistic character. It fulfils neither the principle of the participation of all in spirit nor that of national integration. A remolding on a vast scale has begun in Germany, and the result is difficult to foretell. The old is gone beyond possibility of recall. The conservative elements have delivered themselves up to destruction, and so have destroyed their right of existence in their present shape. The German revolution has opened the door to a complete reconstruction of the social order.

So long as National Socialism was connected with the idea of liberation, of freedom, it was a movement of value. To-day it means compulsion, terrorism, suppression, humiliation, enslavement. It means national self-destruction. To-day the conceptions of freedom and liberation are connected with other political principles.

But the conception of Socialism seems also to have lost the significance which it had in the nineteenth century. At least in its doctrinaire form, as a philosophy of history and a theory of society, it belongs to the past century. It has a future in spite of all counter-revolutionary and reactionary efforts; but only in so far as it is really a representative of the general interests of the whole nation and not merely the doctrine of a militant class.

The dictatorship will be overcome without doctrine—not in the nihilist sense but the reverse, the readiness to accept and incorporate all that is constructive and creative. There is beginning to grow up what I might call the ethical *fronde*. Against this *fronde* the totalitarian policy of National Socialism will come to grief. A state, a society, a nation, even the smallest community, has no lasting quality if it is without an ethical basis. A totalitarian dictatorship of pure violence is possible on a basis of nihilism, but it destroys its own foundation in proportion as its principles become general among the masses. The *fronde* that will become dangerous to the dictatorship is not a monarchist or Conservative one, one of the workers or the middle classes, one of soldiers or patriots or of youth; it is an ethical revulsion, common to all of these groups, which will only proceed from the spirit of Christianity. This is certainly not a political attitude, but it is much more. How it may grow into a political resolve, or simply a firm spiritual conviction and power of moral resistance, depends on many things, material and spiritual. It is easy to object that present conditions do not in the least look favorable to the entrenchment of a resolute ethical *fronde*. Beyond doubt many more strongholds of the ethical and religious forces of the nation, and perhaps the most prominent ones, will be evacuated. Nothing, indeed, can be more deeply disturbing to any non-Catholic than the capitulation of the Catholic prelates of Austria before a system whose hostility to Christianity is no mere chance but the essence of its nihilist doctrine of violence, a hostility which its leader and his satraps have voiced again and again in unmistakable terms. Undoubtedly the attitude of the Austrian bishops struck a heavy blow at the slowly developing healing forces of reason. Even the non-Catholic honors in the Catholic church one of the strongest of the historic powers and the incorporation of the Christian doctrine without which Europe would cease to be what it has been and still is. But to the simplest of our fellow-men it is a much more shocking thing that these high dignitaries of the church, who had but recently renewed their declaration of loyalty to the death to the principles which National Socialism has brutally flouted, should have broken faith. That immoral action must damage for years the confidence in an institution which can provide the firmest of all support for the ethical regeneration of the nations. Scarcely ever has a Christian church delivered such effective weapons into the hands of its enemies as the Catholic church of Austria.

This attitude may even result in the destruction of the Catholic church in its present form and constitution. No less fanatical than the determination of the National Socialist leaders to unite all Germans in a Greater Germany is their determination to liberate the Christian confessions from all international connections and to confine them entirely within the national frontiers. The schismatic creation of a national Catholic church is only a question of time. And even this will only be a stage on the journey to the total abolition of Christianity, the fight against which is not a mere philosophical fad of the National Socialists but an iron necessity of their system. Amid this struggle of Christianity for the most elementary rights of existence, rights which are much more seriously jeopardized than by Bolshevism, it is an irreparable injury to the honor and greatness of this faith, and of the institution incorporating it, when it is made visible to all, as happened at Vienna, that decisions are arrived at by that institution on the basis not of the principles of morality and faith but of practical expediency and discretion. This is only a repetition in the church of what happened among the German Nationalists and Conservatives. National Socialism is not to be overcome by coming to terms with it, but only by a clear, open, absolutely unflinching struggle.

It may well be that nothing but the plain evidence of the destructiveness of the nihilist revolution will furnish the ethical Fronde of which I spoke with active political determination. It may be that it will be necessary for the Catholic and Protestant churches to lie prostrate before all men's eyes as victims of this destructiveness. I do not myself feel that matters will come quickly to a head in Germany, though they may. But if they can at any time without the nation having to pass through the total anarchy of complete nihilism, it will only be through the active intervention of this ethical *fronde.* Nationalist ideas are not enough for the shaping and ordering of a nation; nor are Socialist ideas. Neither of these principles can make good the defects of our time, and the imperialism of the nineteenth century is no longer practical politics. Still less can revolution save us from the sequelæ of the ague that shakes Europe. What has now to be overcome is the dictatorship of violence, which draws its destructive energies from the directionless revolution, a revolution merely for revolution's sake. No longer is revolution the bringer of freedom, of ethical progress, and of a higher social order. To-day, in the midst of a revolution that has wrecked the social order, overthrown every standard, and rejected every ideology, deliverance lies in the forces of true Conservatism and in the healing restoration of the spiritual and social forces of our historic past.

Part Two

DICTATORSHIP WITHIN THE DICTATORSHIP

THE POLITICAL ROLE OF THE ARMY IN THE
THIRD REICH

1

From the National Army to the Armed Nation

THE UNSOUND SLOGAN

"It was a point of honor with the Prussian officer to be correct; it is a duty of the German officer to be crafty." This was said, in the course of a discussion in which I took part, by the first Field Marshal of the Third Reich.* It is doing no injury to the prestige of our army or its leaders to touch on the really tragic conditions implied by that statement. In the past we were accustomed to regarding strict objectivity, unambiguousness, and acceptance of responsibility as the mark of the corps of officers. It was not the duty of an officer to be crafty. The very nature of his duties and his whole training demanded of him a crystal-clear correctness.

There was craftiness in the part played by the army in the German awakening, and it produced the fatal degeneration of that movement, nationalist as it was at the outset, into a nihilist revolution. The army leaders were lacking in elementary straightforwardness. This must be said by way of preliminary to a critical study of the many misjudgments and incompletely thought-out ideas that resulted in the complicity of the army in the production of the present German situation.

* Marshal Blomberg.—Translator.

It was the duty of the army either to lead the nation back to the secure order resting on the forces of the past, or to make itself the instrument of a resolute and clear-sighted revolution. Instead, its leaders remain to this day divided and irresolute. It may be doubted whether the army leaders had any idea either of the direction which the general political development in Germany ought to take, or of the direction it was actually taking under National Socialism. What could they expect if they approved that direction? And if they did not approve it, why did they permit it? Did they originally misjudge the trend of developments, and realize it too late to be able to oppose it? Did they, do they now, consider that the process must be allowed to work itself out to the end, good or bad, because a premature interruption would bring disaster to Germany? Did they shut their eyes to the fact that the revolutionary degeneration of the "awakening" into a purely nihilistic movement was leading Germany to destruction on an inconceivable scale? Must we not, indeed, put our question the other way round: was not the army the actual source and prime cause of the revolutionary development? Is not the army itself fundamentally revolutionary in feeling, and virtually nihilistic? Had it not become, through its own military outlook, the strongest revolutionizing influence in Germany?

THE DILEMMA

In the past the German army was one of the strongest bulwarks of tradition—not merely monarchist, but active in the inculcation of patriotism in the best sense. Until the Great War it belonged to the genuinely conservative forces, those concerned for the preservation of a Christian and Western outlook. War and violence were the *ultima ratio*, the last resort, not the first. The new conception of total concentration on preparation for war as the condition of a nation's success in the next war is changing the character of the army. With the conception of the permanent mobilization of the whole nation there is developing in the army leaders the idea of an all-comprehending militarism, in which war and violence must become virtually the one constituent element in the whole life of the nation: the army must swallow up state and society, economic and cultural and private life, every sphere of human life that until now enjoyed an independent existence. A fatal, suicidal conception. "Peace must be subordinated to the requirements of war. War is the secret ruler of our century; peace no longer signifies more than a simple armistice between two wars"—so wrote the official *Deutsche Wehr*. This is the same revolutionary philosophy which Ernst Jünger elaborated as the philosophy of dynamism.

There can be no compromise in the army between the traditional order of the past and this new revolutionary conception, so that a struggle inevitably arose between traditional and revolutionary elements in the army. Little effort was thus needed on the part of the National Socialist leaders to revolutionize the army by external pressure; they needed to do little more than leave it to itself in order to make it the strongest partner in the total and permanent revolutionizing of the nation. It was a development which the National Socialist leaders clearly envisaged at a time when the army leaders had no idea of the interrelation between their own military conception and revolutionary dynamism.

The great dilemma of the army leaders lies in the fact that the experiences of the Great War and the requirements of national security appear to impose a conception on the lines of total mobilization, while this new form of national existence implies a radical revolution which incidentally is bound to destroy the past ethical and moral basis of the army. If, on the other hand, as the strongest conservative force in the nation, the army proposes to retain this former basis and, consequently, its past composition, it must set limits to its military aims and abandon the fundamental conception of war as the permanent condition and normal form of existence, with its practical corollary of the permanent mobilization of the nation.

There can be no doubt that many leading military officers are aware of this dilemma. The vital question, however, goes farther than this: can anything at all be done to bring to an end the revolutionary process which has begun? It may be that the duty mentioned by the first Field Marshal of ignoring certain ethical principles may at any time be declared to be no longer incumbent on the German officers. But it will not be so easy for the army to return from its new revolutionary conception to its past traditional one.

REVOLUTIONARY MILITARISM

This unsound slogan of craftiness and the revolutionary character of the new militarism explain the fatal political course taken by the army. The application of General von Schleicher's formula of "dictatorship within the dictatorship," the camouflaging of a military dictatorship by the National Socialist civil dictatorship, was a disastrous application of the principle of craftiness. All that has followed was implicit in this false start. "Politics must be subordinate to strategy." By identifying itself with this idea of Ludendorff's, National Socialism cut off the retreat of the army leaders to older and sounder principles, and made itself the spokesman of the most radical strategic demands, overriding the objections of the military leaders themselves. The civil dictatorship within which the military dictatorship was to have moved freely became its prison.

There is no field into which National Socialism has carried its disastrous activities that does not show direct connection with the policy of military preparedness. It was only in connection with the practical tasks of total mobilization that National Socialism gained the resources for its revolutionary progress. It was a cunning trick of the National Socialist leaders to appear to be deferring to every wish of the army in releasing the revolutionary forces of total mobilization, while in reality they were pursuing their own aims and were dislocating the close-knit army by immensely inflating it. The relationship in the deal of January, 1933 has been reversed by the clever tactics of the National

Socialists: National Socialism is no longer the cover for the army, but the total mobilization of the nation in the service of the growing army is the cover for the revolutionary aims of the National Socialists, aims similar to those of the Bolshevists. By adroitly relating its propaganda to the needs of the army, the party has wormed its way into the life of the nation under cover of the army until it no longer needs that camouflage. It is the services required for military purposes that have brought workers and employers, the lower middle class and the great capitalists, alike under a severe and levelling state control. The state machinery created for the purpose of this control has been a welcome increase of the party's forces. It has virtually placed the nation under martial law, and so has provided a legal basis for National Socialist terrorism.

In this process a decisive part has been played by the members of the civil government, the political leaders, who, in grotesque contrast to all past governments, have been not a check but a spur to the army, imposing on it their own will to war and their readiness to stake the whole existence of the nation. Thus total mobilization has provided the opportunity for the *Gleichschaltung* of the army, bringing it into increasing dependence on the revolutionary dynamism of the National Socialists. Their benevolent compliance with every demand of the army has enabled the party to secure the utmost possible influence over military matters. Conversely, the military leaders have found the scale of their opportunities continually increasing, and have been correspondingly tempted into adventurousness. The mobilization of the whole nation, by making the army the controlling factor in the life of the nation, has made it also the executor of the revolutionary aims of National Socialism.

THE SUMMONS TO THE RENEWAL OF THE STATE

The resolve of the army to intervene in political developments and direct their course is to be explained simply by the recognition of its duty to guarantee the security and the military efficiency of the nation. There is no justification for attributing to the heads of the army any other motives than those connected with their professional duty, though this always included the summons to the leadership of the nation at a time of emergency. Some of the leaders may have been partly influenced by motives of other sorts, connected with a restoration of the past social and political order; but apart from these motives the internal situation and the dangerous situation in Germany's foreign relations were sufficient to prompt the question whether the army would be acting up to its responsibilities in merely looking on passively. The general outlook was appalling enough to give the military leaders ample ground for the tragic resolves which have given Germany an unprecedentedly strong military instrument at the price of the destruction of her best elements. But did the leaders grasp the full significance of their decision?

I cannot deal here with the grave general military situation which occasioned the decision to rearm after the demonstration that general disarmament was a more or less utopian idea. The coalition of some of the smaller States was bound to imperil Germany's security. In addition to the question of adequately securing her military defence there was a more comprehensive one —how was the repetition of such an internal collapse as the country had suffered in the last war to be avoided if a new war came, a contingency which it was the duty of the army to have constantly in view? How was the response of the nation to a general call to arms to be assured? If Germany was not to become a nation of helots in Europe, fundamental changes were manifestly necessary not only in the State but in the economic structure of the nation, and, above all, in the social, spiritual, and intellectual structure—changes which seemed to be possible only through a revolutionary upheaval.

The same considerations that had brought the Reichswehr the responsibility for suppressing the Spartacist revolt and the lawlessness that followed the collapse of 1918 governed its course at all times—the duty of maintaining order within the State.

Amid the tendencies to general dissolution, the army is everywhere the last refuge of the State. And as the repository of the ultimate moral and material resources of the State, the army comes of necessity into the foreground in the new revolutionary processes; even without setting up a military dictatorship or desiring to do so, it becomes of primary importance in all functions of the life of the nation. In the process of the control of the State by the army, it is inevitable that the State should be modified in accordance with the spirit which is native to the army. This function cannot be fulfilled by the army in the Western States, the victors, with their old political traditions and settled ideas of the State. It can fall to the army only where a nation has passed through collapse, or where the forms and ideas of the State are new and immature.

THE POLITICAL INSTRUMENT

But the army can only serve the renewal of the State in so far as it constitutes itself a means of integration of the State in subordination to the State. In the summer of 1932 General von Schleicher published this statement in *Vorwärts*: "The belief that the intervention of the army in home politics must be carefully avoided has quite specially characterized the attitude of the leaders of the army in recent months. . . . I share their conviction that the support of bayonets is not a sufficient foundation for a Government. A Government in which the popular confidence is steadily diminishing, a Government whose parliamentary basis does not correspond to the actual state of popular opinion, would gain nothing from army support. A Government can continue usefully in office only if it does not turn against the currents of opinion among the mass of the people, but is able to provide itself with a broad basis of confidence in the vital and productive elements of the people." This was a clear declaration that the Reichswehr had no intention either of taking political action itself or of tolerating coups of the type of the Kapp putsch or attempts of any sort at setting up a military dictatorship. The army had no intention of ruling against the will of the people.

This involved the necessity of discovering a political instrument that would permit the army, without coming into the open, to control developments according to its own views by influencing public opinion. A suitable coalition of political forces could provide this instrument. The forming of opinion could take place under the laborious, slow, but honest method used in the countries with long experience of democracy. But the political machinery of a dictatorship could also serve, and there were familiar examples at hand of the way its mass propaganda could quickly whip up public feeling.

The immediate object was a struggle for liberation, the leadership of which ought to have passed openly and publicly into the hands of the army. But the very circumstance that this struggle for liberation implied rearmament in disregard of treaty obligations made it entirely impossible for the army to come forward publicly. It must remain in the background in order to divert the attention of foreign countries from the central task on which it was engaged.

The conduct of this campaign for liberation required strict disciplining of the nation. At this point the disastrous idea came into play of assuring success in the leadership of the masses through modern methods of propaganda, by placing a man of the masses in the center of the campaign. The military leaders had rightly intended to carry on the campaign for liberation only with the support of the nation; but the opinion grew that this could be done better if in place of a genuine popular movement, which had the disadvantage that it would be liable to take charge and follow its own bent, a manufactured one were made use of, as easier to manipulate and keep permanently under control. So the decision was made to accept National Socialism as the propagandist instrument for the staging of the national "awakening."

The National Socialists had more than one quality in their favor. They were more expert than any other group in the technique of influencing of the masses, and their skill in this encouraged the military leaders in the belief that with National Socialist aid they could induce the nation to accept almost any sacrifice. National Socialism had for years been something of a foster-child of the army. And it seemed to have a good deal more popular sympathy than the Stahlhelm or the Jungdeutscher Orden, both of which were tainted with reaction. Above all, it centered on a man of unquestionable popularity with the masses, a popularity unprecedented in Germany. It was also recommended by its ruthless determination, and by a readiness to take risks (a quality particularly to the liking of the military leaders) which the solid middle class members of the Stahlhelm entirely lacked, in spite of all their military bearing. Moreover, it had obviously obtained its great success with the masses with the very slogans which seemed to the army heads to be of special importance. The uniting of Socialist with Nationalist principles was just what the military leaders wanted for the creation and maintenance of the needed enthusiasm for national defence in the whole of the nation. National Socialism seemed to them to have been built up entirely in accordance with the principles evolved by the army command in the last year of the war in order to restore the failing spirits of the nation. It had taken over the idea of patriotic education and the ideas of the Pan-German Union and the belated Fatherland Party, and had developed them further from the point of view of mass psychology. The resoluteness and the novel "realism" of its political methods made National Socialism the very best of political organs. It worked on the well-tried practical principle that only violence impresses the people; it scorned logic and intelligence; and it was a master of the effective device of eternal repetition. All this was a very superficial judgment of National Socialism; and the decision to make use of the National Socialists was a disastrous subordination of broad policy to opportunist considerations of tactics.

2

Error and Complicity

ONE of the main considerations that led to the Government "combination" of 1933 was the extreme urgency of rearmament, an urgency increased by the important assistance it would give to the reduction of unemployment. The limits of rearmament were at first uncertain. The army leaders and the new Government were faced with immense difficulties in connection with its effect on Germany's foreign relations. The whole enterprise was a vast gamble. Would there be intervention, and how soon? That was the most important question. It seemed fairly certain at the outset that the Versailles Powers would intervene. No one could foresee that they would confine themselves to ineffective protests. A plan had thus to be devised which could be quickly carried out, and which would thus, before too long, increase the risk for the intervening Powers to such an extent that sanctions would be unlikely to be applied. This first phase of rearmament had to be so arranged that it would not interfere later with the main scheme or involve too great a waste of material. As a matter of fact, during this first stage of necessarily precipitate arming a great deal of material was used up to no purpose.

The second difficulty lay in the possibility that strong pres-

---

* *Wehrwirtschaft* in present-day Germany means the control of the whole economic system of the country from the point of view of military preparedness.—Translator.

sure might be brought to compel disarmament. In case of a treaty restriction of armaments, it would be well, at least at first, to comply with it. But this would have had the very important result of diminishing the opportunities for energetic pressure against the neighboring Powers, a pressure which was essential if the revision of the Versailles treaty was to be enforced. The limitation of armaments might render fruitless the whole scheme for a national Government, at all events so far as foreign policy was concerned. Thus the political leaders were scarcely less afraid of disarmament negotiations than of any preventive intervention of the Powers with sanctions. As late as 1934 Hitler had in view the possibility of the conclusion of an armaments pact, and in conversation with me he expressed the opinion that a pact which allowed Germany 400,000 or even 360,000 men should be agreed to.

The actual process of rearmament was influenced by the uncertainty whether the other Powers would give the Germans the chance of determining the scope of their armament entirely without interference. Nothing seemed less likely in 1933 than that the foreign Powers would virtually deal Germany all the trump cards and make it possible for her to emerge at once from the first secret phase of her rearmament. It is one of the most remarkable things in modern history that throughout the whole course from the first precipitate defensive measures in armament to the reintroduction of conscription and the remilitarizing of the Rhineland, the foreign Powers got no further than the stage of preliminary studies of the situation created from time to time. The whole process amounted to a great and successful campaign won by the Third Reich, with all its risks but also with the psychological outcome of its success. This outcome was much more than a sceptical assessment of Germany's opponents. As rearmament proceeded, the first objective of the army, the defence of German territorial integrity, gave place to that of victory over the superior opposing forces. It was the inactivity of the European Powers themselves that gave Germany the opportunity of so developing her war machine that the plan of development began to be determined on the lines required for an offensive, with the adoption of *Wehrwirtschaft,* involving the energetic production of substitute materials for the creation of national self-sufficiency (*Autarkie*). This conception, which to-day governs not only military but political and economic policy, has been produced by the actual course of developments, including the absence of any sort of restraining influence. Politically, of course, it offers the great opportunity of upsetting the present European political order by the simple fact of the possession of overwhelming military power, and of enforcing by means of material pressure great political aims which otherwise could only have been attained by years of persistent political agitation and intrigue.

It is in the nature of things that every army should assess the political situation from the point of view of possible warlike operations, and should try to provide itself with the means of success in face of the most unfavorable possible combination of Powers against it. It is for the political rulers to determine whether particular political situations rule out the possibility of warlike operations because they would involve the nation in excessive risks, or because they would require such an increase of its armament as would cripple it in the long run. The National Socialists, however, have ignored this principle; for the sake of their aims in home and foreign policy they have induced the army leaders to take the total mobilization of the whole nation and of its means of production as the basis of their operations. It has been the National Socialist leaders, not the army leaders, who dispensed with political methods of procuring for Germany a leading position in Europe, adopting instead methods of pure violence.

I do not propose to criticize the German rearmament in detail. It has been described abroad as a political, economic, and technical failure. Whether that is so or not, the tremendous pace at

134

which it had to be carried out, and the difficulties involved in the necessary camouflage, make it intelligible that it should not be perfect at every point. An important criticism is that the effectiveness of modern technical equipment seems to have been exaggerated, and that in the long run the trained and versatile infantryman will still be the decisive element. Above all, the expectations based on the ability to make use of perfected technical equipment in order to strike rapid and decisive blows at the heart of an enemy have been disappointed by the superiority revealed by modern defensive armament. This is an argument that must make it especially urgent to abandon total mobilization and seek in its place a new foreign policy. Two considerations are of exceptional importance in connection with armament—the continual increase in the cost of technical equipment, and the growing costliness of adequate defence. The present dimensions of armaments and the necessity of constantly bringing them up to date almost compel their use before they become obsolete. And technical military equipment is being perfected at such a tremendous pace that it becomes obsolete in a very short period.

The military leaders are becoming increasingly sceptical and critical of the economic measures embraced in the Four Year Plan and the whole system of *Wehrwirtschaft*. It cannot be denied that the organization of economic readiness for war is a very urgent task. But the organization of economic preparedness which is being carried on in every country is a very different thing from the vast maze of duplicated over-organization of the Four Year Plan and the accompanying regimentation of private enterprise in Germany. In any case the problem of economic preparation for war is an extremely difficult one. Even a cautious solution of it is bound to have quite unforeseeable revolutionizing effects in internal politics and in economic and social life. And if the economic preparation for war is associated with the production of substitute materials in order to widen the basis of food and raw material supplies, the whole enterprise is bound to have ruinous effects on the existing economic and social system, for the sake of a new system of at least doubtful merit. In view of the vast dimensions of the task, the possibility of success is open to grave doubt: there are too many sources of error and too many potential complications. It is another matter to restrict the use of products containing materials of military importance or involving dependence on foreign countries: this need not have revolutionizing effects if the existing industrial mechanism is used and the character of the economic system left untouched as far as possible. The same is true of the territorial redistribution of industry from the point of view of military security; it is true also of the control of trade, of state accumulation of reserve stocks, and of the development of communications from strategic points of view. But all these things work for revolution if they are made a system and a universal principle as in Germany, and if uneconomic principles necessarily involved in the reorganization are given the authority of a new and "true" order, anticapitalist or whatever else it may be called.

In certain cases, of course, the economic preparation for war requires the overriding of private interests and of considerations of remunerative working. Questions of cost cannot always be kept in the foreground where the purpose in view is the increase of military efficiency. But it is one thing to make an exceptional application of this principle and another to apply it universally. It is not necessary in the interests of *Wehrwirtschaft* to declare the principle of profit-making to be obsolete or to make the interests of the private capitalist a subject of abuse. On the other hand, from the subordination of profit and private interests to military exigencies it is not so long a step to those revolutionary conceptions, for which military exigencies may easily become simply a pretext. In this way a revolutionizing of the outlook of the military authorities themselves is easily produced.

This is exactly what is happening in Germany, where the system of *Wehrwirtschaft*, with its extreme concentration on the utilization of substitutes, its radical control of trade, and its continually tightening control of consumption and production, is beginning to produce a totalitarian, Bolshevist system of economic planning. This economic system is being developed, however, not in the interest of the efficiency of national defence but as a revolutionary phase in the course of the progressive revolution of dynamism. It is not a necessity but a course pursued for its own sake. It does not serve the nation but the continued dominance of the revolutionary leaders. It does nothing to raise the standard of living of the working population or to produce a juster distribution of the products of labor, but at least it enables such measures as the *Eintopfsonntag*, the monthly "one-course dinner Sunday," to be interpreted as social advances, and gradually prepares the way for the standardized feeding which will be celebrated in war-time and perhaps even earlier, as a new sign of the "classless State" and the *Volksgemeinschaft*, the "community of the united nation."

The cardinal question in this whole German enterprise is: is not this a vast blunder? Does not excessive planning and preparation imply a total exhaustion of the nation before the emergency arises? Is not the nation already wearied, and the economic system breaking down? In the *Deutsche Volkswirt* of July 16th, 1937, Major Beutler, of the General Staff, expressed this notable opinion on *Wehrwirtschaft*: "A national economic system that defies economic principles (*die das Wirtschaftsprinzip verneint*) will very quickly be overtaken by the economic systems of other countries, and so will be depreciated also from the point of view of war." This is a sharp condemnation of the present efforts in Germany to form a new economic principle out of the necessity for rearmament and for economic preparation for war. The army should itself have a strong interest in combating the evil of radicalism, because the signs of the exhaustion and crippling of private enterprise are already clearly to be seen, and a state of things thus threatens which will be the exact opposite of the purpose of the economic preparation for war—a thorough debilitation of trade and industry instead of its preparation for wartime efficiency.

Total mobilization is a logical consequence of the totalitarian character of future war-making. The totalitarian war is not an invention of Germany's or of Ludendorff's. It is not a thing to be taken or left at choice: it is an outcome of the revolutionary pace of world developments. For the German military leaders it was essential to consider the country's future perils in the light of the experiences of the Great War. But, it will be objected, do not the lessons of the War lie rather in foreign policy than in military technique? Do not the experiences of the War postulate for the only possible German strategy of the future a fundamental limitation of political aims and of risks to be incurred? Is totalitarian war really essential to victory in the future? Both questions were disposed of as far as the German military leaders were concerned, by the emergence of a novel idea.

This was the idea of a "broadened strategy," in which "psychological weapons" (*geistige Kampfmittel*) play a part of the utmost importance as accompaniments of totalitarian strategy. Just as the time when there was a clear distinction between peace and war is apparently past, so war no longer consists entirely of military movements. One thing is certain: aggression in time of peace without preceding diplomatic tension defeats almost all normal guarantees of security, and so offers great possibilities of success. But it may be doubted whether the element of surprise can be carried to the length of a decisive victory. General Seeckt, however, shared the view that war by means of an attack in the midst of peace, and the strategy of a blow straight at the heart of the opponent, are indispensable. Each stroke should be driven so deep that it produces political disorder within a country and makes it ready to treat. But, after all, other things have also to be taken into consideration. These swift actions may produce counter-

138

coalitions. In order to anticipate them and to blunt the point of their most dangerous potentialities, it is possible, for instance, to seize a pledge. In surprise movements there must be a prophylactic occupation of the key positions for possible strategic operations. That done, it will be possible to await the outcome and express readiness to negotiate. These operations need not necessarily take place in the territory bordering on the Reich. It is necessary to get rid of any idea that future warlike action will take place on lines resembling in the least those of the Great War. Wars of long duration are beyond question impossible for Germany. But in the view of the National Socialists they will not come, even if coalitions should be formed against Germany. Certain political activities constantly going on, which may be described as of the nature of feeling the way, reveal the effort not only to render the tactical situation favorable to a succession of bloodless victories, but also to determine the particular issues which the general political situation may make ripe for settlement in accordance with the aims of National Socialism. These political activities find their explanation in the novel character of the important moves to come—pressure combined with sudden threats, now at one point and now at another, in an unending activity that tires out opponents, enabling particular questions to be isolated, divisions to be created in the opposing camp, and problems to be simplified until they become capable of solution without complications.

It must not be forgotten that we are living amid revolutionary subversive efforts not confined to Germany but directed against the whole European order. The military moves of National Socialism will at all times be simply an aspect of its revolutionary activities. That is the essential new feature. They only become possible when the political situation has so far ripened in the country affected that armed aggression appears to be absolutely certain of success and, above all, of assistance to the revolutionary process. The aim is not simply the expansion of frontiers and the acquisition of new territory, but at the same time the extension of the totalitarian revolutionary movement into other countries. All this is virtually the transfer of the modern technique of the coup d'état, the technique of the formation of revolutionary cadres, the surprise occupation of key positions in the State, to foreign affairs. The military operations have the same function as that of the armed revolutionaries in a coup d'état. Success is dependent on the prior ripening of the revolutionary situation, the general situation prepared by other means. Warlike operations require from now on—such is the conviction of the National Socialist strategists—similar conditions to those required for a coup d'état within a State: the weakening of the enemy by sowing dissension. The age of the segregation of war years from peace years has passed. But it is still possible for political changes to be enforced without bloodshed, simply by means of the weight of armament brought to bear.

Some time before the National Socialist seizure of power, I took part in a discussion at Obersalzberg in which Hitler, whose interest in military matters and in problems of strategy are as well-known as his high opinion of his own abilities in that field, expressed his view as to the nature of the practicable revolutionary modifications in strategy. He rejected at the outset the idea that technical inventions could seriously affect the basic principles of strategy. He rejected altogether the lay conception of the possibility of revolutionary inventions of any sort, and pointed out that in spite of the invention of firearms there had been no change in the great fundamental idea of strategy from Cannae to Tannenberg. But, he said, in a very different field from that of technical armaments possibilities had grown up of the broadening of strategic principles; revolutionary strategy could be carried into the intellectual field. This might justify the risking of military operations which in themselves could only be regarded as senseless and disastrous. As he spoke, his words gathered the suggestive force characteristic of him; then he abruptly broke off. In the past year we have had practical experience in the basic lines of this broadened strategy. The occupation of Austria and that of the Sudeten territory were semi-diplomatic, semi-military operations, a mixture of war and propaganda, diplomacy and subversive revolutionism.

If the army leaders are working on these lines, and it almost seems that they are, then they are making themselves the forerunners of a world revolution which can no longer be stopped. The improvisations of the Great War in the direction of spreading revolution among the enemy are not only being systematized, but the army, in order to weaken the enemy even before the outbreak of war, is making itself the advance guard of revolution in other countries. It is an extremely disturbing idea that the German army leaders should, for reasons apparently of a military nature, have delivered up their own nation and its neighbours in Europe in advance, as it were by way of prophylaxis, to a radical revolution. Is this idea, after six years of the National Socialist regime, so baseless? It would mean that here again there has been a capitulation of the spirit before violence and terrorism.

It must be borne in mind that strategy may include propaganda. But it is also, and in an equal degree, an element involving the ethical character of the supreme army leaders. Can they be credited with the conscientiousness in future operations that is indispensable to success? Are they not departing from the very foundations of the art of strategy in their pursuit of novel expansions of its scope? It is not only a question of the disappearance of the distinction between military and political action or of the addition of propaganda to the military resources. The special strategic conception of the National Socialist leaders consist of a readiness to gamble not hitherto usual, a system of surprise attacks not hitherto regarded as practicable, and an unprecedented indifference to losses of their own. National Socialist strategy will seek to reach a decision in warfare by a single blow of such destructiveness as has hitherto been regarded as inconceivable. It carries to the highest pitch the strategy advocated by Clausewitz, the direct thrust at the heart of the enemy Power. But in the National Socialist conception

141

this "direct thrust" has the resolute and reckless character that marks all operations of the party, with everything staked on a single card.

The danger of this new doctrine of a broadened strategy lies, however, not only in the fact that the army accepts the principle of a revolutionary destruction which sooner or later destroys the army's own basis; it diverts the minds of the political and army heads from the essential question of operations to subsidiary questions. The auxiliary arm of propaganda and the special strategy of surprise operations may be effective, but they have their dangers. The party leadership tends to make of them a universal strategic doctrine—a complete mistake. Similarly with the broadening of strategy to embrace political disruption and the preparation of risings. Each of these expedients is effective and may be required in emergency. Made into a system, as a cure-all, they are capable of producing a disastrous fiasco. The distinction is revealed when we consider the conviction of the party that every aim regarded as politically necessary must be attained by military means. There are political problems which cannot be solved by military means. That was proved in the Great War. Many problems in foreign policy are incapable of solution by war.

It is the characteristic of our time that the normal, laborious method of peaceful adjustment of difficult problems is despised and preference is shown for violent means, which, as the Great War has demonstrated beyond cavil, provide no lasting solution. It is in consonance with the present-day contempt of all spiritual things in Germany that the robust technique of terrorism and oppression which to-day takes the place of German internal politics should also have replaced German foreign policy. Germany's future will depend on whether the army leaders will submit to the degradation of allowing themselves and the army to be used in the service of this substitute for political action, as the officials in the civil service and the law courts have permitted the organs of administration and of justice to be used.

142

The atmosphere of fanatical nationalism, in which all risks are ignored and prudence figures as unpatriotic cravenness, inevitably destroys even in the more responsible minds the clear distinction between the desired and the possible. The sound military principle of always assuming that the opponent will take the most logical course is no longer adhered to. The ill-understood attitude of foreign Powers in face of arbitrary political action on Germany's part has lent support to the view that German political "daring" has been met everywhere abroad with "pusillanimity," so that it has a good chance of succeeding. Unlimited adventurousness and depreciation of opponents hold the field. No one protests: to do so would be to risk the charge of unpatriotic behavior and civilian timorousness. No wonder that in this atmosphere, amid universal spying and purging, nobody ventures to take national problems seriously, no matter how great their importance. Unfortunately not even military authorities are in all cases free from this attitude. In 1934, when Austrian affairs were more and more plainly nearing a catastrophe, I was approached with the suggestion of mediation on the lines of securing Austrian consent to a common foreign policy with Germany, subject to a reciprocal engagement not to intervene in the internal affairs or interfere with the independence of either State. I took the opportunity to seek the support of the officer who later became the first Field Marshal of the Third Reich. General Blomberg gave me this unforgettable reply (a reply characteristic of the attitude of some of the army leaders):

"I have a sort of jester's freedom to say anything I like to the Leader. But I shall never dream of saying anything to him about Austria, and I strongly advise you to steer clear of the matter. It is being decided by the Leader alone. It is a point on which he is not quite sane."*

I retained this reply almost word for word, and made a note of it at the time. It seemed to me to be thoroughly characteristic

* "Diese Angelegenheit wird von dem Führer allein entschieden. Sie ist etwas wie ein Tollpunkt für ihn."

of German conditions in general. Here was the supreme military commander, a former officer of the royal Prussian army, boasting of his "jester's freedom" in relation to a man whose political importance had neither been confirmed by experience nor proved by any genuine achievement. A Minister of the Reich declined, in a question of outstanding importance, to intervene on the strength of his joint responsibility, and yielded to a leader of problematical qualities on a point on which the leader was not quite sane. I must say that few things so disturbed me as this revelation of the pass we had come to. Blomberg's reply went far to confirm me in the conviction that the German nation was proceeding in its National Socialist course to inevitable self-destruction. There was a certain analogy between the conditions in Danzig and in Austria, and I was necessarily concerned that a policy should be pursued in the Reich which would diminish the risks, not gratuitously increase them. I was reduced to discovering that the man in supreme command of the mightiest instrument of State power was apparently allowed no say in regard to the great problems of the nation, and that he was not prepared to move even in regard to political adventures the results of which might easily be irreparable. I found that in Germany policy was being decided not by the question of the important material considerations involved or of the practicability of any particular aim, but by the obsessions of individuals on points upon which they were not quite sane. A few months later Dollfuss was murdered. It was an event the results of which might easily have been irreparable, but it did nothing to enlighten Hitler; it only increased the passionate obstinacy with which he pursued his revolutionary policy.

It is impossible to understand the true situation in Germany without a knowledge of these things. It is deeply distressing to a German to witness this unexampled moral and intellectual collapse. Only desperadoes could pursue such a policy as has been pursued in Germany in these six years. The risk which the military leaders are unwilling to face is taken by the political leaders. The military leaders, however, in their abandonment of the duty of arriving at their own decision, and their capitulation to a sort of idolatry, will have no control of the nature of the victories achieved. They have succumbed in a disastrous way to two temptations: they underestimated the strength of the National Socialists, contenting themselves with the existence of their own instrument of power instead of creating a political instrument ready to strike at any time. And they incurred the most extreme risk that could be incurred by resting the expansion of the army on the basis of the dynamic revolution. After the collapse in the Great War a Reichswehr grew up to continue the observance of all the historic traditions of the old armies. The expansion of the Reichswehr into the National Socialist popular army is likely to produce a force that has thrown overboard every tradition and every ethical principle and has become the resolute instrument of a world revolution. Passion, ambition, personal inadequacy mark the course of a process of destruction from which there will not be a second recovery.

It is said that two generals, both likely to be promoted to the supreme command, were sent a few years before 1933 to Soviet Russia, in order to report on the situation there. One of them gave a brief, sober, realistic account, which made an effective end of certain illusions. The other saw what he had gone to see. He saw in place after place what his chiefs desired and expected him to see. Both of these generals have played a decisive part in recent history. They represent two types of leader. They are now in keen competition with one another for decisive influence in the supreme command. There can be no doubt that the one who belongs to the type that is capable of illusion has the best prospect of success. A very grave factor is beginning to operate in Germany. The country is intellectually so cut off from Europe in every field that reality in Germany is already a different thing from reality in the rest of Europe. The German honestly thinks he is a realist, and mistakes his own illusion for reality. In the growing impatience the realization of plans is regarded as possible simply because it is desired. Here lies the greatest danger to Germany's future. In spite of Cabinet meetings and military discussions, nobody is able to convince the hysterical fantasts of the country of the reality of things they do not want to see. And hysteria is infectious. "We National Socialists do not believe in economic laws; we believe in the creativeness of our race, because we feel in it the dynamic will to creativeness which exists among us." Thus the *Völkischer Beobachter.* The National Socialist not only does not believe in economic laws, he does not even believe in the law of cause and effect. After the victory of National Socialism over the army leaders, and over their deep-rooted opposition to the permanent revolution, we must wait to see how far the capacity of the National Socialist leaders for self-delusion is conveyed to the supreme command.

There is no doubt that among the majority of the army leaders a counter-movement is beginning to make effective progress, a movement that is throwing off the dross of the present materialist epoch and is returning to the spiritual models of a classic past. There is no doubt that this movement, not, as a superficial judgment might assume, from reactionary or class motives, but as the result of the most careful reflection upon the tasks of the army and the conditions of their fulfilment, is taking the shape of a total rejection of the utterly destructive ideas of National Socialism, with its misguided policy, its belief in force, its contempt for reason and for any serious examination of problems.

Yet, even among the high military leaders, there seem to be signs that the gifted amateur has a better prospect of acceptance as a master of strategy than the professional soldier. Even before the arrival of National Socialism in power, admiring stories were told in the higher circles of the party about Hitler's great strategic gifts: he was supposed to have made strategic suggestions of a really epoch-making nature to the East Prussian command, and to have given sound reasons for them. Such things have happened—with Cromwell centuries ago, and Trotsky in our time. More than one of the supreme party leaders aspire to the supreme command in the field, confident that strategic mastery is no more difficult to acquire than the political mastery they already possess. But the question for the professional military leaders is this: is not the whole idea of totalitarian war, the whole state of Germany to-day, a reckless defiance of realities? It is not the strength in armaments, so impressive to the uncritical mass of the people, that matters: the elements of victory are strategic ability and army morale. Both of these things are products of the training of mind and spirit.

UNITY OF SPIRIT

Among certain circles in the highest ranks of the German army it is being said that the army cannot continue to maintain its aloofness from the Party. The revolutionizing of the German nation has proceeded so far that the exclusion of the revolutionary ideas of National Socialism from the army would destroy its fighting quality. It is not, say these officers, for the military leaders to decide from their point of view whether a particular set of political ideas is suitable for the nation; they are concerned only with the defence of the nation. The army cannot alter the nation or reverse the process of its revolutionizing. All, therefore, that it can do is to make itself the instrument of the revolution. That is the only way the fighting quality of the nation can be maintained. Consequently, the ideas of National Socialism must not only not be kept out of the army; they must be actively and energetically impressed on it. The corps of officers must regard themselves as actually analogous to the National Socialist élite. Only so can the army maintain its position as educator of the nation in fighting spirit and as the guiding influence in the nation. Just as many members of the old nobility and the leading social classes sought admission to the S.S., the "Black Guards", without thereby sacrificing their aristocratic character, so now the corps of officers must enter the party. Such agitation for entering the party has been the prelude to every past process of *Gleich-*

147

schaltung. Behind it in this case lies also the recognition of the actual revolutionary rôle of the armed forces and of the universal and permanent mobilization they have to carry out.

But can the past type of German soldier and of German officer continue to be trained and maintained on the basis of the National Socialist philosophy? It is impossible for the soldier to be deprived of the moral basis of his existence and to confine his sense of duty to the inferior basis of loyalty to the nation. It is absurd for other men, but above all for the soldier, since in the last resort his duty implies the risk of his own life, a thing which a man will do only from one of two motives—either in pure devotion to a cause or out of the desire for adventure or material gain. And the mercenary soldier acts neither out of patriotism nor from any other ethical prompting. The mercenary type is unquestionably beginning to develop because the progressive loss of authority of all standards is inevitably affecting those of patriotism and soldierliness with the rest. The growth of the new type, less among the common soldiers than among the officers and non-commissioned officers, is steadily advancing. The army is thus clearly at the outset of a revolutionary change at its very centre. There is little doubt that the army leaders are as loth to admit the extent of this revolutionizing as were the monarchists and Conservatives in the political field. The army maintains the illusion that it is still the essential bulwark of tradition and of the old national standards, whereas in reality it is undergoing the same subversive process which all other elements associated with National Socialist dynamism have long suffered.

The character of the soldier is affected the moment the grounds of devotion to his duty are lost. Those grounds demand an ethical foundation, and cannot exist in a realm of opportunism. Soldierliness as we have known it in the past is possible only in the sphere of a transcendental faith. Any religion concerned only with this world lacks the faith that transcends egoistic promptings, the faith through which alone a man can be ready to sacrifice his life. In the realm of opportunism, in which that is right which serves the State and the nation, the step to the view that that is right which serves the individual is inevitable. On this soil the mercenary soldier may thrive, but the true soldier is out of fashion and out of season. Herr Banse, whose subtle processes of fundamentally irrational ratiocination are far more dangerous than those of the power-adoring pan-German professors of pre-war days, asks how the unheroic racial elements of the German nation can be made and kept willing to defend their country. The real question, overlooked by Banse but vital to our country to-day, is: how can we preserve the fighting spirit of a whole nation when its moral and religious foundations are being systematically destroyed, and replaced by a concocted philosophy brutally forced on it, a philosophy compounded of scepticism, nihilism, misanthropy, and materialism, with a pretended national movement of renewal revealing itself as nothing but the will to power of new leaders?

If I am rightly informed, it is in this vital question for our nation that the anxieties of not a few of the responsible military leaders have culminated in recent years. Those who were in close touch with the corps of officers in Germany before the War know that it largely included elements of genuine piety. These, admittedly, were not universal. The current materialism and the new doctrines of violence and unprincipled "realism" were beginning to appear not only at the top but lower down in the scale of seniority. Among the leading generals, Christianity was beyond question the accepted foundation, not because the Emperor himself desired it but on account of a genuine faith. It is difficult to convey a convincing impression of these matters to the outsider, because this Christian element in the corps of officers was never obtruded, owing to the easily understood manly repugnance to the display of feelings deeply and genuinely entertained.

With this Christian basis stands or falls the character of

the German officer. If the Christian basis disappears, the officer loses with it the essential validity of his other principles. In the past, realism and the harshness of his profession were compatible with a high spirituality which characterized the best men in the General Staff, and with a loyalty to the tradition of the ruling house which was natural to the nobility. The element that gave these characteristics their binding nature in the life of the officer was the Christian heritage of our Western world. Only in the Christian sphere lay the character-forming elements which produced amid the conflicting calls of an officer's profession and the temptations of a life of external splendor, the great personalities in which the German armies of the nineteenth century were not poor.

Mehr sein als scheinen, "Be more than you look"—this motto of Schlieffen's is no motto for a mercenary, but indisputably a bit of the Christian ethic. It is not surprising that mottoes of another type are gaining currency among the corps of officers, when one of their best figures is tilting against Christianity with the violence of a quixotic berserker. With this truly tragic figure of our recent history, with Ludendorff's furious campaign and his secession, obviously painful to himself, from the world of Christendom, the spiritual doubts of the corps of officers in the German army to-day become evident. Here are plainly to be seen the spiritual processes of disintegration which are destroying even the firm traditional foothold of the officer class. In the absence of spiritual directives from which the officers are suffering at the moment, with their two main elements of guidance, the crown and the Christian church, taken from them, they are reduced to spiritual *Ersatz,* cheap substitutes of doubtful origin and efficacy.

Unquestionably, in spite of notable exceptions, the Christian spirit has largely disappeared in the present-day corps of officers. Even in the generation at present in command it is no longer so firmly rooted as in the past generation, the generation of Ludendorff and Seeckt, or the still older one of Hindenburg and

Mackensen, of the pre-war generals, who were firm believers. The generation with whom I sat on the benches of the cadets' college, and who to-day occupy the chief army commands, still possess so much of the essentials of the Christian faith as to recognize the perilousness of the whole course taken by the nationalist movement in Germany, though the careerists among them may have dispensed with scruples and look on with indifference. But the case is different with the younger generations, the young men who are now entering the corps of officers and working their way up in a new and unscrupulous spirit of revolutionism. With their advance, and with such destructive teachings as those of Professor Banse, the total revolutionizing of the corps of officers is inevitably approaching, and with it the destruction of the last firm foothold still left for the historic spiritual and religious elements in the German nation.

I have discussed this question of the spiritual and religious change in the German corps of officers at some length, though still inadequately, because it is only from this point that it is possible to understand developments which at a casual glance seem mysterious and full of contradictions. An élite of officers who showed nothing but contempt for the capable and honorable, if limited, President Ebert, are now yielding to the fascination of a revolutionary fanatic and capitulating at once to the elements of their own destruction. Between 1918 and 1938 lie two decades of a spiritual disintegration which is only now being realized. The last stronghold of the old order has, to all appearance, been surrendered by its garrison.

This leads to the grave and, indeed, critical question—is there still a uniform type of Prussian or German officer? The very fact that this question has to be asked reveals one of the most fatal weaknesses in the structure of the nation. A lack of uniformity in the corps of officers would lead of necessity to a lack of unity in the command. Until the War one of the principal elements of the strength of the German armies was the indissoluble unity of the corps of officers, as a body with firm conceptions

151

of honor, identical ethical and spiritual standards, and the uniform outlook on life of a fully developed professional class. The corps of officers of the Reichswehr, the army of the Republic, remained essentially a uniform body as before the War, though it was inevitable that elements of ambition and materialism should begin to make their influence felt. Since January, 1933, all has changed. The spiritual training in the corps of officers is beginning to lose its unifying and formative influence, and alien elements of thought are showing themselves, producing sharp divisions of opinion. To-day the corps of officers is already broken up into several groups of conflicting outlook and purpose, and it is difficult to see how under present conditions unity could be restored. The corps can thus no longer exert its unifying formative influence upon new arrivals. It is no longer able to preserve the traditional standards intact even among the older officers. Comradeship demands the uniformity of tone produced by a common general outlook, and this uniformity is disappearing. The ethic of the officer is becoming in general what it was only in individual cases of degeneration in the past, a matter merely of outward conformity.

Rearmament, with the resulting rapid promotion, has dissolved some of the old mutual loyalties. It has unmistakably let loose a mass of ambition, produced jealousies, aroused resentment at favoritism in promotion, and, above all, provided opportunities for the exertion of influence upon promotion by elements outside the corps of officers. Not every officer has resisted the temptation to make use of these elements in the interest of his own career. Careerism and unconscientiousness were not entirely absent from the old army. Connections play their part in every army. But in the past this defect was kept within bounds by the unquestioned authority of the Crown. At this point the process of *Gleichschaltung*, completed years ago in civilian life, is beginning to show its unhappy disintegrating effects among the corps of officers.

152

All this is as yet in the initial stage. But for those who have eyes to see, and who have watched the process of dissolution amid the civil community, the corresponding process is unmistakably recognizable to-day in the army. It is taking special forms, but these cannot conceal the essential parallel with civilian *Gleichschaltung*.

Thus we have now to reckon with more or less sharply divided groups in the corps of officers. Relatively strong in influence, but certainly no longer predominant in number, is the group whose members hold to the army's traditional social and professional conceptions, a group monarchist and Christian in outlook. They joined in the adventure with National Socialism only with the purpose of laying a firm foundation for the restoration of a Christian monarchy, by means of rearmament. There is a large second group of officers concerned with little beyond their professional duties. They stick rigidly to their work, and hold aloof from anything calculated to unsettle men's minds, especially anything of the nature of adventurousness. Yet neither they nor the first group can fail to see the signs of the manifestly destructive nature of German developments. Both groups are alive to the present overvaluation of material things, and see in the whole National Socialist drive a vast mistake with incalculable potentialities of evil. They have little knowledge either of politics or of economics, but they declare that the whole work of military reconstruction is proceeding on insecure foundations. They are not convinced of the value of the successes achieved in foreign affairs; in home politics they see that the work of the Party has produced a semblance of unity in the nation without really reconciling any of the national dissensions. They see the economic foundations for the maintenance of large-scale armament more and more plainly dwindling. So they yield to the soporific virtues of endless attention to their duties, which in any case are exacting enough to absorb all their attention and leave little time for reflection on deeper issues. It is almost a flight from reality that is

153

going on in army offices and clubs—a rigorous concentration on the daily growing round of duties, and withdrawal as far as possible from practical political life.

A very different group is the third. It is at present a small one, but it has every chance of a great career. It has much the same prospects in the army as the old party members had in the administration. These are men of the new *condottiere* type. This type is not the creation of National Socialism, but National Socialism gives it a chance of promotion that will never recur—and also a chance of soldiering on an important scale. Here, therefore, we find the boundlessly ambitious mercenaries, brilliant professionally, soldiers who are soldiers to the exclusion of all else, and who intend to show their mettle in any emergency. They are the future type of the revolutionary army, the coming German revolutionary generals. Ruthless, brutal, they are concerned only for themselves, their career, their power and influence; they are out to play as great a part as they can, and to make their way up to high command. For them, rearmament and the coming war are no more than the framework for their own careers. They are the army equivalent of the central and local leaders of the National Socialist Party. They are ready to make any concession whatever to the movement, without the slightest scruple—true revolutionaries, who have discarded character as useless ballast. This type of German is very common to-day; in the corps of officers it is not yet widely represented, but it is to be found in all ranks. It is a dangerous and unreliable type. It will sacrifice National Socialism as readily as it has adopted it, if ever it sees further personal advancement in so doing. These are the most reckless of the advocates of military adventure.

The fourth group is not yet of any great importance, but its importance is growing. It consists of the young officers who, secretly or openly, are resolute members of the party or have a similar revolutionary outlook. These are the new generation, with the doctrinaire obstinacy and unteachability of the young.

They are dangerous because they are fanatical; they are imbued with the new principles of violence and determined revolutionism, and a source of incalculable ferment. In them spiritual nihilism has produced a positive attitude. Their contempt of the normal standards of civil life extends to the traditional standards of the nobility, of the soldier's profession, and of legitimism. They have no more respect for Christianity than for any other "mythology." They have their own conception of heroism, the heroism of the modern mechanized army. They heartily despise their commanding officers as respectable old gentlemen. Theirs is a new form of National Bolshevism, a revolutionism entirely immune to any sort of educative influence because of the confidence and conceit of its representatives.

The development in this younger generation of a new type of German officer, with its own standards and modes of expression, is all the more steady and certain because the old traditions are being passed on generally by inadequate and outmoded methods. Moreover, even the firmest adherents of a monarchist and Christian outlook have suffered a loss of faith in the old standards which damps their own spirit and robs them of all power of conviction in their relations with the new generation. The newly-acquired, would-be-humorous tone of roughness and robustness, and the ostentatiously assumed loftiness of bearing of the older men, cannot conceal from the observer with any insight the real virtues underlying their deliberately adopted mask; but they have no educative influence at all on self-sure, uncompromising young revolutionaries with their "heroic" ideal. A certain seriousness and sense of duty seems to be giving place more and more throughout the nation, and even in the army, to other attitudes, opportunist and not entirely conscientious. It is impossible to escape the strong feeling that under the National Socialist regime some of the finest German qualities are beginning to disappear—the absolute reliability, the seriousness and honesty of outlook, and the selfless devotion to duty. There are many signs that justify the fear that superficiality and indifference to

155

good work are bringing us down from our past technical and intellectual standards. These are bad omens for a new war.

Is it these difficulties that are crippling the activity of the army leaders? We have the astonishing spectacle of generals who, in their own sphere, are hard and resolute and clear of purpose, quickly becoming hesitant and perplexed, and ready for concession or capitulation, in the civil and political sphere. Are they lacking in the courage and the promptness and resolution in action that their opponent possesses? Is there justice in the criticism levelled long ago against the corps of officers, that they have become "civilian" in spirit? Are the German generals no longer anything more than "professors of war," as another critic declares—doctrinaires incapable of practical political work?

Other men are coming to the fore. They will gain control of the army as they have already gained control of the State. It was not for nothing that last year Dr. Dietrich, *Reichspressechef* or head of the government Press department, sang the praises of the military qualities of the Führer in his article on Hitler's 49th birthday: "This tremendous achievement is the work not only of a political but of a military genius. . . . His knowledge is considered remarkable even by experts. And for that reason he is not only the driving force and the soul of German military armament, but also its spiritual creator and inspirer. In his immeasurable labor on the military strength of the Reich, in his care for its defences and its arms, in his anxiety for the military protection of the German nation, he is the true soldier-leader of his people." The party commands the State—that was the slogan under which the *Gleichschaltung* of the organs of civil government was carried out. The party leader commands the army—that is the keystone of the *Gleichschaltung* of the army. It will be placed in position at any time now. The generalissimo of the Great War has given place to the generalissimo for the coming war—that is what the *Reichspressechef* meant in this apotheosis of the Führer.

Fatal and irreparable mistakes have been made by the army leaders. One of the most fundamental, whatever may have been the practical grounds for it, was the moral capitulation in face of the murder of Generals von Schleicher and von Bredow. It was a moral capitulation which has continued to breed capitulation. It has bred the refusal especially of the higher classes of society to "play the martyr," to expose themselves, their position, their families, to any risks, and this refusal is of evil omen for the attitude of the army in the coming crises. The conception of obedience and loyalty has lost its moral basis. It was accepted in the past even by the opponents of the regime, who were ready to sacrifice even their lives in its service. It was bound up with the monarch, and cannot be transferred to an institution that lacks genuine authority and stands outside the realm of traditional loyalties. The new conception of obedience and loyalty has been mechanized and materialized, and, like everything National Socialism has produced in the ethical and spiritual sphere, lacks the creative spiritual roots of free personality.

No one can deny that the army leaders are chiefly to blame for this development in Germany, under which the army is itself being shaken to its foundations. The army leaders fell with the rest into the idea that it was advisable to keep the nation under the pressure of a terrorist regime and under the influence of intoxicating propaganda, instead of seeking a sound basis, perhaps less obvious and more difficult to secure, but all the surer and stronger, in the nation. The army leaders saw fit with the rest to follow an easy path, which evaded the actual problems of political and social, economic and spiritual renovation, instead of wrestling with them and overcoming their difficulties. The army leaders fell with the rest under the influence of the cult of materialism and the pseudo-realism that underlay the whole patched-up solution of 1932-1933. This is the only adequate explanation of their fatally mistaken course.

The grave, perhaps the critical, question for the future of Germany and Europe is whether the German army leaders will

157

succeed in breaking the hold of the revolution over them, and clearing their ideas in sufficient time to arrive at definite statesman-like resolves in regard to their political course before disaster comes. As things are now in the Reich, the only possible rebirth of the State must come from the army, from the purified spirit of a genuinely Christian and Western soldiery, not from revolutionary mercenaries.

Revolution or Restoration

Is it possible to hope that the extremely critical situation in which Germany is now placed, in spite of all her apparent "successes," is fully recognized, and that the army leaders, who, may I say once more, are the proper leaders of the nation in time of emergency, have the will to hold back the nation at the last moment from self-destruction?

At the beginning of last year an event occurred which drew public attention to the true conditions in Germany. It came just in time to stop an open military revolt, and revealed the tension existing beneath the surface of the nominally established order. To attempt to explain this forestalled revolt as an attempt at a coup by a small clique of monarchists, a desperate attempt by members of a sinking social class to maintain their position, is absurd. Beyond question the monarchist principle was at issue, and beyond any question there are monarchist elements in Germany who desire a restoration in order to save the nation from unimaginable chaos and destruction.

Even to the outsider, two things became evident in connection with the crisis of February 4th, 1938.* There is only a pseudo-unity, unity under duress, in Germany. Deep-lying forces are

* On February 4th, 1938, Herr Hitler took over the command of the German armed forces and the conduct of foreign policy. Field Marshal Blomberg was retired from the War Ministry and from active service, and at the same time General von Fritsch, the

at work in the effort to end existing conditions, which are leading to the ruin of the nation. The view that the only way of avoiding revolution and chaos is by the restoration of the monarchy exists to-day far beyond the narrow circle of the monarchists. The opposition of military leaders to the regime is no departure from national unity but the expression of a general revulsion of feeling in the nation, which is groaning under its present moral and material burden. And without the assembling of the constructive elements of the nation behind an instrument of power there can be no liberation of the people from the present omnipotent dictatorship.

No one will deny that there is little probability now of any resolute intervention from the army. It has neither the spirit nor, probably, the material strength for intervention. Many have nevertheless rested their hopes in the generals, but only because they are the last hope. If they fail, as the leadership of *Geheimrat* Hugenberg, the grave-digger of German Conservatism, and the Stahlhelm, failed, then the fate of Germany and Europe is sealed. There must come wars, civil wars, revolutions, a witches' sabbath compared with which the turmoil in China and Spain will have been child's play. It may well be that resolute action by the army leaders in January, 1938, would have cost fewer lives than will have to be sacrificed one day in order to restore the regime which Germany needs.

To-day any intelligent and unprejudiced observer can survey the development of National Socialism and note its essential tendencies without the possibility of error. The events of June 30th, 1934, appeared to retard the logical process of radicalization; in reality the concentration of the elements making for revolution has been all the more determined. We must keep in mind all the men on whom Röhm's Storm Troop organization conferred the rank of Divisional Commanders and Generals Commanding

military Commander-in-Chief, was placed on the retired list. Baron von Neurath retired from the Foreign Ministry but became Hitler's senior adviser and the head of a new secret Cabinet Council. The net result was a complete defeat for the Conservatives in Germany and the subordination of the army to the National Socialist Party.—Translator.

and Inspectors General. These were no mere decorations. These men aspired to the creation of the true revolutionary professional army, independent of the forces of the State and firmly in the control of the party leaders. These personal ambitions continue to exist, and the idea of the party's new professional army was not quashed on that 30th of June. The strength of the party leadership lies in its tenacious persistance in any task, once it has recognized its necessity. And it is altogether a vital matter for National Socialism to possess its own professional army. Röhm was the first of the German Revolutionary Generals, but statements by others besides Röhm in the same sense have come to my knowledge: the innermost clique were clear and remain clear as to the necessity of building up the new army entirely out of the one element of National Socialism, and of giving it the character of a mercenary army.

Röhm was acting on the strength of historic precedents. The French Revolution produced its revolutionary armies with their special character of propagandists of revolution. The clique inferred that the German revolution similarly needs revolutionary armies with which to fulfil its mission in the world; these armies must become the vital expression of the new revolutionary outlook and its principal instrument of propaganda. It has repeatedly been found in the past that revolutionary campaigns cannot be conducted with reactionary troops. Yet other historic analogies set Hitler thinking along these lines. Spengler and other speculative historians have developed the theory that in the new Cæsarian epoch national armies are in any case no longer the type of instrument required, and that the army needed is one of legionaries sworn to personal allegiance to the new Cæsar; only with these can he retain his hold of power and carry to success his gigantic foreign adventures.

The National Socialist plan envisages a professional army on a vast scale, selected purely from the party standpoint, a Præ-torian Guard such as the world has never before seen, and along-side it revolutionary mass militias with the dash and enthusiasm of the French popular armies of the Revolution. Röhm, as a gifted military organizer, had thought out the possibilities of the development of a professional army alongside a universal armed militia. He did not propose, as was generally imagined, that the Storm Troops should be that militia: they were gradually to develop into the professional army, the existing army being allowed to sink to the level of a militia.

I doubt whether the army leaders were fully aware of the nature of Röhm's conception at the time when they were at issue with him. Hitler, of course, knew and approved every detail. He acted because he suspected Röhm of insubordinate activities which would wreck everything. Hitler's characteristic capacity for biding his time and for allowing problems to ripen, a capacity constantly misrepresented as hesitation, has again and again revealed his superiority over the rest of the National Socialist clique. He was justified by the event in this case in regard to the problem of the relations between National Socialism and the army. In spite of June 30th, 1934, the military position of the party is incomparably stronger to-day than at that date. Similarly the events of February 4th, 1938, would have been unthinkable not only in 1934 but even two years later.

This leads to the question how it comes that the army leaders are now almost impotent—prisoners of the revolution, whereas, having possession of the decisive means of power, they intended to be the "dictatorship within the dictatorship." The answer is that the army has become revolutionary in spirit, and has also been weakened by fatal errors in leadership at important stages in the developments since 1933.

There is a picture of which party circles have a deep hatred: Hitler, at the thanksgiving service at Potsdam for the coalition's electoral victory after the Reichstag fire, demonstrating his submission to Hindenburg by a deep and reverential obeisance before the tall, rigid figure of the President. Such was the aspect of National Socialism in the spring of 1933—tamed and harnessed to the monarchist forces, a constituent element in a new State of which Potsdam and Frederick II were to be the guiding inspiration. The tacticians of the German Nationalist Party seemed to have won complete success. Not only was the restoration of the monarchy, which had been steadily worked for since 1929, apparently approaching within reach, but another Conservative objective of continually growing urgency seemed to have been attained. The National Socialists, with their dangerous revolutionary tendencies, a party capable at any moment of turning over from the extreme Right to the extreme Left, had been won over to positive co-operation in the State.

To this day there are Germans who remain under the influence of that occasion. The Potsdam celebrations revealed the direction in which Germany was to have moved according to the ideas of Hugenberg and Papen, the actual progenitors of the deal of 1933. Actually those celebrations marked the end of the Conservative and Nationalist plans and aspirations, and the beginning of a new and different movement, a revolutionary movement that had nothing in common with the ideas of Potsdam. The Potsdam ceremony was a strangely spectral occasion, full of a deep irony that grew yet deeper with the years: its aim was to restore the spirit of Potsdam, and it seemed triumphantly to have done so; in reality it completely subjected Potsdam and everything else to the new "dynamism." Some of those present imagined that they saw their most dangerous opponents, the young men of National Socialism, laid by the heel, chained up as a house-dog to snap at the Marxist rebels and so keep clear the path for a thoroughly reactionary solution of the crisis. Meanwhile the Brown Shirt leaders, thrust into the background with only minor parts at that Potsdam festival, ground their teeth and swore to drive their reactionary rivals out of every position and achieve their own dominance and revolution.

It seems probable, nevertheless, that the National Socialists entered into their deal with the monarchists in 1933 not only with a definite purpose but with their eyes open to the risks they were running, determining, however, to seize every opportunity

163

the alliance brought them; the reactionaries, on the other hand, and the army seem to have been blind to the risks of their association with their incalculable partner. In the autumn of 1933 it became evident that the National Socialist movement was losing none of its mass support through its revolutionary course, but, on the contrary, had begun to strike root very effectively for that very reason; it was too late, however, to counter it without a great deal of bloodshed. The party was firmly entrenched in the positions it had occupied, and had fortified them as the basis of its own power. An army commander to whom I expressed my concern in that autumn replied that if the German people were ready to put up with the treatment they were getting, there was nothing that could be done. With her withdrawal from the League of Nations, Germany had, moreover, entered a zone of very serious dangers. The most urgent task was to pass through it as quickly as possible and to arm in the shortest possible time. It was no time for internal dissension. Had there been any disorders, the army would undoubtedly have been ready to intervene; but it felt no call to act on its own initiative. It had no concern for its own existence; it knew that it was strong enough to prevent revolutionism and subversive propaganda from penetrating its own sphere. In the background stood the unbroken authority of old Marshal Hindenburg, which could be brought to bear at any time to produce a rapid change without risk, should the internal situation really become threatening. The army did not regard the situation as dangerous though the President himself was very much dissatisfied with the course of events, and especially disapproved of the struggle with the churches. The opening of that struggle, the attack on the independence of the Evangelical church, the annulment of the election of Bishop von Bodelschwingh and the appointment of Bishop Müller in his place, and the launching of the German Christian movement— all this was of deep concern to the aged President, and disturbed him much more than political events, of the true scope of which he had little conception, and some of which, including the *Gleich-*

schaltung and the acts of terrorism, he believed to be unavoidable. In spite of Hindenburg's growing antipathy to the National Socialist regime, the fiction of the Potsdam celebrations was kept up; his advisers deprecated any change. Men like Meissner very quickly gauged the strength of the National Socialist movement more accurately than the Generals and the monarchists did. They were ready for a second deal with it, for the sake of the opportunities it offered them. They were concerned for what was to happen after the death of the frail old President.

Hindenburg regarded himself as regent for William II. In his eyes the deal of 1933 was a resolute move in the direction of the restoration of the monarchy; and it was so not only in his eyes but, at first, in fact. Hindenburg had for years been the integrating element that held the State together, and the whole "combination" of 1933 had rested on his authority. Under his authority the restoration of the monarchy seemed not only possible but the logical ultimate objective. But his death not only made the restoration of the monarchy once more a debatable subject but brought the risk of a breach between the army and the monarchists on one side, now a leaderless group, and on the other side the National Socialists with their unscrupulous but strictly disciplined leaders. What should then have been done was to assure the return to monarchy under a new Constitution. But nothing was attempted. It was not even decided by the monarchists whether with the death of the President the moment had come for the announcement of the restoration of the monarchy, or whether it would be better to allow an interim period to elapse, since no one wanted to bring back the exiled monarch, while the candidature of a grandson of his in his lifetime was out of the question. Still greater was the lack of agreement as to the constitutional form of the new State, which must be organized primarily with a view to the one overriding element of totalitarian preparedness for war. Thus the future lay in the hands of the National Socialists as the most united single party.

The Reichswehr looked on at this development, but was itself so divided in outlook that it allowed matters to take their course. The army leaders imagined that they could nevertheless hold the threads in their hands and guide events in accordance with their own views. They regarded the alliance with National Socialism as a temporary measure. They had not the slightest idea of allowing it to become the permanent ruler of the nation. After six months of the new regime the army leaders still regarded the National Socialists as a propaganda body and an expedient for temporary service, readily removable. Meanwhile the army could devote itself to its urgent and exacting task of rapid rearmament.

Under the protection of the army, National Socialism grew formidable. Its leaders knew that it would win. They were determined to establish themselves in power, and they were well aware of the destiny their partners in the deal of 1933 had in view for them. The determination of the leaders, shared by thousands of their assistants, to "dig themselves in" accounts for the many charges of corruption and the countless completely unscrupulous accusations brought against honorable men: the purpose was to render their posts vacant so as to fill them with National Socialists. So the party extended and entrenched its power. Plain advice was given from above throughout the party, down to the lowest ranks, to seize every post that could in any way be got hold of; this was a matter of life and death to the party. While the reactionaries still imagined that they had the means of retaining power because they held the key positions in their hands, many important functions of the executive were being taken over by the National Socialists. While the Reichswehr was organizing the nucleus units of the great new army and providing the nation with the instrument of power, the National Socialist party built up its own power and took possession of the machinery of the State.

That is the explanation of the capitulation of the army, so far as home politics were concerned. But there was also a reason connected with foreign policy. It must not be forgotten that, throughout the years of rearmament, the grave risk of foreign intervention, if Germany showed the slightest sign of internal weakness, weighed on all concerned. There can be no doubt that had a distinction been drawn abroad between the points at which the justified determination in Germany to right the wrongs suffered was revealed, and those at which revolutionary purposes were at work, there would have been a totally different development in Germany.

For all that, I know many of the details, some from my own experience, of the serious effort made by the army leaders, and those in close political touch with them, throughout 1934, and even later, to change the course by radical means, to dissolve the party, to set up a temporary military dictatorship, and under its protection to replace by a true State the machinery of forcible rule set up by the party, to introduce constitutional though not parliamentary conditions, and to restore liberty of the person. There is no need to dwell now on the personal inadequacies and the fatal errors that resulted in the postponement of this plan. Two considerations played a part in the postponement—the undeniable tactical superiority of the National Socialist leadership, with its greater rapidity of action; and the total inexperience of respectable members of society in the conspiratorial methods of proceeding which were necessarily involved. But the army cannot be absolved from blame for its failure: it was unwilling to take the initiative, it wanted others to make the first move, and it wanted the famous fifty-one per cent guarantee of safety. It treated the whole affair, moreover, at a time when success was still possible, with a good deal of lofty indifference and with an equally lofty assumption that whatever happened it would be able to control the course of events at will. One of Hindenburg's East Prussian intimates told me how after the events of June 30th, 1934, the President actually comforted and praised the distracted Hitler, telling him that no birth was exempt from pains and bleeding. It is true that Hindenburg had been given an entirely one-sided picture of what had happened.

Then came Hindenburg's death and the army's oath of loyalty to Hitler. These years had three practical tasks—the completion of rearmament, the breaking of the Versailles front, and the preservation of the German economic system. Success depended on the avoidance of all serious internal political disturbances. The sense of responsibility for the prevention of the collapse of all the efforts that were being made, involving the probability of infinite chaos, crippled the freedom of decision of the army. But the main reasons for its capitulation in August 1934 were the absence of any adequate and clearly envisaged plan of its own and the lack of initiative in high quarters. At least the sovereignty of the army remained inviolate. With the co-existence of two independent realms a tolerable situation was produced, at all events for the period of the building up of the army. No attention was paid, however, to the facts that the nation was slowly but inescapably being revolutionized, its past elements of public order disbanded, and the army itself revolutionized from within. In the years following the introduction of universal compulsory military service the victory of the revolution over tradition, though almost invisible, steadily became a fact, a fact of decisive and vital importance for the nation. With its growing importance as a military instrument, the army steadily lost its decisive political influence. Its incorporation in the "dynamic" revolution proceeded silently but unceasingly.

THE NATIONAL TASK OF THE ARMY LEADERS

No one can yet say whether this means that the National Socialist dictatorship has finally imposed its destructive regime on the army. For the present the settlement of the conflict of January 1938 means that the party has gained time. But does it also mean that the army has gained time? It must be feared that it does not. The only power that exists in revolutionary times is that of a reliable organization that can be called instantly into action at any time. The Reichswehr was an organization of this type firmly in the hands of its leaders, but it was without an adequate special service arm. This should have been provided in 1934, but was not. It is no longer possible to see how the omission can now be made good. It is impossible to improvise special revolutionary or counter-revolutionary units under the eyes of the ruling power in the midst of a state of crisis. The omission is inexplicable, especially in view of the breaking of the army's monopoly of armed force by the formation of the S.S., the party's "Black Guards." This force itself has the manifest function of serving at all times as a revolutionary or counter-revolutionary instrument ready for instant action, a nucleus organization that does in truth make the party unassailable. Clearly there is nothing of comparable strength that can be brought against it.

The present regime seems thus to be in an almost impregnable situation. The S.S. leaders have the advantage of all the revolutionary experience of recent years in Germany and abroad. To all appearance, other bodies took no account of this experience. It seems extremely doubtful whether it is not now too late for the army leaders to develop their own anti-revolutionary tactics, and to create the only effective means of quickly getting rid of the evil conditions in Germany without a vast national upheaval. But has the army really the will to get rid of the present regime and end the revolution, even if it had the means of doing so without a civil war? The desire probably exists among considerable sections of the army leaders (the desire, rather than the will); but other sections, the strength of which is by no means clear, are for steadily pursuing the revolutionary course. Both groups are faced with the great mass of the officers who think only in terms of their own careers, under the influence of the typically middle class anxiety for security, and

169

without a trace of the aristocratic outlook. It may be that the army is holding back not in order to strike at the right moment but simply because of its divisions of opinion. Or it may be unable, and with better justification than before 1933, to decide at what point to move. Is there, in that case, any other means of lifting Germany out of her present situation? Is there any authority which could recall the army to its own traditions?

There is—one, and one alone: the restoration of a German monarchy, which could summon the army and the overwhelming majority of the nation to oppose the nihilist revolution and to seek a just and peaceful reordering of the State, progressively replacing dictatorial powers by new principles and institutions of freedom and justice. It is well known that this solution has already been envisaged in the past. Under it the army would at first be omnipotent, and would then gradually delegate its rights and duties to organs of the State or to self-governing bodies. The National Socialist Party would then be not only a superfluous but an injurious element, with no national function; its dissolution would be the obvious condition for the continued development of genuine organs of the State and self-governing bodies. But the army would be able to succeed in this special task of re-creation of the State only if it had a genuine authority at its back—the authority of a Christian monarchy. It can only exert its renovating influence in the State if it is not purely an instrument of power but also the organ of the historic traditions of the nation. It can end the revolution only through the exalted figure of the monarch.

It was, in any case, the patriotic duty of the army to undertake this national task. It is so more than ever to-day.

The decision that is now taken by the German army leaders will affect not only the destiny of the German nation, the form of its existence, dictatorial, revolutionary, or reactionary; it will be a decision either for peace and the restoration of the monarchy or for war and permanent revolution. The army leaders cannot indefinitely maintain their present position. Time is working against them. Either they will enforce a fundamental change of the whole system or they will be compelled to capitulate. Unless they capitulate and allow things to take their course they must come forward openly with the claim to restore order and must summon the nation to collaborate with them.

The developments of recent years suggest, however, that the supreme army leaders are afraid of responsibility. Is not this the true explanation of the strange developments in the army that led up to the events preceding February 4th, 1938? Must we not speak also of unscrupulousness? Can we, six years after the deal of 1933, separate army and party, the laws and the prophets of one and the same order? Is the army free from responsibility for all that has happened, at least from responsibility for passive acceptance or neutrality? How can its leaders expect to be exempt from blame for their years of toleration of the ruining of the character of the nation with concentration camps and oppressive legislation and miscarriages of justice, with acts of terrorism and every sort of physical and material oppression?

The elements that must end the revolution are ripening slowly and with difficulty in Germany. But while there is no sign of any direct reaction to the horrifying events of these years, they have brought perplexity of spirit and deep qualms of conscience to more men than is apparent on the surface. It must not be forgotten that it was a long time before many of the things that have been happening in the Third Reich became of common knowledge. All those who have had the misfortune to play any part, whether active or passive, in events in Germany have undergone a sort of tragic purification. The new cry for a return to the standards of Christianity and a Christian monarchy is thus not to be dismissed as reactionary: it has deeper and more genuine motives. The army appears to have the clearest conception of the true situation of the German people, if only because it has still the means of exacting a measure of attention to its views. But it also stands to suffer most from the

destruction of the two elements of the Conservative outlook:
it stands or falls with the monarchy and with Christianity in
Germany.

ACHERONTA MOVEBO*

"Things might have become even worse." Such is the soothing
argument with which those who know exactly what is going on
in Germany, but cannot summon up the courage to end it although they have the means in their hands, elude their responsibilities. Such an attitude, amid so desperate a national situation
as the present, is inexcusable. The public need induced the army
leaders in 1932-33 at least to act incorrectly and to prepare the
way for a coup; the present incomparably graver situation must
release all men from their oaths, and all the more so since the
present political leaders have often enough claimed that the vital
interests of the nation override all formal commitments or obligations. One thing is beyond any question: if the army leaders
take no action, they will pass out of existence as certainly as the
other elements of the nation outside the totalitarian party have
done. They must not imagine that in the totalitarian State they
will be of the same importance as in the past. They will not even
continue to exist, they will not be wanted even as instructors.
They will be swept away with the rest of the old order, to make
room for a new organization of "leaders."

That will mean the unhonored end of the Prussian and German armies. Their Generals will themselves have been the destroyers of the glorious tradition of several centuries of German
history. The destruction that not even defeat in the great world
war could effect, the leaders of the army will themselves bring
about, because, as a whole, they lacked courage and pluck, resolution and strength of will. The German armies will come to
their end, but not on the battlefields. The Prussian army will
die the craven death of the suicide, because, apparently, the noble
and soldierly spirit of its officers has been quenched. Its place

---

* Flectere si nequeo superos, Acheronta movebo.—*Aeneid*, vii, 312.

will be taken by a revolutionary mercenary army with neither past nor future, neither conscience nor religion.

War in the world of to-day is not only inevitable, it has come; it is at present in the midst of its first phase. The permanent war of our day began seven years ago, with the first bombardment of Shanghai by the Japanese, at the very moment when the Disarmament Conference was in session at Geneva. Since then the war has continued, spreading into new theatres, dying down there and flaring up elsewhere—until the whole world is being drawn in. This new world war threatens to become an open world revolution, a sanguinary and universal revolution of unending civil wars. National passions may seem to take the place of those of the "class war," but these last will return in full force as an element of destruction. Behind the coming great wars there rises already the figure of world-wide revolution as the one shaper of the destiny of mankind.

Part Three

THE REDISTRIBUTION OF THE WORLD

TRENDS AND METHODS OF GERMAN FOREIGN
POLICY

1

A Peace Policy of Justice

AMONG certain groups in Germany of intellectual conformers to National Socialism there was talk for a long time of a great change in National Socialist policy in the direction of peace. Hitler, they said—until the occupation of Austria—had grown to greatness in his foreign policy. He had long thrown off all the dross of revolutionary recklessness. He held ready in the background a great peace policy, a plan for a constructive reconciliation in Europe. It was only awaiting the completion of German rearmament. Then, on the strength of her indisputable power and her impregnable position, Germany would be ready for a lasting peace and a new European order. This naturally implied the recognition of certain German rights and the removal of certain grievances. But National Socialism had renounced all adventurous plans both in the West and in the East. In two or three years' time an accommodation with the Western Powers was certain to come, a new system of pacts that would bring Europe peace and security, prosperity and the means of growth.

Germany would then be prepared to return to membership in the world's economic system and to re-enter the international credit market; she would devalue the mark to effect the adjustment which must come sooner or later between her currency and those of the Western Powers. She would then, in her recovered position of power, be the center of a permanent European peace.

Then, too, all the internal tasks which had had to be deferred during these years of struggle would be taken up, above all the reframing of the Constitution. It would naturally become possible to relax the stern restriction of the freedom of the person, and all temporary invasions of legality would disappear. National Socialism would be able to turn to the tasks nearest to its heart, the increasing of the prosperity of the people and the ending of social dissensions. It would at last be able to devote itself to housing, which for a time had had to be allowed to fall into arrear, to the return to the land, to the creation of a new farming community, and to all the tasks which it regarded as forming its own peculiar mission.

Thus, it was argued, National Socialism had not the slightest intention of offering the world a permanent revolutionary menace. It was its honorable part to carry conviction by its example and to stir other nations to emulation. Nothing was farther from its intention than territorial conquests. Only in entirely exceptional cases—revolutionary developments, for instance, in Russia, or, perhaps, France—would Germany be bound to intervene and safeguard her vital rights. And such cases could be calmly awaited: National Socialism was now so strong that nothing could bring it down.

This view corresponded to the confident hopes entertained by nationalist and Conservative circles in Germany, and shared by Germany's friends in foreign countries, up to September 1938. Similar considerations manifestly inspired certain efforts made by the Western Powers to assist Germany in the peaceful pursuit of her policy, and to cut short the revolutionary period of her unilateral removal of the last vestiges of the Versailles order by themselves joining in a legal process of more peaceful change. Thus the British and French attitude in the German-Czechoslovak conflict concerning the Sudeten territory followed logically from an evident purpose of defining and meeting within certain limits, as an act of justice, the claims Germany might put forward in respect to the dictated peace of Versailles. The desire of the National Socialist regime for peace would thus be met half-way, or alternatively its lack of good will clearly established.

This is beyond question a bold and patient policy, broadly conceived and certainly just. It is not to be discouraged by arguments concerning the inadequate security of verbal assurances or written pacts; for it recognizes that a nation which is still fighting its way out of so hard a situation as Germany's has a sort of right to proceed to extremes in self-defence even in these political matters. It is true that statements have been made on the British side which suggest that, while this policy has been carefully considered, it proceeds from a thoroughly sceptical view of the assistance rendered by National Socialism up to the present to any future policy of peace. When on September 27th, 1938, Mr. Chamberlain spoke, obviously in reference to Germany, of a nation that has "made up its mind to dominate the world by fear of its force," and when he described the German attitude as "unreasonable," he was clearly under no illusions as to the past Germany policy, but his very candor showed that he was ready to encourage a change in its character, in spite of the British unmasking of Hitler's intentions in regard to the Sudetens, and immediately after it.

It would, indeed, be easy to conceive that, after making an end of what Bismarck called the *injuria temporum*, the weakening and hedging-in of Germany, a great German policy would declare a sincere determination to follow a course of peaceful reconstruction in collaboration with other nations. I am thinking of Bismarck's definition of the limitations of German policy (*Gedanken und Erinnerungen*, Vol. II, page 267): "My ideal aim, after we have recovered our unity within the frontiers attainable, has always been to gain the confidence not only of the less powerful European States but also of the Great Powers in the intention of German policy, once it has made good the *injuria temporum*, the splitting up of the nation, to pursue peace and justice."

But what is the new *injuria temporum?* What is justice in the new work for peace? Is it the formation of a Greater Germany by the incorporation of the German groups in the territories bordering on Germany? Does the Third Reich confine itself to the peaceful use of its newly-won strength; does it see in the past annulments of oppressive elements in the Treaty of Versailles the conclusion of this course of treaty revision in external affairs? In this connection it is worth while to recall another passage of Bismarck's. He says: "We should endeavor to diminish the annoyance which our growth to an actual Great Power has caused by the manifestly peaceful use of our influence, so as to convince the world that a German hegemony in Europe is more serviceable and more impartial, and also less injurious to the freedom of others, than a French, Russian, or English hegemony would be." This should indicate the conditions for a German peace policy in Europe in our own day also. The criterion of German policy lies in the use Germany will make of her recovered influence. If it is used in the spirit of impartiality, of "honorable and peace-loving" leadership, which Bismarck inculcated, German policy will be truly constructive and will attract support, even if at first it meets with opposition and mistrust. No nation need be disturbed by the fact that the older order no longer exists; the only disturbing question is what is to follow it.

But this gives their symptomatic importance to all the constituent elements of political life in the Third Reich. Are these the elements of the new order—these authoritarian devices, this disciplining and restricting and totalitarian *Gleichschaltung*, this regimentation and centralization and bureaucratization, these methods of terrorism and oppression, physical and mental? The political state of a country is not an isolated fact; the standards in internal policy are closely connected with the aims of external policy.

The things that have happened up to the present may be justified by the *injuria temporum,* by the difficult situation of the Reich, by the necessity for the leaders of taking unexpected and

180

unilateral action as the one condition of success. They do not necessarily prove that the regime is and will always remain nihilistic and subversive and filled with unbounded imperialist ambitions. If the permanence of the revolutionary character of National Socialism is to be demonstrated, special criteria must be produced. Do these exist?

CONCLUSION OR PERPETUATION OF THE REVOLUTION?

We have to distinguish between two things. Hitler's will to peace is an undeniable fact. But that does not for a moment imply that he can have no intention of pursuing a revolution of unknown scope in foreign policy and of trying to set up a world empire. The two things are not incompatible. Hitler certainly has no desire to introduce war into the life of the nations as their normal condition, whatever may be the current theories in Germany. His conception is rather the bloodless war for which he coined his phrase of "broadened strategy." And in this he remains true to the doctrine of Clausewitz that as a rule the simple existence of a strong army is sufficient for the achievement of aims in foreign policy affecting a weaker opponent. Thus German peaceful professions may actually be as sincerely meant as is ever possible in politics. Even the renunciation of territorial claims may in a certain sense correspond to real intentions. For what has still to come in Central Europe will be the logical outcome of Germany's preponderance of power, which is such that she can now dispense with territorial changes without suffering any loss of power. Further territorial changes are entirely unnecessary for the achievement of German hegemony, which would be attainable even in the West less through annexations than through the incorporation of existing States in a German federal system.

But the renunciation of warlike operations and territorial changes does not by any means sum up the actual aims of National Socialism. The question is what will Hitler do with the hegemony he has virtually attained in Europe, or at least in

Eastern Europe. What are the actual aims of National Socialism in foreign policy? Hegemony can be exercised peacefully and with moderation, as the passage quoted from Bismarck shows. But it can also have very different implications. And there can be no question that National Socialism proposes to use its European predominance in a totally different way from that envisaged by Bismarck.

What Germany is aiming at is not *revanche*, not the restoration of the frontiers of 1914, but "total revision," "a completely different order" (G. Wirsing, 1934); a *"rerum innovatio,"* a "new rejuvenation of the world," in Burckhardt's words. The German nation cannot "permit itself" "yet another confinement within a small space" in "a period of great spaces, hastening forward precipitately with seven-league boots" (Haushofer).* Does not a rejuvenation take place always through the incursion of crude and misshapen forces, whose subconscious pressure only gradually gives place to a conscious will?

Not the conclusion but the perpetuation of the revolution is the characteristic of the peak of German foreign policy attained in the autumn of 1938. And this elementary fact will not be altered by any treaty agreements, any proclamations, any more than the speech made by Hitler in the Reichstag after June 30th, 1934, ended the revolution within Germany.**

But can there be in the field of practical policy such a thing as a will to unlimited revolution? What useful thing can pro-

---

* Kein nochmaliges kleinräumiges Zurück-bleiben [hinter einer] grossräumigen jäh mit Siebenmeilenstiefeln voran eilenden Zeit gestatten.

** For that matter, Hitler's political declarations always serve as political weapons; they are never simple communications of facts or even of a purpose. I cannot refrain from quoting a few statements on which subsequent happenings have amounted to an eloquent comment. February 1st, 1934: "The statements according to which Germany has the intention of violating the frontier of the Austrian State are senseless and entirely groundless." March 31st, 1935: "Germany has neither the intention nor the desire to intervene in the internal politics of Austria, still less to annex Austria." March 7th, 1936: "Germany has no further territorial claims of any sort in Europe." Everyone will remember how the solemn undertaking to respect the Czechoslovak frontier given at the time of the occupation of Austria was followed barely six months later by the attack on the existence of Czechoslovakia. The practical politician will thus be more inclined to ask himself what is the political purpose of Hitler's peace declarations and peace pacts than to accept them at their face value.

ceed from it? That is certainly the question the ordinary citizen asks of all the incomprehensible measures of National Socialism; and it has led him into a futile waiting for an inner change in the movement, for its ripening. But if ever a phrase spoken by National Socialists was entirely candid and in accordance with the facts, it was Goebbels's phrase about the rare moment having come for the redistribution of the world.

Hitler's realism deceives the onlooker. This man, who can calculate with such icy clarity, who can await the right moment, who feels his way forward, one might say, with mastery, who is constantly testing and trying the weak spots—a man who so realistically examines everything surely cannot at the same time be a fantast simply out to overturn everything, trusting himself to a limitless movement that is to bear him to some dimly sensed new order. And yet this duality is in fact the essential characteristic of those great "destroyers" of whom Jakob Burckhardt writes. Men of this type are "inventive in destruction," they have a flair for the weak points, the points at which they can apply pressure in order to bring down the old order. And it is their destiny to do this until a really creative will opposes them or until their environment is exhausted. These are the men of great tactical gifts. They are also the men possessed of demons, of second sight, dreamers urged on by visions, who regard themselves as men like unto gods, and who live in an unreal world in spite of all the realism they can assume on occasion.

National Socialist policy has only impulses, no fixed political aims—impulses and a system of tactics. There is no degree of saturation in the political aims of National Socialism: there can be none. Thus, nothing can be more irrational than to ask what are the final demands of its "dynamic" foreign policy.

In particular, therefore, it is not correct to regard the new German foreign policy as simply the final form of the policy of the Pan-Germans. The foreign policy of the Third Reich goes beyond the most extreme limits any nation has consciously set itself in the past. It is supposed to be a "peace policy of

183

justice"—but: "A new peace shall make Germany 'mistress of the globe,' a peace not hanging on the palm fronds of lachrymose pacifist womenfolk, but established by the victorious sword of a master race that takes over the world in the service of a higher civilization." Such is the main political principle of National Socialism as expressed by Rosenberg. Hitler's language is rather more general, but it conveys no less ambitious perspectives.

2

The Aims of the Revolution in Foreign Policy

POLITICAL DEVICES AND TRENDS

IN order to get to the pith of the National Socialist ideas in foreign policy, we must turn to other sources than the popular literature of the movement, *Mein Kampf* and the rest. There is no need even to consider the various groups in the Third Reich that concern themselves with foreign policy. The slight differences between them are of less importance than in the past. Differences exist, indeed, only in regard to pace and, here and there, method. And in any case an inquiry into these differences is a labor we may spare ourselves, for in the last resort it is Hitler who decides and, in this field, does indeed "lead." He is beyond question the master in this field; he is also the only one who has carried to the pitch of virtuosity the pursuit of tactical elasticity.

The old party members, the provincial leaders, play a relatively unimportant part in foreign policy, though here and there are men who are listened to, such as, strangely enough, Hitler's "Benjamin," Herr Foerster, of Danzig, who counts as a sort of expert on eastern questions. Rosenberg, once the party's supreme "expert," counts less, at all events in the determination of foreign policy, than he did during the "period of struggle." His views have long ceased to carry the day. The group around

Hess, together with, for instance, Ribbentrop in spite of some blunders, and Bohle, carry much more weight. The official experts, and such men as von Neurath, are used only as advisers on formalities, on the modification and adjustment of the over-smart policy of the regime, and on polishing the phraseology of drafts. One name deserves special mention, that of Professor Haushofer, retired Major-General, now president of the German Academy. With his school of "geopolitics" he has contributed a great deal to the clarification of the intentions of the regime on foreign policy. Exceptional weight must be attached to his statements, because he has given expression to many aspirations and intentions of the regime with almost criminal candor.

Two errors must be guarded against at the outset. Intensive settlement in the east of Europe in territory won for Germany is no longer the central aim of National Socialist foreign policy. The idea existed and still exists in some minds, but it is no longer of any importance. The impossibility of agricultural colonization in its historic form of eastward expansion has long become clear even to the romantics of the "Blood and Soil" myth; the potential settlers do not exist in sufficient number; and, what is more, that method is inconsistent with the actual imperialist policy of the regime. All imperialisms detach a nation from its own soil and mobilize it. The actual slogan of the "dynamic" policy is not the return to the land but imperial expansion into a Greater Germany carved out of Europe. And, secondly, the idea of making an end of the military power of France in a final struggle, and reducing that "hereditary enemy" to secondary political importance in consonance with its diminishing population, is no longer regarded as a primary political task. These aims, mentioned in *Mein Kampf* and in the older popular literature of the party, have largely been put out of date by the course of events, or at all events have been allowed to fall into the background. They do not touch the essence of National Socialist policy, the popular formulation of which may be summed up in the familiar lines of a marching song of the Hitler Youth:

"Heute gehört uns Deutschland,*
Morgen die ganze Welt——"

"To-day we own Germany, to-morrow all the world."

A further change is that armed action stands less in the forefront of political means. Here as elsewhere we see the ripening of Hitler's political genius since the issue of his standard work: open violence, putsch, revolution, war, are replaced now by subtler methods of application of force. This development seems to be still proceeding, in foreign as in internal policy. The new policy is prepared by means of tactics, of a growing arsenal of political expedients, handled with infinite ability. Here again it is tactics that are the revealing element, rather than doctrines and theories and ostensible aims, or than assurances and solemn agreements, resolutions, pacts, and axes. Tactics reveal the actual revolutionary pressure more plainly than all these day-to-day political expedients.

THE MYSTICAL DOCTRINE OF ELBOW-ROOM AND OF THE PRESSURE OF POPULATION

The prime force in foreign policy, according to the "organic-biological" *Weltanschauung* or philosophy of the National Socialist educators, is the urge to territorial expansion, involving the revolutionary use of the pressure of the population of a growing nation. This pressure takes no account of established conditions or mere legal titles. It is a struggle for existence, brutal and lawless—the right of the stronger to eliminate or subjugate the weaker. Rival national wills and national energies, say these theorists, determine the boundaries between nations and the distribution of territory. All else is fancy. Thus National Socialism, in its return to this primal law and its elimination of false doctrine, is a liberating force, at all events for all nations with vitality. "Plenty of room," said Ratzel long ago, "helps to maintain life." This, comments Haushofer, is "the state-biological

---

* The original version was "Heute hört," etc. ("To-day Germany hears us"), but "gehört" ("we own Germany") is the current version.—Translator.

THE REVOLUTION OF NIHILISM

rule of life put into classic form." There is, he adds, a "natural
right to room to live" which may properly be brought to bear
"against owners of great spaces who have not the capacity to
develop their reserves of space."

Opportunities of expansion for a nation of strong vitality are
provided, we learn, only through the forfeiture of great spaces
by their holders. This forfeiture is the strongest characteristic
of our day. It can be hastened by appropriate methods. This
shows the "inevitability of the struggle for existence" between
nations. "In a world," writes Haushofer, "which is slowly beginning once more to recognize the inevitability of the struggle for
existence . . . only two elements of self-preservation take front
rank* in the mechanism of the world," the net food-supplying
capacity of a nation's soil and the possession of the indispensable
raw materials. Here we have in our hands already the current
small coin of present-day politics.

Of equal importance in the foreign policy of the "biological"
Weltanschauung is the pressure of population. "Excessive pressure of population" becomes "an explosive in the existing world
order." Haushofer writes of a "danger of suffocation of Europe
proper." "The question that concerns us very closely, what to
do with the Germans, Poles, Czechs, who will exist in ten, fifty,
a hundred years' time . . . is plainly quite far from the
thoughts of all who are busy with the petty pursuits of parlia-
ments." The relief of this pressure of population by home colonization is no more than an emergency alternative to territorial
expansion. The breaking up of estates within the country does
nothing to relieve the pressure. It leads quickly to the Chinese
ideal of the small peasant, living at the margin of subsistence
and with no interest in life outside his plot of land. Consequently
National Socialism has virtually abandoned the policy of home
colonization. Since, however, all space in Europe is over-filled,
and even territorial conquest in Europe could not remove the
pressure of population, the "dynamic" policy must never rest

---

* *Stehen nur zwei Grundlagen . . . obenan.*

content with frontier revision and partial solutions, but must seek a general solution, a "redistribution of the world." Only so, we are to understand, can the problems be really solved with justice, giving nations territory in proportion to their vitality, territory which must be taken from the dying nations. Simply for aims of this sort, the sacrifice of the lives of another two million young men may yet again become justifiable—so the Führer has declared, in discussing the eastern territorial policy with his colleagues.

The danger of suffocation through insufficiency of space is coupled with an equal danger of exhaustion of the nation through insufficiency of population. The nation must be kept at its numerical strength; the growth of its population must be promoted by all possible means. It is no paradox, but a relation of cause and effect, that brings the specter of racial extinction close behind territorial constriction and over-population. Over our present European civilization hovers the nightmare of the downfall and depopulation of the ancient world. Japan artificially restricted her population for centuries by means of strict social regulations; but this policy is no longer possible for Japan, which has shown such unexampled growth during its imperialist epoch, nor for the European nations. "Precisely in the coming quarter of a century," says Haushofer, "increase of population and provision of room to live . . . are of critical importance for the future of a people in competition with the rest of the human race." The course of events since 1914 should make it perfectly clear to every German "why he must pursue a racial policy." Thus lack of territory cannot be compensated by birth restriction. Any nation that wants to endure must promote the growth of its population by all possible means, no matter how small its territory. The possibility of renewal and rejuvenation of a nation, says Haushofer, is a fact. Thus foreign policy also yields not only the need but the possibility of a "doctrine of racial permanence through racial preservation." The tasks inculcated by this doctrine, which may be summed up as the tasks of the "racial State," are racial eugenic selection, racial hygiene, and, in so far as territorial policy is affected or conditioned by these, not only the provision of a healthy balance between town and country within the existing national territory, but, above all, the expansion of this territory.

The dying-out of a population through birth restriction would certainly solve the territorial problem and many political problems bound up with it, but only at the price of the self-surrender of the nation. In England, according to these racial theorists, the prospect of sinking to the level of a small nation within a century is found actually attractive; but, they declare, a nation full of vitality and of faith in its future will see in the steadily increasing number of its members the guarantee of its future and the seal of its dominion. Once more, as under mercantilism, population is regarded as the great element of wealth; but now it is not population in itself, but the racially purified, homogeneous population of a nation. The growth of the nation is demanded not only by its will to live but by its will to power. Without growth the dynamic pressure it can exert ceases. Without this pressure its dynamic policy is crippled. So the ideas of this policy move in a great circle and revolve upon themselves. The dynamic policy grows out of the pressure of population and the effort at expansion. But if this policy is to be continually pursued, a population policy is required in order to increase this pressure.

National Socialism does not confine its doctrine of the vital need for territorial expansion to Germany. Herr Goebbels envisages the rare moment when a redistribution of the world will come. The advantages of this revolution, he considers, would be open to all nations that have less to lose than to gain. This is the fanfare with which the dynamic foreign policy of National Socialism goes into action.

THE LOST DOMINION AND THE DYING NATION

It is not idle to pursue these ideas. They are not mere word-stringing or fancifulness. They are attractive and in their materialistic simplicity full of meaning for the masses. They are fundamental to National Socialist foreign policy. They are fundamental also for its judgment of its opponents. Accepting the "biological" basis of its foreign policy, the consideration of the diminishing vital energy of Western Europe must produce quite definite conclusions. Here are excessive spaces, with exhausted nations occupying them, or at all events nations troubled with a birth-rate falling to nothing. Sooner or later, therefore, these nations must yield before stronger ones and cede their excess territory to them. Here are the regions destined to forfeiture, —here, and not in the East with its big birth-rate. Here, inevitably, policy will become negative, devoted merely to holding on to possessions, to assuring existence, a policy backed by no power of resistance. The political leaders of the upward-striving nations may count confidently on this weakness, running scarcely any risk in tactics of unlimited daring. The situation is similar to that of the middle class population of Germany, which capitulated at once to National Socialism. Here again it has nothing but the pseudo-great to bring down. And the secret of success is to have recognized the absence of substance in their power. Only along these lines is the confident judgment of the National Socialists on the weakness of the British position, and on the inevitable doom of France as a Great Power, intelligible.

What changes of population there have been, for instance, since the classic period of French predominance, three hundred years ago! Then France had as many inhabitants as the whole of Europe east of the Rhine and west of the frontier of the Russia of that day. Then the empty spaces were in the East. During the Napoleonic wars the situation was still favorable to France. But to-day she has only half as many inhabitants as Germany.

Undeniably National Socialism has touched the weak spots in the Western nations with such arguments as these. M. Flandin, an ex-Prime Minister of France, has recently made use of the same arguments. Regarded from the point of view of population, the great nations of the West have no future. This gives the nations that are still growing their certainty of victory, and

191

their tremendous ambitions for the future. It was not so much any marvellous tactical ability or vast intelligence service that enabled Hitler to carry out his bold policy of the late summer of 1938 with success, as the confidence of judgment resulting from the knowledge of the biological facts.

Scarcely any other opinion is given currency by the National Socialists with such diligence as their belief in the doom of the British Empire; they regard its downfall as already an accomplished fact. "As an imperial body the British Empire is as dead as the Roman," said an American journalist, N. Pfeffer, shortly after the Great War. The Germans go farther. They no longer ask with Pfeffer what is the strength of the spiritual bonds that hold the Empire together; they come straight to the recognition of the fact of the "subsidence of the British main islands after the fashion of Venice," as Haushofer expresses it. It is the last and almost inevitable stage "in a curve of dismemberment." The "aging Empire" has grown "tired." "Does it still possess the energy for so great a resolve?" asks Haushofer, " . . . or is it resting already with flagging energies on the enjoyment of rights?" An inclination to pacifism at the wrong moment is, in Haushofer's view, a special "symptom of the flagging English will to empire."

Haushofer, like many other of the National Socialist "intellectuals," never tires of variations on the theme of the doomed British Empire. England has lost the "flair for rule" in the old, genuine sense. This, at all events, was the interpretation given to the placing of the Dominions on a basis of equality in 1926— "the most conspicuous surrender of power." "While apparently at the height of power in territory controlled and in population," the Empire suffered a "drastic change of form into a more and more loosely developing association of States." Haushofer's "geopolitical" disciples return again and again to the fundamental importance of this fact, of England's passive renunciation of world dominion.

German public opinion is, on the whole, kept free from anti-

British feeling by the present regime; since Munich it has been decidedly pro-British. The party leaders consider that the old *"Gott strafe England"* is no longer needed. England has lost the Great War, and cannot venture on another. She is no longer in a position to defend her rule by arms. The time has come, therefore, to admit younger elements to world rule. The new Germany might be ready to take upon her own shoulders the "white man's burden" which has grown too heavy for England's tired shoulders. But Germany's junior partnership must not mean merely that the German nation would fight England's battles for her; it must be a partnership in which the younger partner takes over the actual conduct of business.

"England needs peace; only if peace is maintained can she continue for a while to hold her greatly shaken position in the world." Such was the opinion expressed years ago by General von Seeckt. It has long been a foremost political axiom of National Socialist foreign policy that England can no longer venture on a war, and that she may therefore be offered any affront with impunity. Von Bethmann-Hollweg used to say as Chancellor that he regarded his highest task as that of "appeasement" (*kalmieren*). This, it is considered by the party leaders, is to-day the only maxim left for England. And there seems good reason for supposing that the policy of "appeasement" will be equally ineffectual in this case.

Every policy depends on some initiative that has to be kept up for a considerable time. The British initiative was the voluntary disarmament which was kept up for years. After this course, which must be interpreted as the expression of a flagging determination, further developments followed logically step by step. A voluntary abandonment of the means of power at a time of the rise of new Powers is more than remissness; it is the symbolic expression of a voluntary abdication. "The two territorially mightiest *pan*-ideas of the world are attacking the continuance of this empire," says Haushofer; and yet England cuts down her armaments. In face of these developments the only

193

"long-range aim of the British world empire is the maintenance of its position in culture, power, and economic life." This, says Haushofer, means the extinction of the will to live, the surrender of the will to power.

One of the essential features of National Socialist relations with England is the fact that, alongside a certain sense of racial kinship and the desire for an alliance, there exists a very plain dislike of England. Yet the political conviction is repeatedly expressed in *Mein Kampf* that Germany needs to maintain friendly relations with England. In this respect rational reflection is countered by deep-seated feelings, not only among the party leaders but largely throughout the party! The German dislike of England is derived directly from the ideas of anti-Semitism. The Englishman in his Puritanism, saturated with the spirit of the Old Testament, has become the chief representative of capitalism which, in the eyes of National Socialists, is the principal Jewish achievement; thus, the British Empire is a Jewish empire, an empire in which the typically Jewish way of thinking, guidance by economic considerations, the spirit of profit-making, dominates. The liberalism of the English mind is the essential and almost insuperable obstacle to an alliance between Germany and England. In the past the English were despised (and imitated) as the nation of shopkeepers; their cant and "perfidy" were denounced; but the present regime in Germany goes farther. The English through their Puritans have become the nation that appropriated the promise to Israel, and they are Judaized through and through. England is to blame for the dominance of the Jewish spirit in Europe. England has made this identification of economic success with the blessing of God the ethical framework of her public morality and civic virtues. England is Judah. This is the character the national propaganda against England will one day assume, when it is found necessary in the Third Reich to prepare for a struggle. Until recently the regime was currying for favor, but already the lines just described are being followed among National Socialists in private discussions of Albion's latest perfidy. England, they are sure, can no longer hold her ground if the German-British issue is put to the test of fire and sword. That is the great and decisive improvement in Germany's position as compared with 1914. England is now only a pseudo-Power. It will be well, if possible, to make an end of her fictitious power by peaceful evolution. But if there must be an appeal to arms there is no need to fear it. The very day war broke out, it would become manifest that Great Britain had already lost her world dominion.

France is a "dying nation," both physically and politically. A charming people, likable, perhaps even happy, relieved now of every political task. But a nation with no purpose and therefore of no importance. There is no animosity in this assessment. German feelings have changed radically from the pan-German hostility of pre-war days. France's past friends in Germany, and even her friends of to-day, share the general view. An East European politician spoke to me rather rhetorically of the odor of death over Paris—"not yet actuality, but prophetic." The French nation, say leading National Socialists, is no longer the nation of *esprit* and *élan*, but a sober, tenacious, economical, and with all its grace a dry and humdrum people, with no uplift, no passion, without the magnificence and the ambition of the classic French. It is no longer the nation that made French history, a small nation with a great spiritual and political heritage: it is merely a second-class nation on the periphery of Europe, long since excluded from the European centers of future dynamic development, and forced on to the defensive. In any case, an attractive nation, deserving of pity, a nation that may be left to itself, since time is working inexorably against it. The Franco-German question will settle itself one day—on the day when it is demonstrated that France, too, is only a pseudo-Power, incapable of assisting her friends and allies.

Mein Kampf expressed the National Socialist view that "the destruction of the French military power in the West" was necessary as the "condition for a free hand in the East." When

Mein Kampf was being written, France's power was still regarded as so considerable that an armed conflict between France and Germany seemed indispensable in order to gain "security in our rear . . . for the increase of living space for our people in Europe." To-day, after a few years of National Socialist foreign policy, it seems possible that a final war with France for hegemony in Europe may be unnecessary. In a few years, said Hitler in 1934, Germany would be in a situation enabling her to reap by bloodless means even in the West the fruits of her rearmament. Ten years ago he had said that the Germans could not accept the existing order in the West, and France must be ruthlessly destroyed in a "final decisive struggle." Now, however, there are entirely new chances for Germany to induce France, the dying nation, voluntarily to abandon her past rôle in Europe. This sober and sensible nation, no longer dreaming of glory and heroism, a nation of petty bourgeois, would be much too clear-headed to fail to see the uselessness of a renewed struggle with Germany.

It is known that this line of thought has for a long time ruled among the leading members of the party, and that it largely determined the policy pursued against Austria and Czechoslovakia. There is no hatred of the French nation. On the contrary, even among persons whose weakness does not lie in the direction of impartial judgment of opponents, I have found the French referred to with unqualified respect as soldiers. But it was joined to an equally great contempt of the political aims of the nation. France's importance in history, it was universally considered, had come to an end with the Great War. The nation was no longer capable of anything beyond a heroic resistance in national defence; it would never again develop readiness to take the offensive. Its *élan* had been broken for all time. It was inconceivable that French expeditionary forces should play a part of any importance in a foreign war. There was no longer, a prominent politician said to me, any need to isolate or encircle

France, as Germany was suspected of intending; France was voluntarily isolating herself. She could do nothing else. And this estimate dates from years before the autumn of 1938. In his purpose of destroying France, or at all events decisively vanquishing her, Hitler stood alone, said my informant, among the German people. A war with France would be extremely unpopular. There was no feeling in Germany of hereditary enmity or desire for *revanche*. The intention was simply to try to weaken France without bloodshed, to manœuvre her out of her positions, perhaps to declare her Government to be the enemy of the people, but to show sympathy with the people. Internal tension and dissension may be expected. There is finally a possibility of coming forward as "liberator" of the French nation, just as Napoleon marched into the old Germany. And the destiny of the French military power might well be the same as that of Czechoslovakia—capitulation without the Maginot line having the opportunity of demonstrating its strength.

CHANGE IN THE IMPORTANCE OF SMALL STATES

Bülow recalls in his Memoirs a conversation between von Jagow, State Secretary for Foreign Affairs, and Jules Cambon, the French Ambassador at Berlin, in which Jagow expressed his opinion in regard to the future of the small nations of Europe, particularly Belgium, a few months before the outbreak of the Great War. He did not suggest that Belgium's great colonial empire was too heavy a burden for so small a State, but he regarded it as certain that, in the coming recasting of Europe, the small States would no longer be able to lead an independent existence as in the past. The peace treaties applied exactly the opposite principle, that of the right of self-determination of nations. But, says Haushofer, this "step back for the benefit of the small-area States" is only apparent. Ratzel's laws of the territorial growth of States and the movement toward continually greater areas remain in force. "Small-area formations" are for Haushofer "forms of dissolution and evaporation." Their tendency to "large-area amalgamations" is "one of the surest signs of the prevalence of processes of acceleration in world politics." "In regard to the assessments of size of such independent areas, world politics have undergone a development of enormous power and destructive force in a relatively short time." It is a gross illusion to regard the "bits of States" of the "Central and Intermediate European zones of wreckage . . . as really independent existences in world politics." "Inadequate world-political extent of area," says Haushofer,* is a curse. The shadow of inadequacy of this sort lies, according to Haushofer, "over the nucleus countries of the Belgian and Dutch colonial empires, to say nothing of Portugal; over Denmark, the Baltic States, Switzerland and Greece: all of these, in view of their extent of area, are no longer capable of really independent world politics." The small States are faced inexorably with the choice between deciding to place themselves under the protection of the Western Powers, which have enough to do to protect themselves, or to federate with the new dynamic Powers. An independent existence is practically denied to them from now on. As regards protection from the Western Powers, it is becoming increasingly doubtful how far they can rely on a policy of collective security even for their own protection.

Can the small States play any part of their own amid the interplay of imperialist forces in the future? The change in the importance of the small States is a fact of revolutionary political significance, and one which is being vigorously publicized by National Socialist propaganda. The treatment of Czechoslovakia turned this fact to practical effect. The smaller States are no longer politically independent in reality: the Munich conference demonstrated that beyond cavil. And that revolutionary precedent has laid the whole structure of Europe in ruins. What happened to Czechoslovakia may happen to-morrow

---

* *Die unzulängliche weltpolitische Raumweite.* These quotations from General Haushofer are in the curious language of "geopolitics." "Intermediate" means between Germany and Russia.—Translator.

to any other State, no matter how long it has been in existence. This means in effect that the great areas now being carved out must be recognized to be the one and only structural element of the future. But, since it is recognized that there are degrees of sovereignty, the small States are required henceforth to seek the friendship of a protector.

PROTECTORATE AND SOVEREIGNTY

For the isolated small States, with their narrow individualism, there appears now, say the "geopoliticians", to be only one means of salvation, a pseudo-independence, purchased by the friendship of a protector and subservience to him, within an amalgamation of wide areas under the leadership of a Great State. Union can only be brought about by superior force. That is the teaching of the twenty wasted years of the independence and undue significance of the many small States of Europe. An agreement can be achieved by other means besides good will. No one knew that better than Bismarck. In his footsteps, but by methods that differ radically from those by which he created the second Reich, the small States will be forced by a more or less voluntary protectorate into vassalage to the resolute dynamic Powers that are now rising. It may be decidedly open to question which is the more lasting, an *Anschluss* out of love or compulsion. One thing, however, is certain: a State without greatly superior force has no power of attracting States of less power; for they want two things: not only respect of their independence but above all a buttress. Thus they are inclined to seek the strength they lack from a State more powerful than their peers. The practical politician will therefore easily agree that, for instance, Count Kalnoky was right when he said that the friendship of the South Slav peoples was an uncertain factor, and that a union of fear or of material interests works better than a union of love, since those motives are more reliable than love, which in any case always comes in the end.

Thus there comes into existence for the great and resolute

nations a new idea of leadership and the opportunity of peaceful expansion across neighboring territory. "How can we return to our old torn-up territorial right?" asks Haushofer. "Hand in hand with the right of self-determination and in respect for it; or in opposition to it, in worship of force, as has been alleged against us?" It all depends on how the right of self-determination is interpreted. There are some new and very "realist" methods of interpretation in currency.

THE SHADOW OVER THE OLD COLONIAL POWERS

The destruction of the old political order has also affected, we are told, the great areas that are only independent in appearance. The day of the old-style colonial Powers is past, just as is that of the small States of Europe. Such is the view of the National Socialist politicians. Not only is the British Empire beginning to break up, and its member States to drift in other directions; the French colonial empire can no longer be maintained intact. Least of all can the small Powers with vast colonial possessions count on continuing to hold these possessions while great European nations are left to suffocate in their confined situation, without the smallest colonial possession. These contrasts cannot but produce an explosion that will shatter and revolutionize the existing order. The old colonial Powers are "no longer able to set forth distant aims; they can only maintain retrospective claims to rights based on past robbery," to quote Haushofer once again. These Powers no longer have sufficient forces to defend their possessions. Still less can they defend them morally. They are entirely without persuasive ideas; their insistence on rights is so thin and feeble an argument that it illustrates the entire hollowness of the existing world order. Powers which are no longer capable of continually adding, materially and spiritually, to their possessions by superior will and creative energy, are ripe for abdication. The fate of the old colonial Powers is, therefore, independently of the growing material difficulties of maintaining their rule, sealed through their spiritual sterility—they are unable either to take up a resolute stands as masters of colonial territory, or to turn to use such ideas as those of the movements for union among the colored races. They are allowing the primacy of the white race of rulers to fall out of their weak hands, instead of subjecting the colored world in the colonial territories to the European white race, by means of new ideas, under new forms of domination. New principles of order can proceed only from the revolutionary dynamic Powers. Such principles proceed from Italy's Mediterranean conception. They are still more manifest in the ideas of National Socialism. These will be summoned to the reshaping and reordering of the political structure of the world, far beyond European territory.

The self-determination movement, says Haushofer, "is destroying colonial rulership" (*Herrentum*—the gift of ruling as lord and master). "The self-determination movement, at first conceived only as a lying means of fighting Germany, and as one that would be easy subsequently to bring to an end, is now on the march as truth, and is destroying colonial rulership wherever it spreads in lordly style over alien territory." The process of the formation of national States is extending now to colonial territories and to the colored world. "There can be no going back on this critical change." "To-day these great areas are fighting a hopeless rearguard action in the world." Only a new rulership and racial sense can be of any help. Thus national States and other great territorial formations are growing on what has hitherto been colonial territory; and they will shake off not only the political but the economic domination of the white nations.

The economic system has taken almost everywhere the form of State Socialism. Thus in Turkey, Persia, Afghanistan, the economic system has been reconstructed through the nationalization of minerals, and through monopolies and customs tariffs, in the interest of political liberty and independence. The whole complex of semi-sovereign States and nations will follow along this path of national revolution, with the aid of economic reconstruction on the lines of State Socialism. These will provide new centers of propaganda by example, which will inevitably exert a subversive influence on the existing colonial territories.

What has been written here of colonial territory applies with still more force to the Russian realm. Soviet Russia, as a revolutionary Socialist State, is the enemy of the National Socialist forces of order; but it is more. As a great territorial formation, it is a standing menace to Europe. The principle of self-determination applies also to Russia. The Russian problem can be solved only in accordance with European, that is to say, German, ideas. The great process that began with the German victories in the World War, and with the truly historic secession of the western territories from Russia, a secession of world importance, must be carried to the conclusion that was prevented by the loss of the War and by the Bolshevik dictatorship. Not only the Russian border territories but the whole of Russia must be broken up into its components. Those components are the natural imperial territory of Germany.

THE RENOVATING POWERS

Germany's revolutionary task embraces the West as well as the East of Europe. It concerns both the colonial territories and the great Eurasian hinterland. It will also embrace the great American spaces which are still far from political and social, racial and economic equilibrium. For the German nation is faced not with a mere set of petty political tasks but with a new ordering of life. Germany is the leading renovating Power.

The distinction between the "renovating" and "resisting" Powers, the *Mächte der Erneuerung* or Powers working for renewal and the *Mächte der Beharrung* or Powers merely holding on to what they have, is one of the most effective principles of National Socialist foreign policy. The latter Powers are charged not only with weakness and inactivity but with holding possessions to which they have no right. This distinction has unquestionably an important propagandist efficacy. It is combined with a sound psychological estimate of one of the principal weaknesses in the present general constitution of Europe. It seizes the bull by the horns, so to speak, in connection with one of the main European problems. There is undoubtedly a certain identity of destiny between the have-nots of the Danube basin and the east of Europe which might bring them into community of interest with Germany. It is clear that, in Haushofer's words, "the members of Central and Intermediate Europe, cut off . . . alike from oversea and overland territorial gain . . . sit on the same bough with the German national soil* in territorial policy, and are unceasingly . . . proceeding toward the same cramped destiny." National Socialism, "extended as a dynamic doctrine throughout the world," would simply mean "either freedom for every duly qualified emigrant to migrate throughout the planet, in all areas still free and undersettled, which he can raise to a higher level by his arrival, or equitable reallocation of unused areas to areas already national-socialistically organized (*nationalsozialistisch durchgegliederte Räume*)." In this way the renovating Powers become virtually "restorers of natural right." Needless to say, "the Powers of holding-on and possession will have furnished themselves with every legal claim . . . and the restorers of natural right will be denounced as breakers of the peace." These are plausible and generally effective phrases. "A matter of course, returning again and again in world politics for thousands of years past," is the replacement of the Powers that are holding on to their possessions by dynamic landless Powers with a determination to make their way in the world—as England and France once, when they were rising Powers, tore scraps from the body of the Spanish world empire and the Habsburg monarchy. Only when placed in relation to these broad historical processes does the revolutionary will of dynamism in foreign policy reveal itself. "The preparation for achievement," for the hour of realization of these aims, as Haushofer calls the total mobilization and armament of the

---

* *Mit dem deutschen Volksboden raumpolitisch auf einem Ast sitzen*—Trans.

dynamic Powers, arouses "fear for their foreign policy among all those who have a bad conscience; this means, of course, the past lords of wide, undeveloped spaces."

What can the resisting Powers do to defend themselves from this new creative will? What, after all, are these Powers but encirclement associations? "From this fear," says Haushofer, "there come encirclement associations against the bearers of every demand for the future, whether Bulgaria, Germany, Italy, Japan, or Hungary." The "resisting Powers" are above all England and France. On them depend at present the small States of "Intermediate Europe," the small, buttress-needing colonial Powers, the Scandinavian States, and Switzerland. Actually all new States or States that have grown greater through the world war belong to this group: the Succession States of Austria-Hungary, the Border States, Poland. But in the Near East and the South-east the resisting tendencies, consisting in the defence of unearned possessions acquired through Germany's defeat, cut across dynamic tendencies existing in the same States in their quality of young nations, tendencies arising from their pressure of population, their constricted territory, and their poverty-stricken existence. There is thus every probability, indeed it is virtually certain, that all these dependent States, these unsatiated small nations, will sooner or later enter the ranks of the renovating Powers, because it is only so that they can have prospects of a tolerable existence. They will join the dynamic Powers even if this involves a restriction of their sovereignty or the sacrifice implied in certain frontier revisions.

It is obvious that a foreign policy on this sort of basis can have little intention of seriously coming to terms with the resisting Powers. It is uncertain in any case whether England could not ultimately be attracted to the side of the renovating Powers. A good many elements in Great Britain have remained undemoralized by the democratic poison. England might still be capable of renewal in spirit, and might find her way back to the great driving forces, the will to rule, out of which the grandiose creation of the Empire proceeded. England is not comfortable at the head of the resisting Powers. This is beyond doubt the reason why her policy has been so full of inconsistencies and weaknesses in recent years. To bring over this "evolutionary" England, "always ready for metamorphosis at the right moment," into membership in the front of renovating Powers, alike by friendly advances and by menaces, is the persistent effort of important groups in the new Germany. The English nation too will regain health from contact with the new dynamism. For the possessing Powers are sterile. Their thinking and their policy are confined to rigid juridical categories. They have shut themselves out of the creative life that is movement. Their inevitable fate is extinction and the loss of their possessions. Their policy is an anxious clinging to what they have, barren of ideas, passive, defensive. In a world of unceasing revolutionary movement, they will automatically grow steadily weaker. Defence in their case is the first stage of defeat. The renunciation of expansion is renunciation of life itself. Consequently the resisting Powers, the "demoplutocracies," are doomed to ultimate liquidation and the transfer of their effects to Powers which are able to do useful work with them and make something of them.

THE NEW DOCTRINE OF RULERSHIP

What are the conditions of dominion? Is it possible for great areas to be ruled as the possessing Powers are trying to rule them, without the heavy hand, without the will to dominion, without the sense of a world mission? World significance and the call to rule over great areas emanate only from "the will to rule over alien territories and people," is Haushofer's reply. It is doubtful "whether such a will to rule exists at all among the resisting Powers. It seems more likely that the essential characteristic of the resisting Powers, which also explains their hesitation and weakness, is the lack of a will to rule." In all world empires founded, says Haushofer, "in addition to the imperial idea or simply the idea of economic exploitation there lives also a philosophic or religious sense of a world mission . . . without such an ideological content all efforts of this sort come much more quickly to a stop." Both signs of capacity to rule great areas are lacking in the possessing Powers—the will to rule and the spiritual sense of a world mission. Both signs, on the other hand, are evident in the dynamic Powers. A nation's urge to expand is the natural expression of its healthy growth. The sense of a mission is a legitimate manifestation of the will to rule. It is the will to the spiritual domination of the world. National Socialism is busy setting up this very domination.

National Socialism recommends itself to a nation of rulers so old and experienced, but temporarily weary and slackening, as the British, especially by the effective political element of a new doctrine of rulership. Behind the make-believe of its nationalist and Socialist doctrines, National Socialism unquestionably sets out to be a new ruling element, capable of providing the ideological basis for the ruler's standpoint in colonial territory. It may even be that it is not too much to say that the new German policy is meeting with approval in certain realist political groups in England for the very reason that it expresses a clear will to rule, in contrast with the doctrine of equality, with all its corollaries of self-determination, national dismemberment, and concern for all shades of national and religious thought, a doctrine that weakens every empire. The National Socialist foreign policy is able to represent both elements—a new doctrine of rulership and at the same time the subversive principle, entirely destructive of European rule in the colored world, of the right of peoples to self-determination. The German statements make it very clear that it would be Germany's mission in her own interest to place herself in the colonial territories as elsewhere at the head of the proletarian nations, and that she would do so if hindered in applying the new doctrine of rulership to her own as a ruling race.

The doctrine of race, as yet developed only in regard to Jewry, offers inexhaustible opportunities of domination and of providing an ideological basis for a realist will to power in colonial territory. Only on the basis of the doctrine of race can democratic ideas be ideologically combated, only this basis can provide the strength of will, the ruthlessness, and freedom from all "humanitarian folly," necessary for the control of great territories and the defence of the privileged position of the white race in the world. The new political doctrine facilitates, so to speak, the work of ruling. The racial doctrine, the doctrine of the inequality of men and races, sweeps away all the sentiment acquired under the burden of centuries by so reflective and sensitive a race of rulers, rather feminine in their sensibility, as the Anglo-Saxons. If they still like to consider it their special mission to bear the "white man's burden," nothing is better calculated to facilitate their task than the new racial doctrine, the new rulership of the dynamic nations.

It would be instructive to regard the persistent policy of anti-Semitism from the point of view of this idea of a doctrine of rulership. We must distinguish between a popular conception for the masses and a special interpretation for the élite. Among the S.S. and the leaders of the S.A., anti-Semitism is deliberately regarded as a "school of rulership." The Jew is the "colored man," the *déclassé* of Europe, the politically disfranchised "subman." A humane attitude toward him is the sign of unfitness to rule. For this reason insensitiveness and absolute cruelty are deliberately practiced. Soft-heartedness has to be driven out and brutality provided, so to speak, with a good conscience.

There is a right to brutality—the Pan-Germans used to declare this unequivocally. "France, the dying nation, can be so prostrated by us, that she will never rise again, and we shall do it! England, if fortune is kind to us, we can reduce to an innocuous island-State"—such were the German war aims as defined by Class. But need we define the new doctrine of rulership in such foolish terms as this tragi-comic pan-German

Justizrat? Haushofer sketches the new style of colonial policy cautiously, as a policy that should have nothing to do with exploitation and oppression, but would find its justification simply in the ideas of leadership. A leadership, it is true, that has nothing to do with the old "trusteeship" for the colored population. What is advocated, with brutal candor, by National Socialist politicians is a policy of depopulation. With this, as a harsh but necessary expedient of the new will to rule, goes the "shifting of population," an expedient by means of which social or national minorities are now beginning to be destroyed by administrative measures. As yet this expedient has found practical application only in regard to the Jews. Perhaps we shall next see it applied to the Czech population of the remainder of Bohemia; old National Socialist plans provided for the removal of the Czechs to Siberia, in order to secure room for colonization by a solid German community.

GERMANY'S ROLE AS A WORLD POWER

New rulership, world influence, world transformation, world hegemony—this is the direction of the principles of German foreign policy thus far considered. But they do not aim at a Greater Germany, they are not content with the place of Germany as an element of order in Central Europe; they are not by any means confined to "overland" conceptions, as Haushofer calls them. The "faith in a rôle of leadership in world policy" inspires the German activities. The "mystical faith in a world mission which . . . at times of slowly crippling pressure throws itself into an unheard-of inner strengthening and steeling, in order to be ready at the given moment for the highest achievement," is Haushofer's description of the actual nerve of the new German political purpose. "For we have not much more time to allow the energy of movement of the world Powers and the speed with which they are marching toward their immediate and remote objectives, and their thrust, already begun, through the old Great Power groups . . . to pass us by, without being clear in our minds that in this approaching settlement the destiny of our people and Reich will be determined for centuries, perhaps for ever." The German situation leaves the nation no political choice. Dynamic movement is necessarily more important for us in world politics than a static condition, a condition of holding on.

Again and again in her past history Germany was prevented, says Haushofer, from gaining her "full stature." Early in the Middle Ages there began for the Reich the process of dismemberment which may now be observed in the British Empire. Thus, Germany found no satisfactory solution for the Baltic territories; the result was the existing irrational territorial system. So in the past with the separation of the Netherlands from the Reich, the transfer of the Flemings to the Romance empire, the cutting off of Switzerland, of the Danish territories, the old federative German Empire, from which all these members wrested their independence, came to ruin through the lack of the will to rule. The lesson the National Socialists draw from Germany's past is that dismemberment can only be prevented by rigid centralization. The developments in the British Empire seem to their historians to be a repetition of the error of the old German Reich. The second Reich, the Germany of Bismarck and William II, tried to avoid that error. National Socialism sees its own great significance in its gift to the nation of imperial ambitions. The Germany of William II threatened British life at its most sensitive points. But it lacked the actual sense of a mission. The essence of the German mission to-day is the consciousness of being the chosen people with a permanent and universal task. Germany no longer menaces Britain; she is seizing the leadership only because the British nation has become feeble and weary. The young German imperialism of pre-war days was an attempt to solve our pressing population problems without suffering a continual loss by emigration; the new German will to world hegemony is the definite resolve to transform the world order under German leadership.

Germany's new growth is breaking all the resistance of rival

Powers, as the germ will split the hardest stone. But that which is growing up with Germany is not an imperialism of the style of the end of the nineteenth century. The coming order will be an upheaval of dimensions at present inconceivable. It will not be the empire of a single nation, spread over subject territories and races. It will be a common achievement of all nations, disciplined under the rigid leadership of the one chosen nation in a common realization of a world mission. The new hegemony of the leading World Power of the future has nothing to do with the ideas of a liberal imperialism based on economic exploitation. The old songs may still be heard. But those have deaf ears who cannot hear something different, something deeply in earnest, something demonic and impelling now underlying the favorite slogans of the right to a redistribution of the world, of Germany's mission, of the feeble old hypocrite England, and of the "finished" France. The creative will now intervening manifests a harshness in its ends and its means that Europe has not seen for centuries.

NATION AND EMPIRE

It is no longer a question of an imperialism built up by a national State. The forces of the Liberal national State have become inadequate for the dimensions of the tasks to be coped with. Another mobilization of forces is required. The new great organized territories crystallize around Powers that are prepared to undertake the protection of others. The qualification for forming great new imperial territories is the capacity of a great State to weave around itself a garland of protected associate States. Only when that has been done can there be any talk of a world court, "the miserable farce of which is being played today," says Ernst Jünger, "by the League of Nations." A true League of Nations will grow up round the new imperial Great Powers—a real accumulation of power centrally exercised.

Once more it becomes necessary at a critical point to distinguish in National Socialist policy between that which is make-

210

believe and that which is reality. The actual political aim of National Socialism is a domination stretching far beyond all national limits. The recognition of this throws an entirely new light on the reincorporation of Austria and of the Sudeten territory in the German Reich. The Holy Roman Empire of the German nation—"it has really come!" So, in an ostensible outburst of romantic candor, Hitler brought the National Socialist Congress of 1937, the "Congress of Work," to a close. That which centuries of German history and many generations of despairing patriots had longed for and tried to win, was now, apparently, attained. But this was no more than the propagandist camouflage of a practical policy with altogether different aims—those of territorial expansion and increase of power. The immediate concern behind the scenes was for the conversion of Austria into what Germany had already become, a submerged population, the obedient subject and instrument of dynamism. The ordinary middle class German still imagines that the nationalism of National Socialism is essentially that of the nineteenth century. But National Socialism has usurped ideas and phrases in order to bring into existence other things than those for which they have hitherto stood. The Greater Germany of National Socialism is most certainly not what we and our forefathers envisaged. The earlier movement for national unity and expansion, the Greater Germany movement, was inspired by an idea of liberation, a free union of related elements amid respect for alien ones. The ostensible national unity of to-day, the *"Volksgemeinschaft,"* is a unity under duress. It is a summons to the individual from a merciless regime. It has nothing to do with liberation either of the nation or of the individual; on the contrary, it is the sharpest disciplining and *Gleichschaltung*, or forcing into conformity, of nation and individual. It also means the claim to dominion, and the ranking of nations in accordance with their population and power. It means the rule of force and a regime of privilege. In this sphere there is no development of liberty, no federative association, but only the central power exercising hegemony and the garland of subordinate nations round it. Greater Germany becomes not the peaceful center of Europe, but the starting-point of a coming vast empire. It is not the self-fulfilment of the nation at long last, but the claim that it shall lose itself once more in the adventurous pursuit of a monstrous world dominion.

Thus there is nothing romantic, visionary, unreal and childish, about these activities. They are, on the contrary, a cool utilization of the political slogans of the opponent in order to build up and extend the power of National Socialism in such a way as to defeat in advance any reasoned objection. It is certainly impossible for this expansion of power to be challenged by the States that stood at the Peace Conference for the principles of the national State and of the right of peoples to self-determination. Yet the whole purpose of this Greater Germany is the expansion of power. Its creation enables the dynamism of the Third Reich to apply its policy of expansion at the point that permits the strongest and deepest blow to be struck at the heart of the opposed order. In this national policy Hitler may have been moved partly by certain romantic ideas. What is more important is the fact that this policy of make-believe was able to exploit a national movement.

German policy stands to-day, says Haushofer, "in the shadow of the Holy Roman Empire of the German nation," just as the great shadow of Rome looms up at the back of the new Italy. "The fear of its return in some of the territories it formerly overshadowed" is still, he considers, a vital element in world policy. This shadow, he says, lies not so much over the Southeast of Europe as "in the West of the German national soil (even if we take no account of France), at least over the language frontier that lies to-day far beyond the frontier of the Reich and the defensive frontier, which embraced Flanders—German Belgium—Luxembourg—German Lorraine and Alsace. Beyond these, however, lay . . . the present French West Flanders, the Burgundian heritage, the recollection that imperial power once ruled here as far as the Mediterranean, that Besançon, Lyons were cities of the Empire, Savoy an important pass country of the Empire, Switzerland . . . a part of the Empire." If we follow this outline of a Greater Germany with Haushofer, the National Socialist plan of national union is evidently not fulfilled either by the reincorporation of Austria or by the incorporation of the Sudeten territory, to say nothing of a few little groups of Germans over the frontier. Flanders, Burgundy, Alsace, Luxembourg, Lorraine, Switzerland—these are not Greater Germany; they represent the empire of a race in Europe. National Socialism claims that the national unity of the German nation can only be achieved by the formation of a European empire on a German foundation: no humanist League of Nations, no pacifist, anemic pan-Europe, but a Greater Germany, on which non-Germanic nations may lean in so far as they adjust themselves to the political forms of the National Socialist type of domination. That is the National Socialist conception of the achievement of German unity.

This unity need not involve sanguinary struggles. It needs none in the view of the creator of this conception. It will be for other States to recognize the inevitable necessity of this Greater German Empire, and peacefully to look on at its formation.

CAPACITY FOR SELF-DETERMINATION; CELLS OF EUROPEAN DEVELOPMENT

The European revolution of National Socialism and the recovery of Germany would have made no progress if Italy had not acted. It seems to be entirely due to certain chance developments, perhaps we may call them mistakes of the democratic Powers, that Italy is to-day one end of the world-dominating axis. But is it mere chance? Haushofer asked, not so long ago: "Where does Italy stand? Where is she going? Is she really entirely a renovating Power, as her Fascism declares, or is her Mediterranean situation forcing her back into the ranks of the old-style colonial Powers, to the Geneva League?" But Italy herself could not have developed alone into a renovating Power. Thus the meeting between Italy and Germany was of fateful importance to both. Their union is irreplaceable, perhaps also indissoluble. Italy gave dynamism political style and rhythm and inner control. But Germany first gave it the consciousness of its great revolutionary task in foreign policy. Only the association between the two provided the opportunity of action on a grand scale. These circumstances are illuminating, but the inference is rarely drawn in Germany that the country's advance would have had a substantially different aspect without this axis alliance, which was by no means a foregone conclusion. This shows how weak and casual were the foundations of this whole policy.

What is astonishing is Hitler's foresight in working for the German-Italian association. He met at first with almost a disdainful reception from Mussolini, but he did not allow himself to be deterred by that. He even overlooked the hurt to his own feelings. It was unquestionably German dynamism that was the suitor in this German-Italian alliance. So there came into being a sort of league of the proletarian nations against the possessing Powers. It was only with the alliance between Germany and Italy that the sterile political talk of revision turned into the political determination to achieve a total reordering and redistribution of the world.

"Cells" or points of departure "of future European development" is the name Haushofer has given to the political problems of interest to National Socialist dynamism, including the problems of Lithuania, Hungary, and the Ukraine. In contrast to these points of departure there are those small national groups of the past which have regained their independence. The conception of "capacity for self-determination" must be given precedence over a merely theoretical "right of self-determination." For "bits of country" (*Teillandschaften*) cannot exhibit any capacity for self-determination. This applies to all "spatially constricted, small and thinly-peopled forms of life," * such as are revealed by most of the "States of the western and eastern European intermediate girdles." The "wretched state of Germany's relations with most of eastern Europe and the way Intermediate Europe has been split up" are mainly due to the failure to perceive the lack of capacity for self-determination of these "bits of country." Haushofer demands, accordingly, "a well-conceived political and publicist handling of these two conceptions: the right of self-determination and the capacity for self-determination." For it would offer great opportunities of success and might reveal very dangerous weaknesses. In this connection he comes to one of the most important points of departure of dynamic development, a "skeleton in the cupboard," as he calls it, affecting the Soviet Union, Poland, Czechoslovakia, and Roumania—"the Ukrainian, Ruthenian, Little Russian, or Red Russian question." It has much the same importance as had Poland when that country was partitioned between Russia, Austria-Hungary, and Prussia. "The territories, if any, out of which new solutions of the Ukrainian question could arise are of Eurasian dimensions," he says, laconically. For the forty million Ukrainians, "sections of whom have disappeared as short-range aims in Poland and Czechoslovakia and Roumania, while the largest section exists in semi-independence within the Soviet Union," would nevertheless play "a part in certain long-range aims of Great Powers against the Soviets." This raises the wartime ideas of making the Volga the backbone of the Great Russian State and the Dnieper that of a Ukrainian State. As long ago as 1917 the German army command in the East had declared in propaganda literature that anyone who wanted to liberate Germany permanently from the Russian menace must turn his thoughts to the Ukraine and awaken that country into independent life. But it must not be associated in any way with Poland. It may incidentally be mentioned that these ideas date from long ago, and were discussed during the Crimean War. At that time their purpose was to counter Russia's eastern plans. Bunsen wrote a

* *Volksschwachen Lebensformen.*

memorandum on the subject. It was the time of anti-Russian orientation in Prussia under Moritz August von Bethmann.

Thus the points of departure of future European dynamics are subject to the two principles of capacity for and right of self-determination. This offers an excellent means of forcible solution under the guise of obedience to a just political principle. Either argument may be brought into the foreground at will—the right of self-determination if the German group in Czechoslovakia is in question, or the lack of capacity for self-determination in such a "bit of country" as Lithuania or White Russia or Slovakia; even of the Czechs, indeed, within a rump State of Bohemia. Rid of its German group and cut off from its Slovak section, this Bohemian torso might be capable of functioning only as a dependent "bit of country" within the Greater German Reich. The provisions of the treaties of the Paris suburb set up no permanent order but were only a vain and now collapsing attempt to revive "vestiges of the past." Cells of future development exist wherever the revolutionary dynamic will can intervene politically, that is to say, wherever the past order can be destroyed. "Opportunities of advance" can come "for those who have been cheated of room to live" only out of the forfeiture of "excessively large areas." Or, it might be added, out of the union of non-independent "bits of country," which could not be allowed a right of self-determination because they have not the capacity for self-determination. "In this sense the final aim of National Socialism," says Rudolf Hess, "is certainly the application of sound common sense." So says Haushofer; and Hess is his disciple.

DEFENCE UNION

It is useful to recall the political ideas of the War years in order to find an explanation of the present aims of National Socialism in regard to the east of Europe. Professor Sering, in the introduction to his book, published in 1917, on the significance of western Russia to the development of Central Europe

(*Westrussland in seiner Bedeutung für die Entwicklung Mitteleuropas*), writes that it would be contrary to German intentions to try to set up an empire; "what is proposed is rather to unite the States of the sections of Europe around the nucleus strengthened by the War, for the joint defence of their independence. In such defence unions lies the basis also for the participation with equal rights and the free development of the smaller nations." These are exactly the practical ideas of the future political activity of the Third Reich outside the central German national territory for the formation of a sort of federation of States. The "strengthened nucleus" for the joint defence of the independence of these States is the Greater Germany within the frontiers temporarily fixed after March 13th, 1938, and after September, 1938. This nucleus is strengthened by the national discipline of National Socialism and the principle of the new control. Thus strengthened, Greater Germany is in a position to offer a real support to all States joining her, and the guarantee of their independence, subject only to a few servitudes. After the protection on paper offered by collective security has proved an illusion in face of the "realist" aggression of the dynamic States, the powerful protection of a guarantee offered by Germany in a union for joint protection and defence makes an end of an intolerable situation of insecurity for the smaller States.

"The defence union," continues Sering, "will require completing by an economic alliance for those nations which comply with the conditions for this closer association through their proximity and interdependence." Here it is necessary to proceed cautiously. "Much will be attainable by the elastic forms of free economic associations." It may be expected that after the completion of a temporary stage in the formation of the nucleus of the new order, attempts will be made by Germany, on the lines of these or similar ideas, at an extensive reorganization of Central Europe and the Near East. These efforts may be entirely analogous to the peaceful efforts to set up a Zollverein within the German Federation. Pressure and menace on one side, material advantages offered on the other, will quickly induce States left to themselves, and consequently in a difficult situation, to come to terms. "There is no other real safeguard against the empires that are being built up, and no other guarantee of the peaceful preservation of equality of rights, than the construction of a permanent economic, military, and maritime equilibrium." So Sering, twenty years ago, idealized the task of the defence union and its future peaceful efficacy. It is easy for National Socialism to make the task of insuring against the world revolution threatened from the East and against the liberalistic decay advancing from the West its exclusive task in the coming new federation of States.

Germany has done her utmost to delay the dynamic solution of the problems in the east and north-east. These are by no means confined to Danzig; they include Memel and the whole of Lithuania, the Baltic States, and influence in the "cornerstone of the expanded Central Europe," Finland. The primary task is the safeguarding of the Baltic and of the "glacis country" facing Soviet Russia. The great question here is how the necessary safeguarding of the German north-east flank can be reconciled with similar tendencies on Poland's part, arising out of her "geopolitical" situation. Can Poland allow Lithuania to fall under German influence? Is a peaceful solution possible here, similar to that between Germany and Italy in the Danube basin? This could only be so if Poland resolutely joins the dynamic front. It has been assumed in many quarters that Germany and Poland have already come to an agreement on certain lines, that Germany wants to develop in the south-eastern direction, and that in consequence she is leaving to Poland the organization of the north-east, and of an intermediate girdle between Russia and Germany as far south as the Danube. I think these ideas go too far. But the future of Europe will depend very largely on whether Poland becomes a partner of the axis Powers, and whether Germany renounces her aspirations in the north-east in favour of Poland, finding her own security for the north-eastern flank in the introduction of Scandinavia into the German sphere of influence.

The fate of Danzig and of the Polish or rather the Vistula corridor will then be no longer a problem of any difficulty. The great difficulty, and the fundamental change since the War, lies in the fact that Poland now belongs on a basis of population to the great States, and that her incorporation in a "defence union" is scarcely possible. She has very deliberate Great-Power aims of her own, and could at most be admitted to partnership in an extended axis, with admitted rights if not equality of rights—assuming that she follows her own "geopolitical" lines of development. It need not be assumed that German policy could not be sufficiently generous, in view of greater and more comprehensive aims, to allow Poland a free hand for expansion in the zone of power "geopolitically" natural to her.

If Poland were definitely brought within the realm of dynamism, Germany would have to give up her aspirations in the north-east, the so-called "Prussian task," and also all idea of reducing Poland to the rank of a *Mittelstaat* or secondary State, to the dimensions envisaged by Germany in the Great War. It does not seem that the National Socialist leaders are ready to agree to an apportionment of interests with Poland in the same way as with Italy. The past twenty years of Poland's existence as a State have confirmed in the opinion of some influential groups in Germany the view formerly held in another political quarter, that Poland is suffering above all from the size and unproductiveness of the territory under her rule, which involves her in expenditure beyond her means in maintaining her position as a great military State. In any case, the National Socialist policy in regard to Poland is neither clear nor consistent.

Above all, to permit Poland to play the part of a Great Power in the east would conflict with Hitler's "Testament," in which he declares that he would never "tolerate" the existence of a second military Power in the east. There would be little point in manœuvring the greatest military Power in the west, France, into voluntary capitulation, only to allow another to grow up in the east.

The conception of a novel alliance on an essentially military basis and with rigid authoritarian leadership, not to say domination, from a center, is only possible through the overwhelming superiority of power of the central State over all its allies. The existence of another Great Power garlanded with States under its leadership would lead to a repetition of the historic relation between Austria and Prussia in the old German Federation. Consequently, in spite of all territorial assurances, German hegemony implies the necessity sooner or later of reducing Poland to her barest ethnographic frontiers, with a population of eighteen to twenty-two millions.

ANTI-EUROPE

But this new federative principle of the defence union will also embrace the girdle of States in the west and north of Europe. The new "Teuton Empire of the German Nation" will include both the "sub-Teuton zone of fragments" of the east and southeast, and also the original areas of Teuton colonization in the north; in addition, it will include the western members of the old Reich, the Holy Roman Empire, which were lost through weakness. In the zone of fragments the process of history resulted in an atomization down to the smallest national units. It was impossible for a separate State idea to establish itself here. The expedient of a dynasty, to make good the lacking State element, is now out of date. A State can thus only be made by means of the two elements, overwhelming power and a special political ideology, represented by National Socialist Germany. In the smaller States of the north, on the other hand, remains are discernible of past historic processes; these States owe their independence to the balance of power between the rival Great Powers. It is natural that they should lose their independence the moment an overwhelming will to power makes its appearance. Here again it is the new power-center of the Third Reich that intends to make out of the petrified elements of a superannuated process living members of a new order. For these States also there is only one solution that can "liberate" them from the sterility of isolation within petty confines—annexation.

In west, east, and north the German nucleus-Reich is surrounded by national States of semi-sovereign character. All of them depend on the State in their center. From it they receive their impulses. They are no longer state individualities; they form a collectivity. It is not a "union" that results, not a federation; it will be a "following," precisely in the sense of National Socialist home policy. And the discipline of this union results not from free agreement but from the principle of leadership and of absolute authority. In return, the members of this union gain great material advantages. It is taken for granted that the colonial empires brought in by some of these States will be administered for the benefit of all members. The advantages of the great area of the union and of its adequate possession of raw materials must be shared by all alike. Economic advantages will be offered in compensation for the sacrifice of political rights. There will be not a few who will welcome this development, especially when the effects of the social policy of the regime on the standard of existence of the masses, at present overshadowed by the Four Year Plan, are revealed.

This would, in very truth, be the territorial and spiritual dissolution of Europe. A few of the principal links in its past unity would be thrown back on themselves—France, and England. Italy would form the nucleus of an empire of her own in the Mediterranean area. Europe would cease to exist. And, indeed, the National Socialist policy is deliberately directed toward the destruction of the historic, political, and economic unity of Europe.

There is logic in the idea of the political destruction of the conception of Europe. Only with the banning of this conception is the way really clear for entirely new territorial aggregations, stretching far beyond the limits of the Continent. The first nation to found its power almost entirely on territory outside Europe was the British. In this way, according to the National Socialist view, England was the first European Power to break away spiritually from Europe. The other Power that does not belong to Europe is Russia. But Russia has not so much politically broken away from Europe as been driven out, to form an Asiatic Power. Thus in its idea of politically banning Europe National Socialism can quote historic precedents. The firmest bulwarks of the pre-war political system were, as Zehrer has expressed it, the solidarity of the Great Powers and the idea of equality of rights; and the essence of the National Socialist destruction of Europe is the refusal to recognize either solidarity or equality of rights as constituent principles of the political order. The Power that re-entered active political life with the declaration that it intended to regain its full equality of rights among the possessing Powers has thus become one of those that deny the validity of equality of rights as a political principle. This denial determines its attitude to the small nations, and gives it the means of fresh activity in the colonial sphere. But this denial also destroys the structure of Europe, which rests on the idea of the equality of rights of nations independently of their population or power. The denial thus destroys the solidarity of the European nations, which in any case was deeply shaken by the Great War. Perhaps it may be said conversely that, because equality of rights and solidarity stand in the way of the rise of National Socialism to new world empire, Europe as a political reality must be destroyed.

THE NEW CONTOURS OF THE WORLD

Are the new contours of the world becoming clearer to-day? It is a mistake to regard National Socialist policy as confined to central and intermediate Europe, the Near East, and the German groups over the frontier on east and west. The German-Italian-Japanese *bloc* reveals decidedly different political tendencies.

These tendencies embrace the whole globe. To adhere to the text of *Mein Kampf* and think in terms of eastern European colonization would be to have an entirely absurd misconception of the scope of the political aims of National Socialism. We may be thoroughly sure that the political leaders of the Third Reich are far too clear-sighted not to be well aware that for more than a hundred years the face of the German nation has been turned westwards, and that it had given up the idea of territorial acquisitions in the east long before the War, in spite of all the efforts at colonization of the Prussian Settlement Commission. It is pure utopianism to figure a German *Drang nach dem Osten* in the form of solid German colonies newly set up in the Russian or Siberian steppes. The urbanized Germans can no longer be induced to undertake the hard labor of pioneering in the wide spaces of eastern Europe, far from civilization, in sufficient numbers to Germanize those territories. What is possible is, perhaps, German large-scale farming with the labor of alien races; or industrial expansion; or, perhaps, agricultural settlement in the thinly populated but economically and climatically favored areas of eastern and northern France. Imperialism does not mean a return to the land, at least for the ruling nation.

From the mass of new plans there emerge the outlines of a radically changed world. North Africa, Asia Minor, the Near East seem naturally to tend towards the new Mediterranean empire. Northern and eastern Europe, and northern Asia beyond them, tend toward the German sphere. But this does not exclude the possibility that new imperial lines may develop in the direction of South and Central Africa, South America, and the Pacific.

There are two conceptions in the Third Reich that demand special attention. They are not made the subject of industrious propaganda, but they may be deduced from statements made by political leaders which deserve to be taken seriously. One conception is that of overland expansion—the Danube basin, Turkey, Asia Minor, India. The other is indicated by the "geopolitical" line from Flushing to Vladivostok. Both conceptions are connected with the search for raw materials, for strategic and economic key positions of hegemony, or of a wide-spread empire. The first conception would collide with Italian ambitions. It has few supporters outside the quarters of the old German Nationalists and Conservatives. The second, however, is possible on the basis of a practical division of interests not only with Italy but with England, which could in this way be brought into the community of the renovating Powers. The first conception would have to be carried out at the expense not only of France but of England; the second would, so to speak, open the way to a possible new distribution of the world which would enable England to be brought in as a partner. The contours of this new distribution would run more or less on these lines: the British world empire overseas; the Mediterranean-Africa-Asia Minor empire of Italy, including as dependents all the French African territories, Pan-Arabia, and all the countries wished by the Mediterranean; finally the American continental *bloc*, and the Pacific empire of Japan.

Until recently, the National Socialists were ready to admit England as a partner on equal terms in the redistribution of the world; but not France. In the National Socialist view Germany, Italy, and England were alone of approximately equal rank as European Powers. Their territorial possessions and ambitions could be defined without collision of interests. Europe is to be partitioned into the Eurasian continental coalition, under German hegemony, and the Mediterranean area, exclusively under Italy; England is to be excluded from Europe and to renounce interest in European problems, retiring with her once European island kingdom and transferring her empire entirely to her oversea possessions and her Dominions. Whether England will be required to declare herself disinterested in the Mediterranean, in Asia Minor, and in the Arabian and North African regions is left to Italy to determine. England will probably be ready to do this as soon as France has been defeated, if not before. Such countries as Spain and Greece fall entirely into the Italian sphere of influence. The new delimitation of frontiers will pass through France and Switzerland, which will lose their unity as States. Other countries, like Yugoslavia, will be taken out of double spheres of influence and incorporated in a single one, in this case that of Italy.

Such are the broad lines of the colossal foreign policy which would correspond in dimensions and in forcefulness with the colossal buildings and rites of the dictatorial regime. Only these dimensions, as Hitler has declared outright, justify the effort of a whole nation until exhaustion threatens. Those who heard this conception developed, at a time when preventive wars against Germany's armament seemed to threaten, could only regard it as absurd bombast. I confess that that was my own feeling. To-day it seems less unlikely to be put into practice.

The continental area under German leadership demands the liquidation of Russia in her present form. This aim needs ideological camouflage. The enthusiasm of the masses must be aroused. And it is necessary to gain allies, and to divert attention from preparatory moves. For, before Russia can be liquidated, the French pseudo-hegemony must be liquidated, the Russo-French "outer fort" Czechoslovakia must be destroyed, and France must be isolated and partitioned. And it is no less essential to bring effective pressure upon the States of the intermediate European girdle, in order to set up a new common structure before the dissolution of Russia permits the new great Eurasion federation of States to be formed. The Reich will certainly be ready to maintain the existence of the States joining it, with a few exceptions, in a restricted form.

But—and it is important to bear this in mind—if National Socialism fails in its first aims in Central and Western Europe, in the isolation and partition of France, and the bringing of England into the front formed by the renovating Powers, it will be able instead to ally itself with Bolshevik Russia and to undertake the partition of the world from the opposite pole. There are many well-known political elements who desire a solution of this sort, as avoiding the loss of time involved in proceeding by way of Central and Western Europe. If Germany and Russia were to join together, the Western Powers and the small States would be compelled to capitulate without a struggle. There is a good deal of evidence that this policy might prove attractive for reasons of internal politics. In any case, dynamism sees in the volte-face of an alliance with Soviet Russia a last chance which might be of incalculable revolutionary effect.

But yet another question arises: can the dynamic revolution stop at a sharing of the world? Must not the struggle for existence in foreign politics continue until the final world domination of a single nation? The triumvirate sharing the world in the age of Cæsarism is always no more than a preliminary to the decisive final struggle for exclusive rule. Thus at the back of Germany's continental empire stands the will to absolute dominion in the world, the technical means of which are no longer lacking as hitherto. England, crippled as a European Power by the occupation or *Anschluss* of Holland and Belgium, will not escape the dismemberment of her empire even by concluding a pact with the Third Reich. Italy, even as a vast Mediterranean empire, will not be equal to a crossing of swords with the Germanic union. And America is already at the outset of internal convulsions produced by a war of ideologies. Here, too, a change may easily come, incredible as it seems as yet, which will convert American opposition into willing discipleship. In the National Socialist view the political situation in America is unstable and can be developed into an outright revolution; to do this is both a tactical aim of National Socialism, in order to hold America aloof from Europe, and a political one, in order to bring both North and South America into the new order. By its ubiquity and its tactics of universal menace, National Socialism is preparing to occupy the key positions for colonial domination, for domination of the great sea routes, and for the domination of America and the Pacific. The German aim of a solid Central

African colonial empire emerged a considerable time ago. All this explains how the initial Anglophile attitude of National Socialism is turning into a continually growing antagonism, which is due to much more than simple resentment over Chamberlain's restraint of Hitler's aggressiveness in 1938. Already the breaking up of the British Empire is becoming clearly outlined as one of the fundamental aims of the National Socialist policy of world revolution.

When Goethe witnessed the cannonade at Valmy, witnessed its cessation and the retreat of the coalition armies, he knew that he had been present at a turning point of world history. Had the French a similar feeling when the German armies marched into the Rhineland? If they did, they had incomparably more reason for it than Goethe had. For they were at the outset, it would seem, not only of the disappearance of France as a Great Power, and the downfall of the British power, but of the breaking up of Europe. But is this anything of which the Germans can be glad and proud? In their new world not only Europe but the great individual nations will disappear. With them Germany herself will perish.

3

The March to Revolution

PRACTICAL PROBLEMS

ALL this arsenal of political weapons, these plans and objectives of National Socialism, will be regarded with some scepticism. What do they all amount to in practical politics? Broadcast with exaggerated candor, and brought in the German professorial fashion within a pseudo-scientific system, all these "geopolitical" doctrines may amount to no more than an attempt to provide for a section of the German educated public a rationale for political aims of expansion, and to prepare this public for willing self-sacrifice in the interest of the nation. The redistribution of the world, a vast imperial territory reaching from Flushing to Vladivostok, utopias of this sort may be useful as elements of propaganda, but they cannot be regarded as actual political aims with any title to be taken seriously by politicians. What, then, are the broad lines of the real National Socialist policy?

To begin with, this vast candor is of the very nature of dictorial foreign policy. It has justified itself in practice. The impossible, the incredible succeeds: the open declaration of actual aims proves their best camouflage.

Let me mention that I am speaking from experience. On more than one occasion, contrary to my own warnings, I have been forced to admit that a sovereign contempt for all discretion has been rewarded in foreign policy with complete success. The most candid of revelations of aims in foreign policy have been dismissed as "going off at the deep end" by the very people who, for their own sakes, had the best of all reasons for listening with careful attention. The propagandist character of National Socialist tactics requires a broad and popular exposition of the aims of the regime. The listener abroad finds it inconceivable that anyone really entertaining such plans could have the innocence to avow them. But it is not innocence—it is the subtlest cunning. It is just as effective, in the opposite direction, as the practice of the famous maxim of *Mein Kampf* that any lie will be believed if it is big enough. Any truth will be disbelieved, if it is big enough.

National Socialist policy is in any case much more candid than that of the democracies, with their Governments' secret diplomacy and cautious and elaborate shepherding of public opinion. We must therefore make up our minds that all the aims and tendencies described in the preceding section represent actual practical intentions. This applies especially to the principal aim, the redistribution of the world. Simple and popularized as this aim sounds, and impossible to take seriously as practical politics, it represents nevertheless the actual purpose of the regime. This is what makes any interpretation of National Socialist policy so difficult: there is no rational approach to its essential elements. Perhaps one needs to be a National Socialist in order to grasp the full destructive menace of the movement.

I should like to mention here, by way of elucidation of the actual revolutionary path of National Socialism, certain practical problems with which I came into contact. I must mention at the outset that those of us, whether National Socialists or Nationalists and Conservatives, who had to work with the regime, were by no means clear at first as to the direction that was intended to be taken, or rather was bound to be taken. I cannot say whether any of those members of the Cabinet, and diplomats and civil servants in responsible positions who are not National

Socialists are still in any doubt about the course that is being pursued. I cannot assume that any of them are, for it was plain to all thinking persons as long ago as 1934. But it may be that those who in the past were opposed to this course have been reconciled to the National Socialist revolution because it has brought certain successes for the nation. For my own part, it was the gradual recognition of the destructive tendency and the growing radicalization of National Socialist policy as a whole that led me at Danzig ultimately to dissociate myself from it. In the Reich matters were different in so far as almost down to the present time there has been an expectation that the army would enforce a change, and those who were in favor of a more rational policy felt that it was particularly incumbent on them to remain in office to serve as a corrective for any excessively adventurous policy. These attitudes are intelligible, but they are mistaken, because they ignore the revolutionary character of the movement. What was needed was a resolute stand against it and a counter-revolution before it was too late.

There were really only two possible methods by which Germany could burst the bonds of the Versailles Treaty and regain her due place in Europe. One may be called the European solution—to make Germany the protagonist of the ideas of right ostensibly but not really underlying the League of Nations and certain treaties. This would have involved placing herself at the head of the small nations of Eastern Europe, but without any "Eastern Locarno" under the guarantee of the Western Powers, who had arrogated to themselves the position of a world judicature. The collective pact system of Geneva did no more than perpetuate an intolerable situation in Eastern and Central Europe. But a number of bilateral pacts between Germany and her neighbors would have removed the dangers of war, recognizing frontiers or regulating them by peaceful agreement, and permitting Germany to establish her economic and political influence over the partner to each pact. It would have been right and reasonable for Germany to be granted economic and political advantages in return for her renunciation of claims for frontier revision.

It may be objected that this is the National Socialist policy. It was originally, and had it been adhered to it would have brought Germany assured and lasting successes; but it was given up for a totally different policy, one of revolution. The essential question for the future was the spirit in which Germany would pursue a policy of accommodation of this sort, whether the terms of alliance would be equitable, leaving Germany's partner full sovereignty and full participation in the benefits of the treaty, or whether Germany's purpose was to set up a dictatorial "protection" of States reduced to semi-sovereignty.

Until late in the summer of 1933 the general lines of the foreign policy of the German leaders were not clear to anybody. No decision in any direction seemed to have been taken. What happened at first was day-to-day policy inspired by no great conception, directed merely to making sure of rearmament, getting rid of the pacts, and preventing any important coalition against Germany. The leaders were pursuing tactical aims alone. The agreement with Poland was one of these.

Was there no possibility, at least in the autumn of 1933, of a "European" settlement of outstanding political questions in the foreign policy of the Third Reich? At Geneva Dr. Goebbels, the Propaganda Minister, asked me to see him at his hotel, in order to discuss the possibility of intensifying German-Polish relations; and I tried to put before him on this occasion the lines of a general "European" settlement. Colonel Beck had made a point of publicly showing friendly courtesy to the German delegates, in order to emphasize the possibility of an agreement between Poland and Germany. I invited him to lunch at Beauséjour; he came, and soon afterwards there took place a meeting with Goebbels which attracted a good deal of notice. Goebbels, who had been praised as a man of "Latin mentality" by some of the foreign papers, had sat for a short time on the front center benches at the Assembly of the League, his slight figure contrasting with that of his neighbor, the jovial Baron von Neurath; Goebbels was there as Hitler's observer. At that time sections of foreign opinion were still ready to regard the National Socialist activities as no more than the crudity and awkwardness and extravagance of vigorous youth. General Smuts, as president of the Assembly, had praised the new national discipline which some nations were imposing on themselves. Goebbels had spoken at great length to Paul-Boncour, through an interpreter, at a dinner, and explained to him the peaceful social and political aims of the German movement. He had also spoken to the Press—a speech that aroused a good deal of interest but was on the whole disappointing.

I gave Goebbels my impressions of the possibilities of German-Polish treaty relations, and went on to the subject of a peaceful, evolutionary solution of the Eastern European problems; but I was met with entire disagreement. I pointed out that Poland could virtually serve as the key to a broad conception of German foreign policy; Goebbels talked down to me with his characteristic arrogance and air of intellectualism—the alliances that mattered to Germany, he said, were in an entirely different direction. There was no possibility of an evolutionary emergence from the fetters of Versailles, because it was not the Versailles Treaty alone that had to be got rid of. He went on to pour contempt on the League Assembly. He talked of the "hollowness" of the whole enterprise, the general irresolution and ineffectiveness, which would permit us to go much farther, which, indeed, simply invited strong measures. These people could only be impressed by brutality: they were too anemic to resort to brutality themselves.

Soon after this Germany withdrew not only from the Disarmament Conference but from the League. "C'est la guerre," shouted the angry journalists in the lobbies. The members of the German delegation to Geneva were themselves dismayed. They had to pack up and go literally helter-skelter. This was the first important event in the National Socialist style in the field of foreign policy. The pace was set by Hitler. There were violent quarrels behind the scenes. The decision to leave the League was forced on the professional diplomats against their strong representations, amid the wildest temperamental outbreaks. Members of the German delegation at Geneva with whom I was acquainted were at their wits' end. This was the incursion of dynamism into a world of fictitious security.

But is not every state of legality, every treaty relation, a fictitious security? It was not the fact of Germany's withdrawal from the League that marked the beginning of the revolutionary course in foreign policy, but the way it was done. Germany had decided for drama, for dictation, for surprise moves, for marching. The withdrawal from the League was thoroughly characteristic of the National Socialist Führer. The move and its manner were a frontal attack not on the Versailles treaty front but on the principles of legality and faith in treaties.

Nothing would have been more natural than to follow this resolute turning away from Western European political ideas with an attempt to create another system of treaties of alliance, which would be a positive achievement to set against the "fictitious" system of Geneva. The affairs of Danzig kept me at Geneva after the German delegation had left, and I had the opportunity of observing the international effect of Germany's move. The psychological effect seemed to me so menacing that I felt it to be of importance that Germany, while rejecting the ineffective principles of the League, should declare her adhesion to the idea of firm and unambiguous treaty conditions on the basis of the inviolability of legality. It seemed evident that in this way she could have separated Great Britain from France. With some States calling for war and playing with the idea of preventive sanctions, it seemed to be particularly advisable, as a matter of prudence, that Germany should remove every territorial occasion for war, sterilizing the frontier problem by building up a system of pacts on the basis of the inviolability of frontiers.

On my way back from Geneva I took the opportunity of pointing out to Hitler in Berlin the precarious situation in which Danzig was placed by Germany's withdrawal from the League, and of urging that the sharpest discipline should be required, in consequence, of the party formations, since only the avoidance of incidents would enable us to emerge in safety from the danger zone which had now been entered. I found Hitler in a state of extraordinary optimism, though Germany's situation seemed to offer little warrant for cheerfulness. In this mood Hitler is simply out of reach of critical argument. Our *tête-à-tête* lasted for more than an hour, but I only succeeded in getting in a few words about my anxieties. I objected that the abrupt withdrawal from the League seemed to expose the German armament and national policy to unnecessary risks; Hitler replied with long expositions of the need for a liberating act, which would restore Germany's freedom of action once for all. What was wanted was not careful consideration of what logic might seem to dictate, but an act that carried people away, a clear and straightforward "No" in reply to the lying intriguers, evidencing the resolute determination to make a fresh start. Whether this was discreet or not, the nation only understood acts of this sort, not haggling and bargaining. The nation had had enough of being led by the nose. He went on to talk of the "poison of Liberalism." The old democracies had, perhaps, more or less got used to it, and so might be able to stand it. But for Germany, a young and still uncontaminated nation, the poison was fatal. It was like syphilis. When that disease first came to Europe "from America," it had almost always proved fatal. But where it was reintroduced again and again through generations the body might, he said, acquire immunity; the disease would become harmless. It had been necessary to tear the German nation away from all these poisonous, dangerous associations if it was not to perish after all. He then went into the subject of "tectonic collapse," the eruptions and landslides in the European social system—far-flung geological similies, with which he illustrated the need for Germany's emergence from the isolation of a quiet zone in an environment of the utmost activity.

It was a new experience for me to find, instead of a matter-of-fact discussion of the risks facing us and the steps to be taken to deal with them, that I had to listen to a vehement monologue, in which the subject on which I had asked for an audience came only now and then to the surface, and, even when it did, rarely for any practical purpose. This, however, is a deliberately cultivated technique which I found employed also by others of the great. It is a deliberate method of preventing any rational consideration of a question. It places the visitor in a subordinate position in which he is reduced to listening, with very little opportunity of making any effective use of the arguments he has to offer. He is put off with an emphatically administered lecture conveying an opinion already formed and fixed, in comparison with which his faintly ventured objections are loftily dismissed as entirely superficial. This technique at all events establishes the superiority of the personage granting the audience.

The situation at Danzig in the autumn of 1933 was particularly precarious. Incidents had been produced by the lawlessness of the Storm Troopers which would have given legitimate grounds for the intervention at any time of the Polish army. It was well known that Poland had prepared a plan for the restoration, by three stages, of constitutional conditions in the Free City, and that she was in a position to carry it out whenever she thought fit. The German forces were not then strong enough to prevent Poland from doing this, or to justify the risk of an armed conflict with Poland. I had consulted the German military authority concerned, and he had made it perfectly plain that this was so. The situation had by no means been improved by Germany's withdrawal from the League. Germany was pursuing a very dangerous course. In this situation the sanguine spirit of the Führer was not so much the outcome of magnificent resolution and faith as of a readiness for a gamble that needlessly jeopardized the future of the nation. That it succeeded is no answer to the criticism. The reasons why Germany's opponents did not intervene, and why they induced Poland not to upset the Versailles system of peace treaties by any act of violence, are plain now for all to see. One was an erroneous estimate of National Socialism, which was not seen to be the directionless revolution that it really was, with a camouflage at that time of nationalism. It was supposed that it would give place to a more moderate nationalism and would quickly divest itself of its evil elements. The bourgeois partners of National Socialism in Germany had shared the same hope. In this interview, however, Hitler's sovereign contempt for every argument in favor of caution made me suspect that Germany's withdrawal from the League was not so much a clever political move, aimed at gaining freedom of action, as the beginning of a revolutionary course that would tear Germany once for all out of the existing social and political order, the beginning of revolutionary dynamism.

On the morning of that fateful day at Geneva I had met a well-known American journalist, von W., who knew Hitler personally. It was being rumored that Germany intended to leave the Disarmament Conference. Mr. von W. declared that Hitler could obtain by ordinary means everything, absolutely everything, he wanted, and that it would be a vast blunder to enter a revolutionary course, which would inevitably lead just where the first German imperialism had ended. But the irrevocable launching of the nation on a revolutionary course was the sole purpose of that abrupt and much-misunderstood step. The great danger for National Socialism was an early ripening of moderate nationalist ambitions. That would have made National Socialism a superfluity. Its leaders were forced to launch the nation on an incalculable wave of revolutionism in order to maintain their own power.

Later on the day of my audience with Hitler it became perfectly plain to me that this was the explanation of Germany's withdrawal from the League. I had the opportunity of taking part that afternoon in a "leaders' conference" in the Prussian Herrenhaus or House of Lords. I had the satisfaction of finding that the Führer had paid attention to my representations; he emphatically demanded absolute discipline on the part of all the party formations: absolute correctness was essential in order to give foreign Powers no ground for aggression. He declared that if anyone jeopardized Germany's armament by insubordination, he would have him shot, regardless of persons. But for the rest the Führer's declarations showed that he was prepared to go to any length. Never, he said, should Germany return to the corrupt and putrefying company of the democracies, doomed as they were to death and destruction. Germany had cast herself adrift from that world for ever. Arguments which were advanced only years later in public speeches were put at length before this meeting—the arguments that Germany was preparing the way for a gigantic revolution; in this struggle all things must be permissible; the nation must be ready to put up with losses; what had to be done was not to act "reasonably" but so as to make the whole nation ready for unhesitating obedience; what had to be done was to act not reasonably but all together. He had torn to pieces the whole fabric of treaties of a lying, fraudulent, criminal system. The world would have to make up its mind to follow Germany.

Hitler had told me that morning what was his view of the value of treaties. He was ready, he said, to sign anything. He was ready to guarantee any frontier and to conclude a non-aggression pact with anyone. It was a simpleton's idea not to avail oneself of expedients of this sort because the day might come when some formal agreement would have to be broken. Every pact sworn to was broken or became out of date sooner or later. Anyone who was so fussy that he had to consult his conscience about whether he could keep to a pact, whatever the pact and whatever the situation, was a fool. Why not please other people and ease one's own position by signing pacts, if the other people thought that got them anywhere or settled anything? He could conclude any treaty in good faith, and yet be ready to break it in cold blood the next day, if that was in the interest of the future of Germany.

In this connection the Führer spoke of the non-aggression pact which had been concluded with Poland the preceding May. He had concluded it, he said, as a matter of course, and it had been a useful step. I took the opportunity to return to the subject of the possibilities of stable relations between Germany and Poland, on which I had already touched. I mentioned the statements Polish statesmen had made on the subject of the supposed German aspirations in the Ukraine, and on Rosenberg's ideas, which were open to strong objection, and I tried to emphasize the importance of preventing any threatened encirclement, which in my opinion could at that time be done only through good relations with Poland. The arguments made more impression on the Führer than they had done at Geneva on the Propaganda Minister. Hitler seemed to see in Poland a rival whose realist assessment of the general European situation and whose freedom from Western European democratic ideas might make her dangerous. As for the Western European politicians, he could not say enough in contempt of their unimaginativeness, hypocrisy, cowardice, and irresolution. He repeated his desire, which he had already conveyed to me earlier, for a personal meeting with Marshal Pilsudsky.

POLAND

The National Socialist policy in regard to Poland was an improvised policy. That it was possible to take such a line is remarkable enough. The party leaders went deliberately outside their program. The agreement with Poland was in entire contradiction with the apparent aims of any nationalist German foreign policy. But, in spite of this beginning of an undeniably important development in foreign policy, National Socialism failed to make of it what it might have done, a firm collaboration with Poland in a number of important elements of policy, in comparison with which the frontier issues were of minor importance.

As early as the summer of 1933, after my state visit to Warsaw, the Führer instructed me to convey his desire for a meeting with Pilsudsky. This confidential mission was certainly outside my sphere, but it might be possible for me to come to the subject on an unofficial visit to the Marshal. I had tried to arrange this in connection with the affairs of Danzig, soon after the conclusion of the first agreements between Danzig and Poland, in order to assist the progress of the negotiations for the settlement of outstanding issues. In spite, however, of official and unofficial suggestions, nearly four months passed before a visit to Pilsudsky became technically possible. In the meantime there had come the dramatic German withdrawal from the League; there had been incidents at Danzig, threatening tension, and ideas of taking action against Germany. At the beginning of December the situation had cleared sufficiently for the visit to take place.

The Marshal, bearing already the visible traces of incurable disease, gave me the opportunity of a thorough discussion. On his side the conversation was mainly concerned with National Socialism as the new political form of the German nation; he spoke with notable candor. It seemed to me that he was seriously considering the question of closer relations with Germany, but was critical of her and as yet undecided, evidently sharing the doubts expressed to me by many Polish Ministers: what were Germany's real aims and intentions? He made a very direct reference to certain particularly striking features of the National Socialist regime, expressing doubts in connection with them as to the stability of the conditions in Germany; this suggested that he would be glad to join in a serious effort to achieve a settlement of German-Polish issues, if conditions really were stable in Germany, and that his only hesitation was due to the character of the National Socialist dictatorship. Herr Hitler, said the Marshal repeatedly, was taking too many risks. He had not changed the German nation, and would not change it by the methods he was adopting. He might seem to be doing so, but all the difficulties remained; they had only been driven below the surface. In due course they would reappear.

The Marshal referred to his own difficulties in training the Polish nation. He had been trying for years, but he could not say that he had succeeded. His arm was too weak. He added that he was kept fully informed of events in Germany and in the National Socialist Party. He went on to speak of a fundamental mistake made by Hitler: he came too much into the foreground, with the result that in the end he would have to bear full responsibility himself. Only once had he, Pilsudsky, come farther out of his reserve than he intended. Since then he had had to come more into the open than was desirable. Reserve reveals the master: he repeated this phrase of Goethe's again and again, and declared that moderation was the only path to lasting success. The taming of a people demanded, of course, a master. He recalled the classic story of Alexander and Bucephalus, and said that a noble horse will willingly bear a good rider, but will throw off a bad one. No doubt the Marshal did not mean to say that he regarded the leader of the National Socialist Party as a bad rider, but the way he referred to the revolutionary movement in Germany, to the excessive use of dictatorial measures, indicated that he saw the real weakness of the regime in an unnatural and unhealthy exaggeration of measures which in themselves might for a time be salutary. He softened his criticism by the reference to his own mistakes. But the way he referred to his action in 1926 suggested that he had most carefully avoided what Hitler had carried fanatically to excess—out-and-out dictatorship, which Pilsudsky regarded as injurious and insecure, because it destroys all the regenerative elements. For the rest, the Marshal found means of declining the Führer's suggestion of a meeting. Hitler's idea was a meeting at the frontier, from car to car; and Pilsudsky considered that there would be "technical difficulties."

There might be something that could be learned from an opponent's remarks; in any case, I felt that I ought not to keep from Hitler the criticisms made during this conversation. His reply was characteristic. With a notable determination to delude himself, he referred at once to events in East Prussia, where a cheerful civil war was blossoming at the time, with all sorts of party formations involved. Pilsudsky, said Hitler, had been influenced by the temporary disturbances in East Prussia. So Hitler waved aside all serious objections, refused to take the trouble to consider them. I have heard of other cases in which the Führer refused to listen to criticism. I assume, therefore, that my experience is not unique. This romantic trait in Hitler's problematic nature, this cry with Kleist, "Don't upset my intuition!" the determination to rely on the certainties provided by auto-suggestion, has been made good use of by the place-hunters and sycophants in the interests of their own careers.

After my report Hitler asked me abruptly whether Poland would remain neutral if he got to work in the West. I confess that I was rather agitated by this question, after Germany had only just come safely through the first danger zone, the danger of a preventive war in which Poland had a particularly close interest. With relations with Poland still obscure, such a question was entirely idle. The only practical question would have been how treaty relations could be established with Poland so as to cover Germany's rear even without pressure on Poland from Soviet Russia. I took the opportunity to put before Hitler my views on the possibilities of further improving the normal conditions now arrived at with Poland, after a period of latent conflict, by concluding a positive pact. The answer I received was: "I am, of course, very glad to be able to pursue my eastern policy with Poland, instead of against her as in the past." That cut short my opportunity of discussing the possibility of a policy of alliance with Poland, an alliance which might well have been attainable both then and later. Poland had very practical reasons for such a policy, if her partner were not too eager to pluck its fruits, which would have taken a considerable time to ripen. At my first official visit to Warsaw, in July 1933, I was asked by the Polish authorities to use my influence to prevent the public discussion of such stupid ideas as those of Rosenberg on the Ukraine. They were, for that matter, by no means Rosenberg's alone. No less inconvenient was the ventilation of the idea of "exchanging" the Corridor for, say, Lithuania. Perhaps the German-Polish frontier issue could find a solution later; it was certainly not the question on which to begin. The first aim in a policy of peaceful revision, in which Germany could naturally bring her weight to bear, would be economic and political collaboration, and the frontier problem would come at the end if it ever became necessary to discuss it.

If, on the other hand, the deferring of the frontier problem were regarded as merely a camouflage imposed by the precarious political situation, and propaganda were carried on on that basis, it would never be possible to follow up a non-aggression pact with the creation of really tolerable relations. Here again National Socialism threw away its chance. In its propaganda it not only never made any secret of its revisionist aims, but never even troubled to make out a plausible case for them. This is true in spite of occasional formal promises to recognize the Corridor. And while a German will compare promises of this sort with subsequent performance, the foreign politician can do the same.

Behind the Polish readiness for an accommodation with Germany stood the same motive as with Germany, the fear of isolation. In Poland's case there was also, perhaps, the element of disappointment at the inactivity of the Western European Powers and their lack of understanding of acts regarded by Poland as necessary to her security. The first moves in her new policy were accompanied by a rather emphatic demonstration that she could do without the patronage of Western Europe, and could pursue her own path in the opposite direction to that of the past, if she were left in the lurch by the League of Nations and the Western Powers in regard to her most urgent needs. But this was no reason why Germany should not try to arrive at an understanding with Poland, so long as excessive expectations were not entertained. She could have promoted the drifting away of Poland from the Western Powers by offering her clear economic and material advantages. Poland, with no colonizable territory to spare and few important raw materials, could not be of anything like the importance to Germany of the South-east of Europe; but her political weight was very considerable. A real political understanding with Poland would probably have had very important consequences in the area known as "Intermediate Europe," the area between Germany and Russia. The first condition for this was the abandonment of any claim to hegemony and the clear demonstration of readiness to remove grievances on both sides, even those concerning the frontier.

Such an agreement could have produced a very serviceable "axis," which might have formed the nucleus around which a greater "union" could have crystallized in the East and South-east, with results of the utmost importance. It would have opposed to the Soviet Union another union in accordance with Poland's own ideas. No doubt the Polish idea of a pact with Germany was inspired not by these ideas but by that of diverting German pressure to the West and the South-east. That this would actually have been its result has been proved by the fact that Germany's occupation with the South-east of Europe has sensibly lightened the pressure on the North-east.

The fundamental element in German-Polish relations is the rivalry between the former Prussian ambition, taken over by the new Reich, and the Polish: both claim the same territory. Neither ambition is nationalist, and the only solution for either is the creation of a super-national State or federation. This does not exclude but, on the contrary, absolutely demands co-operation between the two States in a common "protectorate"—to use Haushofer's word (*Obhut*)—over this territory. But Poland has not been assessed at her true importance by Germany. In order to rebuild and extend the old German influence in the East, it would be essential to gain Polish friendship and prevent the formation of a great Slav bloc in between Russia and Germany, with a population equalling or exceeding that of Germany.

In none of its political ideas does National Socialism reveal more clearly than in its Polish policy, which is regarded as a masterpiece of the Führer's, that it is depriving itself of the fruits of its efforts and achieving the opposite of what it set out to achieve. It may be taken as certain that Poland is farther than ever from any inclination to conduct a common policy with Germany, and is cautiously but tenaciously pursuing her own plan of an independent organization of the "intermediate" European territory, the territory between Germany and Russia, and is thus in process of excluding Germany from the East. Germany could not even have counted with assurance on Polish neutrality in her political conflict in the past summer with the Western Powers. Had she candidly renounced frontier revisions, Germany might in past years have gained a political influence which would have far more than outweighed the sacrifice. As President of Danzig I advocated by speaking and writing the idea of a "sterilization of the frontier." I took an opportunity of placing my ideas of a constructive policy in the East, particularly in regard to Poland, before Dr. Schacht, President of the Reichsbank, and at the time a man of great influence. On another occasion, in a lecture to an invited audience at Essen, I tried to show the economic side of an agreement with Poland, and to bring to the fore a rather more broad-minded conception than that of the maxim that it is high treason to be of service to a rival. Frequently on such occasions I was faced with the question whether I wanted to reverse the policy which Prussia had pursued for a century and a half. The obvious answer was that the time had passed for talking of "Prussian" policy. Schacht made it plain that his interests lay mainly in the South-east; but he declared himself ready to grant long-term credits to industry for the intensification of economic relations with Poland. This policy would have demanded patience and delicate handling; but it very soon became clear that this was fatal. National Socialism demanded immediate returns and could not wait.

What, then, were Germany's real aims in the East? Nobody knew. Hitler had no desire for any clear conception to be formed. The Polish policy remained improvisatory, a policy of merely seizing each opportunity of getting what there was to be got. Here again Hitler's policy is in reality much simpler than the outsider would imagine. It is directed to gaining time, settling nothing definitely, and "meeting the requirements of the moment," in Colonel Beck's words. This may be called realism by those who prefer the term, but it is more accurate to call it opportunism, a policy of taking advantage of every opportunity for revolutionary development. It shows the total sterility of National Socialism, which can only destroy.

But if the German policy was not clear, was the Polish policy any clearer? Poland, too, as is now plain, was out to gain time. It was expected that the National Socialist movement would soon work itself out. It was also, it would seem, hoped that Germany would continue her successes until she was so glaringly in the wrong that a coalition would come into existence against her and would settle the outstanding problems with no advantage to Germany. Thus, to gain time was in any case a useful achievement.

The attempt at National Socialist practical policy failed in the case of Poland, or at all events made no progress, because the extremist character of the revolution permits no limitations, and so carries the day even against the political leaders. The same failure attended the Danzig policy. And in this case the opportunity existed of a broad attempt at a practical solution of the special political problems, a solution which would have cost National Socialism nothing, if revolutionary destruction at home

245

and abroad had not mattered more to it than all the advantages of a far-seeing conception.

The political plans for the East remained in suspense; Germany's relations with Poland did not ripen. Against Russia there developed a wild propagandist campaign that made any German-Russian alliance temporarily out of the question. With Italy, Germany came only slowly and painfully to terms, in spite of the assumed sympathy between the two dictatorial systems. The prospect of good relations with England described in *Mein Kampf* as essential grew remoter instead of nearer. The road to the Southeast seemed to be blocked by Austria. What direction could be taken by the revolutionary course abruptly entered on at Geneva?

It took every direction. It established countless *Stützpunkte* or key positions. New ones came constantly into existence. No place was too remote for the revolutionary course, which was directed at the same time to the centers of power and influence. The rejection of the legal and treaty basis of Geneva was not the prelude to any great political plan, but to the propaganda of revolutionary National Socialism. This was a carefully planned step, and politically a very clever one; it owed its effectiveness to the inconspicuousness of its organization; even where this was noticed it was dismissed as due merely to the National Socialist desire for publicity. When its real intention became evident, it was too late for effective counter-measures. There was repeated in the field of foreign policy what had happened years earlier in home politics—a slow, unnoticed development, quite ineffective until a favorable political situation brought the years of effort to sudden fruition. National Socialist strategic doctrine teaches that a blow must only be struck where the revolutionary situation is ripe. But the ripening in a foreign country is not to be merely awaited but promoted by all possible means. Warlike action begins in peace time with the establishment of revolutionary

Stützpunkte, or key positions, all over the country concerned. But every country is concerned. No country is without importance as a field for the promoting of the dynamic revolution, whether Brazil or the Pacific islands, China or the United States. I may recall Hitler's indication to friends of the "broadened strategy," which armed National Socialism with the elements of victory on a hitherto undreamed-of scale, and decided the issue of war while there was still peace.

Nothing is more characteristic than this march of the German revolution through the world; nothing, perhaps, marks the revolutionary character of National Socialism more plainly than the sending out of apostles under the leadership of Herr Bohle, the head of the National Socialist *Auslandsorganisation* (Foreign Organization). The march into the world did not take place by chance, or simply through the ambition of young men to play a part—though the National Socialist leaders always take careful account of ambitions and personal rivalries. This march into the world was organized with immense resources. It resulted in the formation of a vast network, an international propaganda and revolutionary organization, making use of middle class personages who were not initiated into its actual purposes; that was not essential.

This universal preparedness has already brought National Socialism an undoubted tactical success. But the real successes have yet to come. The extent of the network is shown by participation in politics of National Socialists in Spain and Brazil, in the Far East and in Africa, in Asia Minor and in the United States, and, of course, in all European countries.

At the back of this policy of *Stützpunkte* lies the deliberate plan of promoting revolutionary dynamism all over the world. This is the actual plan of National Socialism in foreign policy— universal political unsettlement. Not everywhere is the aim military or strategic, as in Spain or Scandinavia. But ultimately the military situation is affected everywhere. And it is only by its ubiquity, its interference in every problem of the world, that

National Socialism can attain the maximum of power and influence which is its aim.

Inevitably the nationalist partners of National Socialism and the official German diplomats failed at first to comprehend this plan. The introduction of Bohle, the head of the *Auslands-organisation*, into the Foreign Ministry marks the decisive victory of the "dynamic" style of carrying on foreign policy over the style of the professional diplomats. Among the National Socialist leaders there are some who have doubts of this policy; Rosenberg is one of these, and it is certainly this that has resulted in his falling into the background. Ruthless dynamism has won against all other political conceptions of aims and methods. This is the natural outcome of the doctrinelessness of the whole German revolution. The foreign policy of National Socialism consists simply of universal unsettlement: it is revolution for its own sake. And this characteristic prevails over all else, over all that might confine the revolution within assigned paths and to definite purposes. Accordingly, all day-to-day arrangements, axes, friendships, pacts, even enmities, are only of tactical importance. And the party pushes into the background those of its members who are insufficiently "revolutionary," insufficiently elastic to see power as the one aim of the movement, and universal unsettlement as its one method.

In this connection I recall a discussion concerning the importance of the creation of unrest as a weapon of the movement, at a lunch with Hitler in the summer of 1933; Hitler himself, however, took no part in it. Among those present was Prince August Wilhelm, who almost always lunched with Hitler at that time; with him were Goebbels, Schirach (the youth leader), Hofmann (Hitler's friend and photographer), Hanfstaengl (Hitler's press secretary), and other prominent persons. The conversation began with the Ukraine; it was claimed that here the creation of internal unrest would easily provide an opportunity of intervention. So far as I remember, there was a discussion of the entourage of the ex-hetman, Skoropadsky, who was held in reserve for any emergency by certain political circles in Germany, but was not entirely approved of by the National Socialists. Someone said that in every State discord should be stirred up to such an extent that the State could easily be brought down. Objections were raised, but it was contended that it was all a question of money and organization. It cost more in the West than in the East; that was the only difference. There were no convictions in democracies, real convictions, for which men would stake their existence. That was the point at which to work—fear or the hope of gain would sooner or later bring capitulation in every case. There were plenty of men to be found in any country, as many as were wanted, to launch any particular movement; plenty in every grade of society and of every degree of education. Once a beginning had been made, each country would look after itself. The people without convictions were always defeatist: it was useless, they would say, to resist. No money spent in this way was wasted: it meant that fewer army divisions would need to be sent in the end.

Democracies, it was pointed out, were helpless against this sort of attack: it was in the nature of things that they should be, for the only way to prevent it was to become authoritarian. Dictatorships were largely protected against these weapons. This placed them in a stronger moral position which might go far to counterbalance inferiority in armament. It was objected that this set limits to the efficacy of this political expedient, since very serious conflicts might come with non-democratic States which were immune to this device of stirring up discord. A characteristic conclusion was drawn from this consideration: our opponents would always be democracies and democracies alone, for the simple reason that they were vulnerable. We must always go in search of weaker opponents, and make friends of the dangerous ones. This sounded rather like a cheap joke. The man who said it, in all earnestness, was Hanfstaengl, next to whom I was sitting. Not until later did I discover that he had only been trying to give in a simpler form the views of the

Führer. I never heard a more naïve admission of the character of the "dynamic" political movements.

It is the Germans abroad that are made the medium of these activities, directed from the German Foreign Ministry by Herr Bohle. They are forced in a new and highly revolutionary way into political action, as bearers of "dynamism" into the country whose guests they are, and as *Stützpunkte*, key positions, for the preparation of revolution. And in the East and South-east of Europe, where streams of German colonists have flowed for centuries into the territory of other nations, this peculiar element of Germans abroad is manifestly trained, and at times used already, for the organization of control in what is to become a great alliance of States, and for continuing in a wider field the work the party has done within the German Reich upon State and society. They are to be a factor in the *Gleichschaltung*, the forcing into conformity, of the population among whom they live, disciplining, watching, and influencing down to the most intimate details of private life. They are to be the propagators of unceasing "training" in the National Socialist philosophy. The most recent developments in Czechoslovakia, since the Munich agreement, have demonstrated that the long years of preparatory propaganda and organization were intended to serve the aim, only now revealed, of German hegemony.

For those politicians who are convinced that the German nation, and with it the Germans abroad, will have to struggle for existence long after the National Socialist episode in German history has ended, this policy of ruinous exploitation of the groups of Germans abroad—whether these are still of German or even of foreign nationality—is a cause of deep anxiety. The Germans abroad, especially the German national groups in the States of the South-east of Europe and the Near East, have been a magnificent asset in the policy of alliances, which is alone worth pursuing; and for this very reason they should be spared from political interference, and kept free from all German chauvinism.

The National Socialist conception of universal unsettlement

may, perhaps, not unfairly be described as both political tactics and a political aim. Means and end are here one and the same thing. This is the characteristic expression of the doctrineless-ness and directionlessness of National Socialist revolutionary "dynamism." Rosenberg, as already mentioned, is opposed to this: he has a fixed conception of foreign policy with clearly defined aims. His unfortunate excursions into practical politics are beside the issue: he is not a man of action, an organizer, but his political ideas form a logical system. His picture of the world is a connected whole, and it has had a decided effect on the many people who in their youth had come under the influence of Houston Stewart Chamberlain. Whatever the value of his ideas, they are consistent with one another. But consistency is of no interest to "dynamism."

Hitler has manifestly moved away from Rosenberg's ideas, just as he has moved away from the ideas of the first economic "experts" of the movement. The radicalization of National Socialism into dynamism is like Salome's dance: one veil of ideology is cast off after another. Rosenberg's foreign policy is too dogmatic, too static, to be in tune with the present day. Hitler's policy to-day is entirely a policy of stirring up universal unrest, with the actual aims of the regime kept undefined. This absence of principle suits his gift of recognizing and promptly seizing every political opportunity for increasing his power.

For all that, Rosenberg's ideas continue to count. In this book I have repeatedly made use of them in describing National Socialist tendencies in foreign policy, without always actually quoting him. His conception of a Nordic Pan-Europe is generally accepted where definite political aims are still considered necessary. "Nordic Europe is the solution for the future, with a German Central Europe, a racial and national State, as the central Power on the Continent, a safeguard of the South and South-east; the Scandinavian States with Finland as a secondary alliance for the safeguarding of the North-east, and Great Britain as the safeguard of the West and overseas, at the points where this is requisite in the interest of the Nordic man." Such is the main feature of Rosenberg's conception as expounded in his *Mythos des XX. Jahrhunderts*—a "German-Scandinavian coalition," and "an alliance between this coalition and England." This political coalition is directed against Russia, "to prevent the materialization of a Mongrel peril in the East." The positive aim is "to provide soil for a hundred million Germans." Here we have everything that characterized the early National Socialist ideas in foreign policy: the anti-Russian attitude, the idea of the preservation of the Germanic race, the coalition of Nordic peoples, the alliance with England as racially akin, and the "Eastern territorial policy," providing a free path and territory for the *Drang nach dem Osten.*

All this unquestionably belongs to the past of National Socialism. It is much too unambitious, unrevolutionary, respectable, static, to interest the politicians who to-day determine the tactics of the Third Reich. It is the policy of a settled order, with definite and limited aims. It is national, racial, not dynamic. And it has been overtaken by the pace of revolutionary development.

As leader of a special Danzig "Kontor" or section in the Lübeck "Nordische Gesellschaft," I had occasion in 1934 to come into close contact with Rosenberg and some of his colleagues at a "Nordic Congress" at Lübeck. The meetings were of the most insignificant sort. An authors' hostel was opened for the cultivation of Nordic-German cultural relations. There were two speeches in the Lübeck market-place, and a private session in the town hall. At this last Hildebrandt, provincial leader and an ex-farm laborer, delivered an abstruse speech; another delegate spoke, with endless repetition, on the subject of the economics of imperialism, and other speakers delivered thoroughly "respectable" addresses. This thorough "respectability" marked all of Rosenberg's demonstrations. I remember another, a solemn announcement of the idea of the "orders" as the fundamental idea of the State. Classical music, by candle-light, introduced and followed a respectable, literary lecture by Rosenberg on the history of the Teutonic Order in Prussia and the modern idea of orders; it was all read in the style of any of the despised provincial politicians of pre-National Socialist times. But the environment was thoroughly æsthetic—flickering shadows in the arches of the former guest-chambers of the castle of the Order at Marienburg; midnight music in the Marienkirche at Lübeck, the exterior of the church being floodlit. Thoroughly respectable æsthetic glamour, early twentieth century.

No, Rosenberg is no revolutionary, and those who study him gain an inadequate idea of National Socialism, in spite of all the revolutionary temper of his writings. The radical dynamism into which National Socialism has developed is a dangerous, destructive fever, which spreads at an uncanny rate. Alfred Rosenberg's National Socialism would have been a harmless armchair adventure, if it had not had the dangerous influence that proceeds from the German habit of omnivorous reading in connection with a "system."

I mention this to show that National Socialist policy has grown much more radical, so that it would be a mistake to rely on its literary apostles. In foreign as in home policy the Third Reich is in the midst of the second phase of the nihilist revolution, in which the "racial" element has largely been thrown off. The nihilist foreign policy of the National Socialism of today uses ideas only as a mask, and has no philosophical basis.

The vehemence with which National Socialism pursued its "racial" policy of bringing the German groups beyond the frontier into a "Greater Germany" misled opinion as to the true character of its dynamic foreign policy. Its policy is anything rather than a belated recapitulation of political ideals of national unity carried over from nineteenth century liberalism. It is, indeed, a conversion of familiar and recognized political motives to other purposes. Any examination of the practical proceedings of the National Socialists will confirm this. No more revealing example of the simply anti-historic work of National Socialism could be conceived than the "fulfilment" of a pretended centuries-old national aspiration in the occupation of Austria, with the cynical extermination that has followed of a historical heritage dating back 700 years. Austria has been treated under the German occupation precisely as any military occupying force treats its occupied territory, with complete indifference to its national individuality, as a means to the ends of the occupying State.

The same is true of the "reuniting" of the Sudeten Germans with the Reich. It is possible to regard the founding of a Czechoslovak national State with a good deal of scepticism. It is possible to be sceptical with regard to the "fiction" of a Czechoslovak "nation," in view of the historic divergences between Czechs and Slovaks. The very arguments brought against us Germans, that blood relationship, common origin, similarity of speech, are not politically overriding elements in face of centuries of state and other historic associations with other nations, may be brought against the claims of a united Czechoslovak nation. But even if there does not seem to be any compelling reason for maintaining the existence of the Versailles-made Czechoslovak national State, which contained in miniature all the problems of the old Austria-Hungary, the National Socialist policy against Czechoslovakia can only be described as self-destroying. It was obvious that it was intended to occupy and partition the whole of Czechoslovakia, as has since been done; and this was bound to prevent the very thing which could alone be of service to a German policy which aimed at gaining, through the growth of confidence, something more than merely a frontier territory with a few millions of Germans.

Any observer of the methods preferred by National Socialism is driven to the conclusion that the actual ideal of the regime is domination. The idea of a peaceful territory controlled by treaty relations under German leadership is given the lie by these methods of violence. The methods of National Socialism reveal its true tendencies with documentary clarity. No commonwealth of nations can be produced by these methods, but only a regime of domination over oppressed nations, oppressed like Germany's own sister nation, Austria. If the methods of military occupation cannot be dispensed with in the case of Austria, still less, obviously, could they be in that of the Slav peoples. Who can believe in any German intention of pursuing the method of peaceful federation in Central Europe?

It was precisely these considerations that an Austrian friend put before me in the spring of 1934, asking me to use my connections with the Führer and other persons in the party in the interest of a peaceful arrangement with Austria. The methods of the National Socialist campaign in and against Austria could only destroy, he said, the possibility of the continuance of the German nation on its past historic lines. There was no difficulty about forcibly annexing Austria; sooner or later it could be done without risk. But what would have been achieved by that? Germany would simply have given a clear indication of the lines on which she proposed to proceed in the future. This could not but throw away, trifle away, all that she was in process of gaining by her rearmament and her recovery of the means of political activity. Anything else might be endurable, even a long estrangement between the two German States; but one thing must at all costs be avoided—a forcible solution. That would destroy the future of the German nation. It would have to continue on that path, the path of violence. And every thinking person knew where that would lead.

The man who laid these anxieties of his before me was one who would recently have been called a *Betontnationaler*, one of the group who described themselves as of "emphatically national" outlook. He was ready for the pursuance of an identical foreign policy by the two States, but independently of one another. He pointed to opportunities of a gradual but sincere improvement of German-Austrian relations. He emphasized

255

Dollfuss's good will and approachability. It is beside the question that he was optimistic in regard to the possibility of moderating National Socialism. The essential point is that there was no one in the Reich who succeeded in making use of this or any similar attempt at mediation in order to compel the leaders of the party to seek a solution of the German-Austrian problem on reasonable lines. I have already referred to my own failure to induce the army leaders to move in the matter. A year before my attempt, shortly after the imposition of the $250 fine on all Germans visiting Austria, a fine imposed against the opposition of the Foreign Ministry, I had had the opportunity of noticing how emotional was the Führer's attitude to this problem, how gratified he was to have the opportunity of a quarrel with Austria, how delighted to be using force against her. What subsequently happened in Austria, in 1938, and the way it happened, was a self-condemnation of National Socialist policy, a clear revelation by the leaders themselves of purposes and methods which to this day have not been candidly admitted.

Now, in the complete destruction of the Czechoslovak State, six months after the formal agreement not to occupy the Czech territories, we have in effect a completely cynical admission that in this revision of European frontiers no importance is attached either to considerations of national kinship or to those of the past history of a State, or to anything but imperialist pursuit of power. Germany's future policy will remain permanently compromised by the destruction of Austria and Czechoslovakia.

In these acts Germany has stamped the character of her whole political course. She has heaped up a mass of suspicion and, indeed, of hatred of her, which can be no trifle even though, as the National Socialists demonstrate at every step, they can afford a brutal candor about their aims and have at their back a nation robbed of its power of judgment. Germany has, moreover, set herself entirely in the wrong even where she had the advantage of unanswerable moral claims to the restoration of her sovereignty. She has given the moral advantage to her opponents in every outstanding issue, and provided them with startling arguments in the "moral war" against her, with which to weaken the unity of her people in any new armed conflict.

How close we were to such a conflict, against a united world coalition, was shown by the developments preceding the Munich agreement, and will be shown even more clearly by the developments following the occupation of Bohemia and Moravia. Were it not for the English will to peace, Germany's situation would be so desperate that only a radical change in her foreign policy could save her.

THE RUSSIAN CARD

But was not a chance of this sort, the conclusion of an alliance with Soviet Russia, always held in reserve as a resource in extreme emergency? The anti-Soviet policy of National Socialism seems so much a matter of established doctrine that a return to the old pro-alliance conception of the Reichswehr might seem impossible for the Third Reich. But, as I have frequently indicated, that is not so. The new Thirty Years' War in which we are engaged may, in spite of its supposed ideological character, become the war of permanent changes of front. And it may well be that, sooner or later, Germany will deliberately seek an alliance with Soviet Russia. And not with any Fascist "Young Russia," as many German politicians imagine, seeing in the relations between Stalinism and the monarchist Young Russian émigrés a logical phase in the development towards a new Tsarism with which they could treat.

The dividing lines between the various dictatorial ideologies are, in any case, very indefinite, no more than a matter of convenience of interpretation. In the spring of 1937, before the huge crop of executions in the Russian army, a number of provincial German newspapers were surprisingly busy with Russian events, which were being interpreted as revealing a new development of Nationalism in the Bolshevik State, and its purging of Jewish elements and of doctrinaire revolutionists. There were full accounts of Stalinist anti-Semitism, and much was made of the alleged emergence of the authoritarian idea of a new Tsarism, together with a new Nationalism. I do not know whether all this was a kite flown by the Propaganda Ministry or a gamble by other groups. But nobody who has had any insight into the elasticity of the unscrupulous power-policy of the regime will have any doubt that a right-about turn in foreign policy would not be a matter of the slightest difficulty either for the Propaganda Ministry or for any of the masters of the completely muzzled German nation.

The continuation of a Russian policy was by no means unpopular among the National Socialist leaders. Apart from Rosenberg, there were few prominent members of the party who would not have preferred a Russian to the Polish pact. I had several discussions with Koch, of East Prussia, one of Gregor Strasser's men, a keen supporter of a Russian policy, on the limitations and possibilities of that policy. The party never, indeed, cut off all connection with Russia. My own view was that, at least in the economic field, the connection should not be allowed to be completely broken off, and I found Hitler in entire agreement with this. But, he argued, I should never get anywhere, and certainly never in politics. The Soviet leaders were a set of pettifogging Jews, and there was no getting anything out of them.

The Bolshevik leaders defended the strange plan of an association between the Soviet Union and Germany, in discussing it with members of their party, by arguing that it could only benefit the proletariat if capitalist, militarist Germany built up the indispensable armaments industry for the Soviet Union. But in 1933 any close alliance with Russia for aims of offence was only to be had at the price of a "second," a Socialist, revolution in Germany. I assume that Hitler recognized this, and that he considered that the time was not ripe for that revolution. Undoubtedly there are important military groups which would not shrink from it. For many of the younger generation of Nationalists there is no longer anything alarming about that perspective.

Hitler's aversion from an alliance with the Soviet Union is due, however, clearly to another consideration—that if the National Socialist methods of domination are, perhaps, the equal of the Bolshevik methods, they are in no way superior to them. A German-Russian alliance would certainly bring the danger of the conversion of a National Socialist into a Bolshevik hegemony. As yet Hitler has found no opponent who could stand up to his political methods. This gives him the sense he personally needs of absolute superiority. Soviet Russia would be as dangerous as a partner as it is as an enemy; it would be a partner immune to the wiles of National Socialism, as the bourgeois world is not.

The army was enthusiastically for the alliance, which offered the inestimable advantage of covering Germany's rear. It favored an alliance for practical reasons, just as the Western democracies are trying to-day to avoid the formation of ideological coalitions and are in favor of political collaboration with National Socialism, independently of any revolutionary consequences that might result in the event of war. The Reichswehr, similarly, is not deterred from accepting the practical advantages of an alliance by the risk of the revolutionary infection of Germany in wartime.

Hitler was compelled by the political intrigues of the early years to trim his sails, until he had full possession of power and could venture on a revolutionary course in internal politics. Now, however, with *Wehrwirtschaft* and *Autarkie* (the subordination of the whole economic system of the country to military requirements and, as a part of this, the organization of national economic self-sufficiency as far as possible), the economic system and the social order have been largely approximated to the Bolshevik system—with, it is true, certain important exceptions. There are thus no difficulties left in the way of alliance with the Soviet Union. That alliance is the great revolutionary coup in foreign policy at which controlling elements in the National Socialist leadership have long been aiming.

But such an alliance with Russia, at a critical moment like that of September 1938, would in any case have meant the proclamation of the second, the Socialist, revolution, which Hitler, in spite of his declaration in 1934 that the revolution was over, still holds in reserve. (Everybody who heard the secret interpretation of the events of June 30th, 1934, is aware that he does so.) This alliance may also be brought about by difficulties in the internal political and economic situation, or simply by a slowing down of the revolutionary development essential to the maintenance of National Socialism in power. The decision to offer this alliance has been closer, and will be closer in the future, than is suspected either in Germany or abroad. The decision is the easier since it is that favored by the military experts, who are not alive to the wider issues involved, just as they were not at the time of the "combination" of 1933.

A German-Russian alliance means simply the confluence of two streams which run toward the same sea, the sea of world revolution. National Socialism will submit to *Gleichschaltung* with the Bolshevik world revolution, or will subject that revolution to *Gleichschaltung* with itself: it amounts either way to much the same thing. It will be no ordinary coalition between two Powers for normal practical purposes. Germany and Russia, if they come together, will radically transform the world. That alliance is Hitler's great coming stroke.

THE ROAD TO THE RAW MATERIALS AND KEY POSITIONS OF
DOMINION

This policy does not mean the end of the past eastern policy of National Socialism. But that policy will no longer be pursued for its own sake, as proposed in *Mein Kampf*. It will provide one of the means of a comprehensive world policy, the policy of access to raw materials. Behind the romanticism of the *Drang nach dem Osten*, with its reminiscences of Marienburg, of knightly orders, of trekking peasants and continual fighting and adventure and travels among pagans, lies the very real necessity of finding a way out of the problem, hitherto insoluble, of the completely inadequate food supply of the German nation. Without a sufficient food supply the nation would lead a shadow existence, politically unfree, robbed of the roots of its power.

Criticism of National Socialism has often been easy because it has been directed merely to the ideological surface and has paid no attention to the underlying motives, which would probably repay consideration. Beyond question there lie beneath the principal short-range aims of National Socialist policy vital problems of a military, strategic nature, or concerning the elementary safety of the nation. When these problems are put forward in the purely scientific way in which the army leaders present them, it is difficult to see how the short-range practical policy of National Socialism could be directed along any very different lines from those which are being pursued. The method adopted may not be necessary, but the practical aims could not be different. It was Ludendorff who during the Great War regarded the "grain route" as of such importance that he adjusted his strategic conceptions to it. Thus, after the Roumanian declaration of war, Wallachia was occupied on account of the food situation. So with the "oil route." Here again Ludendorff states that it was for the sake of oil that he had in the end to occupy Transcaucasia. It is the "raw material routes" that determine the short-range aims and some of the long-range aims of National Socialism. This is a heritage of the Great War. And these paths are compulsory so long as the method of assurance of victory has to be determined for the coming second world war by the political conceptions that ruled in the first one.

Here again it is military conceptions that determine National Socialist policy. While the road to the grain, oil, and ore sources determines the short-range German foreign policy, it is the road to the strategic key positions for the domination or harassing of

power-sources and communications that already determines policy in certain regards, and, indeed, directs it in the very opposite
direction to the National Socialist program.

"Confined and frustrated Powers can still pursue distant aims
amid the tenacious pursuit of near ones, and approach the former
—the more closely the less they speak about them," says Haushofer. This distinction between proximate and distant aims is
revealing. To say little is not one of the favorite habits of
National Socialists. But, in spite of the cynical candor with
which the party regularly speaks in public about its compromis-
ing plans, it has said remarkably little about its ultimate aims.
There are plausible reasons for this, and others which are less
obvious. One of the plausible explanations is that the mass of
party members and the mass of the public find it much more difficult to appreciate the reasons for setting foot in Brazil or South
Africa than for a punitive expedition in the East or South-east
of Europe. Distant aims would be thoroughly unpopular, as is
clear from the general dislike of the enterprise in Spain, though it
is of the highest military importance. But there is another reason, a very simple one: the National Socialists do not know what
are their ultimate aims. The universal political uneasiness is
accounted for by the readiness of the National Socialists to intervene wherever opportunity offers, to make use of every opportunity of the increase of their power. There is, indeed, only
one National Socialist long-range aim—to be ready to put in an
appearance, and claim equality of rights, and force compliance
with its claims, in every problem in world politics. The practical
aims are largely *freibleibend*, to use the language of the business
man—subject to change without notice. They will be suited to
the tactical conditions of the moment. They may run to a colonial
empire, or a great continental sphere of domination reaching
from Flushing to Vladivostok, or a South American empire or

one in the South Seas. "Above all," says Haushofer in warning, following Ratzel, "never stake all the plans for the future on a single card." The ideal of high policy, he considers, lies in "discovering the right connection between continental and oceanic periods." There must be no disregard of "oceanic geopolitics" through over-attention to inland problems.

The characteristic of this policy is continual unsettling activity, which gives the opportunity every now and then for a stroke. No order, no balance, no neighborliness between nations is aimed at, but fundamental disharmony. No new equilibrium can be attained, no matter what concessions are made to National Socialism by other nations or what successes it achieves. The essential aim is preparedness, with the determination to push onwards and emerge from central European, continental confinement: an unscrupulous, doctrineless determination to seize anything and to be ready to do anything that serves the increase of power and dominion. It is a *conquistador* policy. With the revolutionary breaking-up of all elements of order in the world, the chances increase of succeeding, if not in every enterprise, at all events in some. National Socialists in high places declare that this is one of those periods that come only at intervals of centuries, a period of revolutionary change in the world, in which, amid the general insecurity, every resolute stroke has good prospects of success. It is the period of a modern type of buccaneer and filibuster, of semi-legalized elements of disturbance who are followed by the flag if they succeed.

Such ideas make it intelligible that one of the main concerns of the "dynamic" policy of National Socialism must be not merely to keep the world in its state of crisis and quasi-revolution but to produce open revolutionary unrest. For it is only in such conditions that the "young" nations can hope to secure their places in the sun. Hence, too, the almost naïve indignation at British "hypocrisy" in condemning Germany as out for plunder while Great Britain owes her own empire to nothing but sanguinary force and cunning. "All life is robbery," declare the National Socialists with Hebbel, and they are unable to comprehend why things that were permissible three and four centuries ago, and down to the imperialist era of the last century, should no longer be permissible.

It is only in its long-range aim that the world-revolutionary character of National Socialist foreign policy is revealed. It is regarded as a shocking aim in the respectable world of the saturated nations, in the offices and counting-houses in which the methods of the buccaneers or even the imperialism of the East India Company have made way for more civilized, but, many people think, no less brutal and sanguinary methods of imperialist exploitation. It is necessary to take account of the whole emotional complex of a nation that for centuries has come off badly, in order to realize that National Socialism is making provision not so much for the belated fulfilment of a constantly frustrated national aspiration to unity, as for the intoxicating adventure of imperialism, the conquest of colored races, the stilling of the hunger for dominion which the nations of the West were able to satisfy long ago, in a less scrupulous age.

Among educated National Socialists such as those in Hess's circle there is an unshakable conviction that the coming epoch of world development will witness a German domination, whereas the last epoch was one of English domination. In the German nation there are a love of adventure and a youthful determination, joined to intelligence and energy, that cannot but be of service in the wide spaces of a colonial empire, and will be of immense importance to Germany. Active young Germans of all classes are waiting for the opening of the gates to a hard but varied and adventurous life as colonists.

With these youths' energies at its back, National Socialism pursues its policy of undefined long-range aims. And this policy is bound to be all the more radically revolutionary in character since its purpose is so undefined, consisting of a determination to keep everywhere on the watch for opportunities of pushing forward and occupying positions, of making headway and building a German empire out of scraps of older empires, just as England and France did with the Spanish empire. This is the purpose of all the preparations for a sanguinary general conflict, of the universal mobilization and the *Wehrwirtschaft*. A new war will not be against European Powers but against world empires, and the victorious continental Power will transfer to its own shoulders the dominions of those vanquished empires.

Confinement to a small territory, says Haushofer, is not a fate with which there is any need to put up. There are examples that show that "only he who thinks in terms of small territories need remain the owner of small territories." Those who look for opportunities of a "large-territory long-range policy" are virtually sure of victory over a "confined-territory and small-territory outlook." Germany, Italy, Japan have "a most important long-range aim in common," thinks Haushofer—"to collect as many racial and national comrades as possible under their flag . . . to assure breathing space for the too thickly crowded population of the mother-country for the future as well."

Just as Great Britain is only attached to Europe, so the Mediterranean *Grossraum* (or wide territory under central control) will lie only partly in Europe. It will unite the European coastal areas of the Mediterranean with North Africa and Asia Minor into a new whole, which will be no more European than is the British Empire. A German *Grossraum* can only be envisaged on similar lines. It has its roots in Central Europe, perhaps it will also bring in northern Europe; in any case, its national and racial basis is of indeterminate size; but its real growth will lie in other continents.

THE WILL TO ANARCHY

The ultimate aim is the maximum of power and dominion. The means is general subversion, the destruction of the existing order so as to have a free hand for the building of a new and greater dominion. But behind this is the intention no longer to be confined to Europe. Obviously it is impossible to state all these aims in precise terms. They are influenced by considerations of military and strategic policy, and by the all-pervading urge to revolutionary destruction; but they are also influenced by just claims to the rectification of frontiers and the expansion of the national life. This whole policy breaks with all customary standards; the political categories of the past are no longer relevant to it. It is idle, indeed, to try to give a rational interpretation to an irrational urge to active interference in every country of the world.

The central ideal of this urge is the redistribution of the world. So at least it is envisaged by the German Minister of Propaganda. And it is no mere chance that it was Goebbels, the Jacobin, who spoke of the rare moment of the redistribution of the world. "Redistribution" is the old ideal of demagogic Socialism. Redistribution, whether at home at the expense of the rich or abroad through the expropriation of defeated enemies—the idea is the same, the magic idea of "sharing out."

This is external revolution, the deliberate application of revolutionary forces to foreign policy. The political method of the "putsch," itself revolutionary, was first employed under the Weimar Republic; now it has become the essence of the regime's foreign policy of universal unsettlement. The aim of this foreign policy is the revolutionary redistribution of the world and creation of a German *Grossraum*, in which everyone will have a share, and the wealth of which will offer very different prospects from those of the sharing out of poor little poverty-stricken Germany, which cannot be made any larger by dividing it up. National Socialism discovers many pretexts for its political actions; but behind them all stands, plain for all to see, the nihilist revolution.

This will to universal unsettlement, this urge to the accumulation of power and dominion, this foreign policy of unbounded dynamism, is, in plain English, nothing else than the expression of a will to anarchy. The unfortunate Edgar J. Jung, von Papen's murdered secretary, noted years ago in his *Herrschaft der Minderwertigen* ("Ochlocracy") an "inclination of Western civilization to anarchy." Anarchy, he said, was only restricted formally by Fascism, not in reality. The same judgment was expressed to me by Marshal Pilsudsky in regard to National Socialism—it altered externals but made no real change. This claim to the redistribution of the world is no longer the just desire of a nation for room to live and move. The mobilization of all the resources of the nation is not for the ending of the *injuria temporum*. Dynamism is the will to anarchy. Not the ending of revolution but the final and complete fulfilment of revolution in Western civilization, its extreme expression—such is the essential aim of National Socialism.

Between this will to anarchy as the first condition for the creation of a new order, and the conservative progress to higher forms of our Western civilization, there can be no compromise. Time cannot bridge the gap between these two tendencies; it can only widen it. Dynamism has performed the unquestionable service of forcing us all to clear our minds and determine our attitude.

For us Germans, the issue is plain and simple. Everyone who is still capable of thinking for himself must know that National Socialism is leading us to self-destruction. The revolutionary character of its foreign policy must inevitably lead to campaigns which will exhaust the nation. In opposition to its boundless aims and revolutionary methods, the plain question must be asked what lasting benefit they can bring the nation. Even if the Third Reich achieves complete success in the redistribution of the world, if after a series of further successes and ultimate victory it sets up its hegemony, in the nature of things this can mean nothing but a permanent military occupation of subjugated territories, with all the accompanying violence and terrorism. But there is no escaping the logical conclusion that the day will come when this effort brings exhaustion and the military occupying force is crippled. This will in all probability happen much sooner than the apparent rapid growth of power might suggest. For the German nation is overtaxed, exhausted by its training before the race begins, and really ill. But when its power is crippled, what then?

4

Toward Maximum Power and Dominion

TECHNIQUE AND TACTICS

LET us survey the technique and tactics Hitler has employed on his temporarily successful course. How has it all been possible? A nation almost unarmed, with millions unemployed, enmeshed in a treaty system that left it almost unable to stir without the risk of sanctions, has now, after barely six years, become the mightiest military Power in Europe, with scarcely challenged hegemony. It has torn up the treaties, and stands unassailable, in the expectation of world empire and of a power growing to an unsurpassable maximum. It is not an achievement anyone can belittle; and the German would have least occasion of all for quarreling with it, were it not coupled with very grave potentialities.

The elements of victory have unquestionably been a firm and tenacious will, enormous elasticity and alertness, undoubting enthusiasm, inventiveness in destruction, and a strength of nerve that withstood every test longer than the opponents; a gift of divination, an impulsiveness supplied at all times with the power for immediate action, for sudden thrusts at enemy positions; a readiness to seize on every slightest sign of weakness and to see it approaching; an ungenerous persistency that allowed no breathing-space and recognized no rules. And all this would have failed of its great success if the opponents had not been ready to accept the fact of Germany's recovery and merely put up occasional resistance to its methods. Germany's rapid gains of territory are also to be explained by the fact that many positions had been voluntarily evacuated by her opponents. Hitler found a situation already ripened.

Is this the full explanation? Far from it, I think. An opponent who does not wish to make a stand—does not that imply much more than his mere recognition that the state of things he was defending is no longer worth defending? Is not Hitler's real achievement his recognition of the actual weakness of Germany's opponents, of the unreality of their power? Is not this the secret of his success and of his unerring judgment? The German nation has no desire for war, or for revolution, or for anything connected with "dynamism." It wants peace and quiet, as the masses do in all countries. But have not all leading nations, in all history, led because a controlling upper class had the ability to hold in check the right and natural pacifism of the masses? And is it not the very sign of their retirement from the making of world history that the Western democracies are without an upper class of this sort that actually controls its nation? It may fairly be said that the recognition of this fact is the essential starting point of the "dynamic" nations— that personal control of technique and tactics in foreign policy alone provides the power to strike a decisive blow. In this way unquestioned personal ability makes use of existing sources of power in the adroit handling of a political situation. Hitler might act to all appearance against nature and against all probabilities; but he always acted in such a way as to have all the actual operative elements behind him and working for him. He swam with the stream.

This is no depreciation of his achievement, and it is still no complete explanation of it. It would be a crude mistake to ascribe entirely to superior and unscrupulous technique things for which there are deeper reasons. Certainly National Socialism had very significant fighting methods of its own, and they go far to reveal its true character. But they would not have been certain of success if they had not had the general political and moral situation in their favor. From "political undermining" to "violent expulsion," as Haushofer says with such remarkable candor, "there are new forms of supplanting in the peaceful struggle of nationalities," and there are new "means of moral warfare with its unsettling effect, new and hitherto undreamed-of means of propaganda."

Haushofer regards it as a particularly effective method in an ambitious and far-seeing German foreign policy to await "the opportunity for a decisive surprise attack" at a "ripe, late hour." *Tout vient à celui qui sait attendre,* he writes, quoting Bülow's favorite maxim. The new policy watches its opportunity for intervention anywhere. It will intervene at any time; and whether it can give a plausible reason or not. It will not be afraid to appear, as in the colonial question, inconsistent. It proceeds from the fundamental conviction that the universal revolution can be kept in progress only by constant activity. It will therefore seize every opportunity of perpetuating political unsettlement, knowing that even the remotest problems are so closely interconnected that this unsettlement in any case hastens the general revolutionary break-up of the old order. Its only care is lest conditions should grow static. For the new German policy there are no longer any political problems that do not matter. Everything is important and significant to it. It cannot declare itself uninterested in any part of the world or in any world problem. It must make it its task to be everywhere, influencing political problems in the direction of general subversion.

The treatment of the Austrian problem, and especially of the Czechoslovak problem, with its technically masterly tactics of continually pushing up the claims advanced until the final moment for claiming everything, shows the tactical method of the Third Reich plainly even to those who have no general acquaintance with National Socialism. But the method has been the same since the National Socialist movement first existed. For those who were familiar with this method, neither the Austrian nor the Czechóslovak settlement brought any surprises, except in regard to the attitude of the other parties concerned. The separation of problems, their isolation from possible complications, the splitting up of each problem into stages with the continual declaration that the stage reached is the last, the immediate advancing of the firing line the moment a position has been captured (we can only describe the process in military terms), the concentration of all forces at a single point —all these are familiar tactical elements. It is not even surprising any longer to find the opponents' ideology used against them, as with the right of self-determination and the principle of nationality. Nor is it anything new to find that the actual aim is never mentioned, that it is never the same as the ostensible aim. The only thing that is astonishing is that all this continues to work, that these devices are not even yet played out. In spite of the transparency of the tactics employed, the opponents of National Socialism still continue to be misled by them. They still enter into negotiations with the National Socialists, although it has been plain for a long time past that, as Hitler himself has said, he who negotiates is lost. Following that principle, Hitler himself at once puts up his price, to the confusion of his opponent. Always to be ready to pounce, never to allow the opponent the initiative, never to permit himself to be pushed into the defensive—all these devices are so transparent that the one and only incomprehensible thing is the eternal readiness of the opponents to be taken in. The readiness to take any risk has brought victory. Already we may speak of a law of diminishing risks in Hitler's future enterprises. Each advantage won reduces the future risk.

But what is the revolutionary element in all this?

It is essential to draw a distinction between Hitler's own highly individual technique, developed and applied by him alone and consequently inimitable, and the actual guiding principle of these tactics, revolutionary and destructive. The personal element, which has rightly established his claim to leadership in the party, and which has made him the teacher of all his paladins, is his infinite dexterity and elasticity and his readiness at any moment to bring a sort of medium's gift into touch with the elements of a problem and to interpret them. Personal also is the iron resolution, the ruthlessness and harshness, wrung from a nature inclined to slackness and in need of quiet for contemplation, and accordingly liable to be carried to excess. The gift Hitler unquestionably possesses of waiting for the right moment, a gift which has been misinterpreted as irresolution and passivity, is only the expression of his inability to come to a decision until an inner voice speaks to him on his problems, and he has the sense that the right moment has arrived. He has the two contrasting qualities of a supreme capacity for cool calculation and the irrational gift of intuition. He has the revolutionary temperament. At any time when he is without all this his technique is unfruitful, and he makes mistakes. It is always opposition, an enemy, that awakes these qualities. This arouses his sense of superiority, on which he is dependent, his confidence in his giant's power over the "dwarfs" around him. Thus he is nothing without his opponents, his *bêtes noires*, the democracies, the "respectable" people, quiet and orderly but comfort-seeking and irresolute. It is these elements that made him. Anyone who has seen how Hitler will almost deliberately grow heated over some small issue in conversation, will raise his voice and begin to gesticulate excessively, so raising himself out of a lethargic dullness in order to say something; how he will grow indignant or rapturous in the effort to fight his way out of mental shackles, will realize that similarly in great questions it is not cool calculation and superior tactical ability alone that bring him success, but that he needs these emotional outbreaks in order to maintain his combative intensity and to gain his power of influencing by suggestion, to which almost everyone who meets him succumbs, the foreign statesman no less than the German citizen.

And so it is exactly with the revolutionizing character of the whole of the National Socialist policy. The revolutionary element does not lie in the use of force, the cunning methods of menace that reduce men to despair, the unscrupulous technique of direct action and of the *fait accompli,* but in the singleness of aim underlying all these means and methods. German Conservatives and Nationalists defended their capitulation to National Socialism by saying that there was much that was open to objection in National Socialism, its methods were reprehensible, non-moral as one Minister expressed it, but on the whole the National Socialist course was the right one for Germany. The truth is almost the opposite: National Socialism has some splendid achievements to its credit, and even much of its work in foreign policy cannot be seriously objected to from the national standpoint, having in view the difficulties with which Germany has had to contend; but its general course is mistaken, unfruitful, and in the long run infinitely disastrous.

Everything it does is done in the spirit of revolutionary destruction, of the "unmasking" of "false" gods and "wrong" systems. And the process is being carried to the length of the "unmasking" of every element of order, until that total anarchy is reached out of which the phœnix of the "biological" order is expected to rise. This is not the constructive work of a great creative spirit, but the cunning capitalization of a process of annihilation. Hitlerist policy lives upon this unmasking process; it fires its revolutionary spirit with the continual discovery of new masks to be removed. The liberation from wrong ideas and principles is certainly no matter for regret. Still less will it be regretted by the German, who suffered years of humiliation under the political ideas for which the Western Powers stood with smug self-approval. But National Socialism is not destroying merely these ideas; it is also destroying the elements of every spiritual order, and preventing the creation of any new one. The secret of its success is the willingness of its opponents to agree with it in this. The Powers are abdicating because they are losing the instinctive sense of their own rightness.

There is no reason to suppose that with increasing knowledge or ripening judgment the Führer will ever revise the ideas that have been operative thus far in the National Socialist revolution. At the back of all the efforts to dispose of National Socialism, to tame it, to give it opportunities of changing for the better, and accordingly to avoid a final struggle with it, especially a moral struggle, for that is what is really in question, lies an arrogant belittlement of what is happening in Germany. At the time of the Algeciras Conference the British plenipotentiary, Sir Arthur Nicolson, expressed the opinion that the Germans were playing a double game, and he said that the reason was that they did not know what they wanted. There have been critics of German foreign policy since January 30th, 1933, who have offered a similar explanation of it. Their inference has been that Germany must be given friendly help in order to induce her to moderate her course. But where under William II there was weakness and lack of definite policy, to-day there are carefully considered and systematically pursued tactics. The German aims are indefinite to-day only because they are infinite.

HITLER'S TRIUMPH

If a German, even one who is critical of the National Socialist regime in other respects, is offered any criticism of its foreign policy, he will be sure to reply with this question: Could any other German policy, especially in so short a time, have so completely destroyed the whole fabric of the peace of Versailles, and so bloodlessly, and, in addition, have created a state unity such as has never before existed in the history of the German nation? Was not this, he will ask, a masterly performance, a historic achievement of age-long importance? A political regime must be forgiven anything and everything if it can show such successes. All the sacrifices, all the restrictions and harshnesses and the loss of liberty, find their justification in what the Third Reich has achieved in six years, an achievement beyond the wildest anticipations. So he will argue.

Naturally I share this approval of all that has been achieved by National Socialist policy in satisfying the vital needs of the German nation in face of an intolerable treaty situation. We are considering here the justification not for the national policy but for its methods and the limits set to it. And, above all, we are concerned with the question whether National Socialist policy can still be regarded as a national policy, whether what is happening to-day and what will certainly happen to-morrow serves the nation or merely the building up of the power of a revolutionary movement which, in the long run, is bound to turn against the nation and rend it. The dramatic events of August and September, 1938, showed plainly the direction in which Hitler is steering. If war did not come (and after initial successes it would in all probability have brought a German defeat), it was due to a readiness to give way on the part of Germany's opponents which to a German is beyond comprehension. A measure of military unpreparedness may have played a part in this, but there were certainly other considerations as well, and these were not what the National Socialists assume. But one thing is beyond any question, that Hitler did not take into account, indeed refused to take into account, the actual situation of a universal coalition against Germany. He went blindly into a situation out of which he was helped only by the desire of his opponents for peace, and in which he played into the opponents' hands all the trump cards of moral superiority, so that it would have been an easy matter for them to mobilize the world against Germany, at a time when Czechoslovakia was intact, with Russia's hundred and fifty millions and a whole world at her back.

For a man of Hitler's past, living in a world of resentment and vengefulness, this autumn of 1938 was a triumph of truly "gigantic scope," to use his language. Three times the Prime

Minister of Great Britain appeared before him, and at Munich, shortly afterwards, the four leading statesmen of the greatest European States except Soviet Russia met to approve and consecrate his triumph. The last democratically governed State in central Europe, the model State among those formed at Versailles, still remained on the map; but it had ceased to count as a military and therefore as a political factor. This happened under the guise of an admission of Germany's just national demands and of obedience to the principle of the self-determination of nations.

Barely six months later the German Führer, with one of the "lightning strokes" of which he is so fond, occupied the capital of that State. He incorporated in the Reich the principal provinces of the State, great and wealthy regions, inhabited by non-Germans. He formed these into a protectorate under his own rule. He presented other parts of the State to its neighbors or took them under his own protection, leaving them but the shadow of independence. And all this in spite of solemn assurances he had given less than six months earlier in regard to the independence and future territorial integrity of this State. At the moment when he gave those assurances, as he openly declared before the Reichstag on April 28th, 1939, he was already firmly resolved to make this fresh annexation. And not on account of the right of nations to self-determination, or in accordance with the principle of nationality, but simply because the annexation was required by the need of the German nation for "room to live"—the real reason being that the step was prompted by his pursuit of power, his imperialist ambition for world hegemony.

This was indeed a tremendous victory. When Hitler recounted in that speech the quantities of military booty he had been able to seize in Czechoslovakia, it was many times the amount of the most famous successes of the war of a quarter of a century earlier. And, to crown the triumph, it had been bloodless.

But there is another side to this triumph. Already it is clear that this last act, the occupation of Prague, has brought into active operation the revulsion of which there were signs beneath all the jubilation over the peace preserved by the Munich agreement. At that time a great war coalition against Hitler was avoided, but the moral credit for that lay exclusively with the allies. That agreement had itself been a breach of solemn undertakings and pacts, but the breach had been enforced by a moral responsibility both for the past and the future. When Hitler drove into the snow-covered streets of Prague and entered the venerable Hradschin Palace, his triumph was already the greatest of moral defeats. The moral trump cards had been played into the hands of his opponents, whose cause was just. He had set himself once for all in the wrong, and had destroyed the German case.

Was this necessary, was it inevitable? Did it serve the vital interests of the German nation? Was it not a flaunting of the fact that what had been pursued was simply power and the conquest of strategic positions, which Germany's "leaders" had won at the cost of the well-being and the future of Germany? These men talked of the need of the German nation for elbow-room and room to grow, of the struggle for existence. Had they not made a most dangerous mistake in attributing the willingness of the Western Powers for peace in those days at Munich to weakness and fear? Was it not likely that there was more at the back of the acquiescence of the democracies than mere lack of resolution?

The whole "biological" basis of German foreign policy is as fallacious as the hobby-horse of "geopolitics." It is not true that England and France have "abdicated." Both nations may well be suffering from weariness, but the German nation should be able to realize better than any other how quickly such weariness can be thrown off by regenerative forces which may give those nations a very different aspect.

The crisis that came on March 15th, 1939, was not the last. And the signs of a great coalition that began to appear after the Munich meeting were not the last. Germany will have to take continual note of them from now on. This coalition may be formed only at the last moment, and may include States regarded by Germany as allies and friends. No one will expect her opponents to be unable to adopt the surprise methods of National Socialism. Then Germany may have no choice but to capitulate or go to war. And capitulation would mean internal collapse. The policy of striving after the maximum of power and dominion rests on the most disastrous misconception of the distribution of forces and of the real nature of effective force.

THE CRISIS

Since the appearance of the first German edition of this book in the autumn of 1938, the political situation has altered considerably. The sketch I then gave of probable developments has not proved ill-founded. "Hitler," I wrote, "may push on in the South-east. With the *Gleichschaltung* of Slovakia he will menace the flanks of Poland and Hungary and will have the means of pushing on into the Ukraine. He will make it more difficult for a 'sanitary girdle' to be created in this quarter, and by action in Lithuania and Finland he could bring down the north-east pillar of the 'Intermediate Europe' between Germany and Russia. But there is no reason to suppose that his action would be restricted to the East and South-east; it may with equal likelihood be directed to the complete encirclement of France until she is immobilized, and to taking advantage of that situation so long as Poland's neutrality seems assured. He may move against Poland herself, in order to rectify the Polish frontier, to improve the strategic situation, and to recover the irreplaceable port of Danzig. Holland, Belgium, Denmark may suffer prophylactic occupation, and may be forced into a close alliance with Germany. As bases for the operations of the German forces, they would completely isolate England and exclude her from Europe; she may even be condemned to the loss of her empire."

The occupation of Prague and the incorporation of Bohemia and Moravia in the "*Lebensraum*" of Greater Germany could surprise no one but those who were still under the illusion that National Socialist foreign policy was capable of changing and ripening. World opinion may see in this step of Hitler's a critical blunder of his, but it is mistaken. This step lay directly in line with his general conception of foreign policy. The only surprising thing about it, at all events for the National Socialists, is the reaction to it abroad: foreign opinion is at last beginning to realize the actual aims of National Socialism and its tactical method. The National Socialists are not to be deterred by this foreign reaction; they merely regret that it places further difficulties in their way. Nothing, not even the threat of world war, will deter them from their course. This greatly increases the risk of war, a risk which the Munich agreement removed for a bare six months. But if it is doubtful whether the efforts to form a great defensive coalition against Germany and Italy will succeed in preventing war; they may limit the duration and therefore the number of victims of a war.

Two things are certain: Hitler has many opportunities of working for increased power and dominion; but his opponents have scarcely fewer opportunities of defence. Germany has improved her position. But her mastery of Czechoslovakia is by no means the mastery of the world. As a base for aircraft, Posen is no farther from Berlin than Prague. The reduction of the "outlying fort" of Czechoslovakia does not dispose of the possibility of similarly strong and equally troublesome resistance developing at other points. The difficulties also are growing for Germany—difficulties which cannot be removed by violence but only by superior leadership. It must not be forgotten that the German has no gifts as a conspirator, while the Slav, whose territory Germany is now entering, is a master of that revolutionary craft. It is true that the hope of entrapping Germany in a convenient quarter by voluntarily permitting her to advance into the South-east is delusive. It would be too simple a solution for the West to leave Germany and Russia, the two great military and revolutionary Powers, to bleed to death in one another's jaws.

Poland's future policy will be of great importance. Will she succeed in welding together the proposed coalition of independent States, and in making it militarily formidable, in time for it to become a factor of importance?

In this connection it was asked in the German edition of this book in the autumn of 1938 whether Poland would be compelled to take part in a campaign against Russia. It was suggested that Hitler might easily be able to force Poland to choose between joining in the march against Russia and suffering a new partition between Russia and Germany. Since then it has been revealed by Polish quarters that in March 1939 a German proposal was actually made to Poland to join in an attack on Russia and share the proceeds. This offer was made in connection with the resettlement of the Danzig question. Evidently, however, Germany omitted to offer at the same time adequate compensation for Danzig, on the principle Colonel Beck laid down in his speech of May 5th, 1939. At an earlier stage Memel might have sufficed, if at the same time Germany had declared her disinterestedness in the Baltic States and the North-east of Europe in general. But since the occupation of Prague it must have become plain to Poland that Hitler would never agree to a genuine partition of interests between Germany and Poland, that all his promises and offers would be no more than tactical expedients, valid only until his next move, and that if he were allowed the slightest chance the military power of Poland would suffer the same fate as that of Czechoslovakia.

The offer of a joint campaign against Russia was made conditional upon strict Polish neutrality if Germany should become involved with the Western Powers. It was a naïve request, for it must have been clear to Poland that if Germany were successful in that struggle she would be at Germany's mercy. Thus the important thing for Poland after the occupation of Prague was that she was no longer isolated in face of Germany, as she had been, for instance, in February 1939; while Germany had no real opportunity of alliance with Soviet Russia. After her understanding with England Poland had a free hand which gave her a new chance of pursuing her policy of creating an independent coalition of States.

On the occasion of his journey to Bucharest in 1937, Colonel Beck authorized his Foreign Ministry to write: "A practical outlook on outstanding problems, which pays attention to the requirements of the moment, is beginning to take the place of the abstract and nebulous conceptions of the past." We are at the outset of a period in which it will be thoroughly realized that all things are in flux in foreign affairs, new situations are developing, and instead of prematurely forming fixed policies the one maxim must be to profit by every opportunity that comes. No one can any longer afford the luxury of doctrinaire fads and fancies. But the "due distinction between the higher ideals of international co-operation and the sense of realities," as Colonel Beck's Foreign Ministry wrote, does not imply capitulation to National Socialism. It needs all the deafness of present-day Germany to the essential nuances in policy to register in such cool language as Colonel Beck's any kinship with the exalted revolutionism of Goebbels's "redistribution of the world." The nations of the East and South-east of Europe will never voluntarily march alongside this Germany; if they join her at all it will be only in order to escape from the danger of aggression in one quarter or another. And in Poland the value of Hitler's assurances is perfectly well known.

In the German edition of this book, it was pointed out that there was a risk that Germany might suddenly find herself faced with an exceedingly formidable coalition, at the very moment when her situation had grown more difficult, as it inevitably would. Her maximum of power would then turn into a maximum of embarrassment and perplexity. This coalition has now become a reality of the first political importance. Its backbone is a new

France, which has experienced a remarkable recovery, almost a national rebirth, instead of the revolutionary dissolution expected by Hitler. This coalition is led by an equally changed Great Britain, aroused out of a certain indifference and now, rather late but all the more energetically, carrying out an enormous program of rearmament including, in spite of past tradition, the introduction of universal military service. As regards these two nations it looks as if National Socialist policy, with its "psychological war" and its tactics of "universal unsettlement," has attained the exact opposite of the result aimed at. No one will to-day venture to describe France as a dying nation or to speak of Britain's lost empire.

Poland has joined this new coalition, taking a clear stand against Germany. But the most surprising factor in this new defence front is the adhesion of the Soviet Union, perhaps the heaviest blow of all, since it makes no longer possible the alliance of the three dictatorships for which there was at least a plausible case so long as Russia was kept at arms' length by the Western Powers. The Entente Cordiale and its circle of allies has quickly been resuscitated. There has sprung up again almost in a night the whole front before which Germany succumbed twenty years ago. The small neutral States, too, forced at present to take a cautious line on account of the dangerous proximity of the Reich, will stand on the side of the democracies at latest on the day of the outbreak of war; they will very likely, in any case, be driven to do so by the pressure of National Socialist aggression. Thus Germany will realize the full extent of her isolation only on the day on which it has become too late for any change of course, and the mechanism of a general mobilization has been irrevocably set going.

Finally, the United States have spoken. In the form of an offer for the preservation of peace, President Roosevelt has made it plain that America's inexhaustible material resources will be at the disposal of Germany's opponents in any emergency. This crushing fact, revealing that once more a main element in the National Socialist calculations had been wrongly assessed, produced a reaction in Germany that was not surprising; but the nature of the reaction was none the less irrational, even if Hitler had no alternative but to reject the offer, since it would have compelled him to negotiate on a plane on which he would have been unable to maintain his footing. No cunning misinterpretation, no open or veiled allusion to President Wilson, can hide the fact that Roosevelt's demand for a guarantee on behalf of thirty States placed Hitler in a difficult tactical situation, forcing him for the first time on to the defensive and into acceptance of the opponent's initiative, a new and perhaps a serious situation for him. He will have no choice but to recognize the peaceful aim of the great new coalition, to make much of his own will to peace, and to cut down his immediate political objectives.

It is quite possible that Hitler will make a show of resigning himself to the situation, and will be ready to offer sacrifice to peace, amid a great flow of rhetoric. On this the Western Powers may make a few concessions, probably of no great importance, and equally probably insufficient to satisfy Hitler even for the moment. In this case it is to be feared that National Socialism will draw back a few steps only in order to return to the attack with increased vigor. But the favorite surprise tactics of the dictators are largely played out. And, while it is doubtful how long the Western Powers can endure the present pace in rearmament, the question of capital importance is how long Germany can.

It may therefore be regarded as probable that, in spite of the great new coalition and of the risk of a new world war, Hitler will make only a short tactical pause, followed by a new lightning stroke, which still has possibilities of success. It seems to be no longer in the power of the National Socialist leaders to decide whether they shall return to a policy of peace and economic coöperation, even if the Western Powers were to come half-way to meet them. The National Socialist regime is now the prisoner of its own system of domination. It can no more dispense with its pursuit of hegemony than with its government by violence at home. It is following the law of its existence, and cannot be diverted from its path either by threats or by good will.

Thus the only chance of the secure re-establishment of peace lies in the removal of the National Socialist regime. It is certain that the Western Powers will not act on this principle; they will wait to see whether the German nation is willing and able to change its leaders. A day will then come when the whole nation will be held responsible for the acts of its Government. Unquestionably the attitude of the West toward Germany has considerably stiffened. The moment does not seem to be far off at which the new coalition will emerge from its present defensive to deliver an ultimatum, not with any purposes of conquest, but to demand guarantees from Germany in regard to peace, disarmament, and the evacuation of certain occupied territories. Such a policy seems inevitable because the democracies are not in a position to support the enormous burdens of a permanent mobilization, and because the cost of armaments is so murderous that it will compel the consideration at least of their potential use in psychological warfare. That means recourse to the methods of menace by superior material resources, the tactics which National Socialism has itself employed being brought to bear against it. When that time comes, it is to be feared that it will no longer be possible to distinguish between National Socialist imperialism and the German nation, and that the nation will be compelled to pay as a whole the bill for its seven years' debauch.

This stiffening of the attitude toward Germany will also find expression in the assessment of what can be allowed to the German nation for *"Lebensraum"*—"room to live." Until now Danzig has been regarded as unquestionably German on account of its national character, and England, at all events, has been inclined to regard its return to Germany as equitable. But the new National Socialist political theory of "room to live," which has just been given a practical demonstration in the partition of Czechoslovakia, leads in a different direction; for it will be impossible to deny that from the point of view of "room to live" a country is not habitable without access to the sea, and that means that Danzig should go to Poland.

The dangers that show themselves here are regarded by the National Socialist leaders as reasons for an early fight. The decisive element in regard to countering any such inclination on Germany's part may be Italy's attitude. Her great opportunity, we may fairly say her only opportunity, lies in returning to the Western alliance system, repeating her move of 1915. In spite of the Gestapo regime in Italy and the German troops on all the Italian frontiers, Italy is no dependable ally of Germany. The relations between the German and Italian peoples are far from cordial; and nothing would be more unpopular in Germany than a war jointly with Italy to enable her, as the masses see it in Germany, to reap the reward for her betrayal of 1915. In addition to this, there are strong divergences of view in regard to the political aims of the two authoritarian States. The natural place of Italy is with Colonel Beck's "sanitary girdle"—Poland, Hungary, Roumania. But such a deviation in Italian policy, which would be a mortal threat to Germany, is unlikely except in time of emergency.

Hitler, at all events, considers that he still has some trumps in his hand. Any temporary slackening in the policy of the Western Powers might quickly induce him to play these cards. The critical point to-day is again Danzig, as at the outset of the National Socialist regime. Even a compromise solution of this problem will only be of a transitory nature. It is not the German city or the German peasantry around it that matter, but the extremely important strategic point of the estuary of the Vistula and the Bay of Danzig. Germany is concerned for the territorial reuniting of East Prussia with the Reich by the abolition of the Corridor. But Danzig is also indispensable to the long-range aims of National Socialism as a naval basis for the domination of the Baltic and a basis of operations against Poland.

It is significant of the unfruitfulness of National Socialist policy that after so many successes this political problem of Danzig can jeopardize the whole work of the past seven years. The reason is that Hitler has not been able to lay the foundation for a really great and lasting success, the securing of Germany's Eastern flank in order to give her a free hand in the West; or the disinterestedness of the West in face of a fair and constructive German policy in the East. Neutrality or alliance could certainly have been secured from the eastern States by even a meagre measure of fairness in regard to their vital needs and their claim to political independence. But Hitler is incapable of a genuinely creative policy; his purely tactical gifts are exhausted in manipulations which produce mere quasi-successes like the German-Polish agreement, or in spasmodic acts of violence like the occupation of Austria and Czechoslovakia. When National Socialism came into power, Germany's opponents were unable to organize a common front against Hitler; to-day this has been produced by the political course followed by National Socialism itself. Thus, measured by the National Socialists' own standards, their whole effort has been in vain.

But the question that is of interest to-day is whether Hitler's power is so great that he has no need of political expedients to assure the neutrality of the eastern States of Europe but can compel it by military means. It may be that this is so. After the Munich agreement Hitler proposed to win the neutrality of these States by a few vague and non-committal assurances, and to secure necessary raw materials by means of pressure and promises. In the first months of the winter of 1938-39 the National Socialist leaders imagined that they could reckon at once (that is to say, without first incorporating the rest of Czechoslovakia, with Hungary and Poland, in the German system of alliances) on the neutrality of the eastern States, and that they could thus strike a decisive blow at the West. The German assurances were evidently in regard to the participation of the eastern States in any colonial territory Germany might gain, and to a "general solution" of the Jewish question, a very difficult one in some of the eastern States. Thus, in connection with an occupation of Holland, and, perhaps, of Belgium, and with action in the Mediterranean, the colonial question was to be brought to the forefront in a great new political campaign.

But here there was revealed for the first time, and in a way that simply disposed of the proposal, the miscalculation in the Hitlerist policy of violence. By his strokes in foreign affairs—in much the same way as in internal affairs—Hitler had burked certain questions of foreign policy, not solved them. They continued to operate below the surface. The factor of insecurity produced by the existence of a Czechoslovakia that had become Germany's mortal enemy in the heart of German territory, and also indications that the neutrality of the other eastern States in the event of war could not be depended on, compelled the regime to proceed further with its brutal policy of violence by making an end of Czechoslovakia and by attempting to encircle Poland, before the operations in the West could begin. This, however, interfered with preparations for excluding England from European politics and encircling France. Unable to hasten the negotiations for the neutrality of the eastern States sufficiently to secure this before the operations started in the Mediterranean and in North Africa which were to cut off England and France from their connection by sea with their empires, the regime was reduced to tackling both of the plans for strategic offensives simultaneously. This threw the political action into disorder. Hitler began improvising; all the problems presented themselves, so to speak, in a body, and complicated one another. The stroke that was to have freed Hitler from every menace, the occupation of Prague, destroyed the opportunity, essential to him, of tackling his problems one by one.

In spite of this, Hitler could still act, taking on himself the full risk of a world war: by threatening England and France in the Mediterranean and from Spain he could progressively improve his general situation by a lightning change of direction of his thrusts, since he still seems to have a monopoly of rapidity and resolution in action. The occupation of Danzig would not of itself make the Corridor untenable; in the opinion of the Polish National Socialists it would, however, place Poland at once on the defensive, throwing her back on the Bug-Narev-Vistula line. Surprise thrusts in the direction of Roumania and Yugoslavia could be carried out with such effect that they might produce the desired result before the coalition had decided what to do. These thrusts would bring Germany raw materials and, in Yugoslavia, the occupation of territories strategically important as outlets. And before the West had had time to face the new situation, Poland would be threatened also from the Carpathians and checkmated. The resources of the axis Powers would then be available for a blow on the West, enabling Holland, Belgium, and Denmark to be occupied in addition to action in the Mediterranean, and bringing fresh triumphs for Germany.

It cannot be denied that in rapidity of action Hitler still has certain chances of success. He will avail himself of them without scruple, and he will take the risk of world war in the event of the Western Powers refusing to give way in face of his lightning blows. For the wresting from France of some of her northern territories is still envisaged; none of the long-range aims Hitler has exhibited in the past has been given up. It is only necessary to glance at the latest literature, maps and instructions, the publications of the Hitler Youth in the last six months, or the latest articles of General Haushofer: the aim is the hierarchical organization of the nations of Europe around Germany, whether past members of the Holy Roman Empire or remnants of the "sub-Teuton zone of fragments" in the east, with protectorates and alliances of various types; the weakening of Great Britain and destruction of her empire, the setting up of a colonial empire in Africa, and thrusts against South America and the Pacific:

union with Russia or annexation of Russian territory; and, in the end, world dominion.

Against all these aspirations it may be contended that Hitler's policy has already been checked by the Munich agreement. In spite of the losses this agreement brought in appearance to the Western Powers, it produced an unanticipated effect against Hitler, especially through a change of feeling in Germany. If he had taken Prague in September 1938, as he intended at the time, and occupied the whole of Czechoslovakia, penetrating to Carpathian Ruthenia, and facing Poland along the Carpathians, he would have overcome all obstacles; he would have compelled the eastern States to observe neutrality if not to enter an alliance with Germany; Poland might have joined the alliance under the influence of the French attitude. Hitler could then have turned against the West. The settlement between National Socialist imperialism and the Western Powers would then have involved the sacrifice of innumerable lives; it is unlikely that operations on the same scale will now or in the future be necessary to seal Germany's defeat. It is evident that the British policy was the outcome neither of weakness nor of insufficient consideration.

What are the reasons for the attitude taken up from the first toward National Socialism by the Western Powers? It has been suggested that they fully expected Germany's recovery, and so welcomed and even assisted the National Socialist movement as likely sooner or later to be Germany's ruin. In certain political quarters, it is suggested, nothing would have been viewed with more alarm than a Conservative, monarchist Government in Germany that had learned the lesson of the errors of the pre-war period and had acquired moderation in political aims and methods: faced with a Government of this sort, the West would have been impotent to prevent German hegemony over the small nations, especially those of the East, which would not merely have accepted it but even have welcomed it. Revolutionary National Socialism, on the other hand, with its absurd and repellent racial doctrines, would be shunned by other nations, and an imperialist German hegemony would meet with the utmost resentment, even if internal disorders did not prevent Germany from ever getting so far.

It is of no great importance whether this policy was actually entertained at any time. If it was, it was a very mistaken one. For a restoration of the monarchy in Germany would, after the experiences of the Great War, have virtually guaranteed stable conditions and excluded any adventurous foreign policy. A restored monarchy would have accepted and adhered to a peaceable settlement that removed Germany's just grievances. The National Socialist revolution, on the other hand, while it must sooner or later end with Germany's defeat, will first have wreaked immeasurable destruction. It would have been disastrous folly to have made to the National Socialist revolution advances that had been denied to a moderate nationalist Government, so preventing the Conservatives and Nationalists from parting from National Socialism to achieve their own solution of a restored monarchy. This much is certain, that the present course will end in Germany's ruin. The only thing that is not certain is the actual road that will be pursued to ruin and the number of victims with which it will be strewn.

All that can be said with certainty is that the pace will grow and the problems to be faced will accumulate, until there will be no way out save by a radical change of course. No revolution can last for ever. Those institutions alone can be permanent that serve spiritual and not "biological" principles, that serve justice and equity, and voluntarily accept limits to their own authority. Not a maximum of power and dominion, but of freedom and justice, is the proper aim of any reordering of Europe.

A EUROPEAN SOLUTION

Not only the tactical situation into which Germany has come demands criticism; the whole idea of an order resting on arbitrary force, of a world empire to be kept together by the methods of domination now practised within Germany, is absurd and entirely impracticable. A permanent system of imperial rule cannot be maintained by such methods. The much-abused England with her imagined loss of dominion has kept up with the times better than the "dynamic" nations, with their parade of brave new ideas which in truth are retrogressive and antiquated. The violent methods of arbitrary rule may show results that for a time are superficially imposing, but in the long run these methods are unfruitful and end in self-destruction. The vital error of National Socialist policy lies in its return to played-out methods and aims, the fruitlessness of which has been demonstrated ages ago. The party has contented itself with re-trying with vastly increased resources a policy that has failed again and again in the past, as though any mistake would succeed if it were big enough. If the Third Reich is to go for inspiration to the old first Reich, the Holy Roman Empire, it might at least, perhaps, usefully recall the essential principle of medieval Western civilization, that the sovereignty of the component States of an empire was not restricted by a universal *potestas* of the emperor, but only by a genuine *auctoritas* which was so strong that sovereigns bowed to it. No one can deny that the British Empire, with its methods of government based on freedom and consent, and with the moral authority of its center, comes very close to an almost spiritual conception of the State and social order.

Undoubtedly the attitude of the present leaders of the German nation is the outcome of twenty years in which the nation felt that it had nothing more to lose. The resort of "despairing patriots" to a radically revolutionary course was not surprising, but it was by no means inevitable. There were plain reasons for the ultimate predominance of destructive over creative tendencies in the foreign policy of German Nationalism, one being the complete political sterility of the so-called victor Powers. This it is, together with internal developments in Germany, that paved the way for the revolutionary foreign policy which to-day is unceasingly being pursued by National Socialism.

The German nation, said Count Brockdorff-Rantzau in reply to the Versailles terms of peace, was ready to face its hard destiny, "if the agreed bases of peace are not interfered with. A peace that cannot be defended before the world in the name of justice would arouse continually renewed resistance." And Philipp Scheidemann said at Weimar on May 12th, 1919: "An unparalleled brutalization of moral conceptions would be the result of a Treaty of Versailles on these lines." It was this Social Democrat, and not a bourgeois Nationalist, who called the peace treaty the most gruesome and murderous of witches' hammers, "with which a great nation is to be pounded into confessing its own unworthiness." It is impossible to ignore the connection between present events and those of twenty years ago. Those events explain not only the objects of the present German foreign policy but its methods. This is not an attempt to shift the responsibility, but it shows cause and effect.

Nothing is more depressing than to realize that, ten years before the National Socialist seizure of power, the Young Conservatives of Germany had a home and foreign policy immeasurably superior to that of the present regime of violence, and envisaged Germany's recovery only in connection with a universal idea of right, with a "European solution." Nothing was more horrifying to conservative nationalists than the gradual recognition that the "national rising," with which they had associated themselves to that end, was in reality a cynical, nihilist revolution, the negation of their own ideals.

As early as the Schober-Curtius plan of an Austro-German Customs union, the ideas of a modern development of federative principles as the means of solution of German-Austrian and Central European problems had been accepted by nationalist opinion in Germany. Nationalists in both countries who had outgrown the idea of German claims to hegemony began increasingly to accept the general principle of federalism, as an alternative to the unsatisfactory idea of "national democracy" of Western Europe. To recall this is to realize the depth of the fall to the brutal operations of National Socialism. The solutions which the National Socialists claim to have achieved, or to intend to achieve, have nothing to do with the vital needs of the nation, even if their economic penetration of the Southeast of Europe succeeds.

The purpose that took Germany eastward was not merely economic, merely a question of markets and raw material sources. Here lay a political mission of a European order of which Germany was at all times conscious. Here the soil was prepared for the elaboration of supernational ideas. East of the Rhine no nation has ripened into a historic State. When the doctrine of nationality emerged in the nineteenth century, no State in this region, apart from Switzerland, was so well established as to withstand the assault of revolutionism. Not even the rigidly organized Prussian State was able to stand against the principle of nationality. The historic meaning of Bismarck's foundation of the German Empire was the absorption of the supernational, superdenominational Prussian State into a German national State which accepted the Prussian forms. In the Habsburg monarchy the idea of the State was too ill-represented and too little accepted to enable that State to be established on firm foundations with the aid of the federative principle, whether the national principle were ignored or incorporated. The historic forces of State-formation have had no more than intermittent play in the East. And it is now too late in this whole region for any supernational State-formation of the type that built up the great States of the West of Europe in the seventeenth century. The national States have ripened into permanence. It is necessary, therefore, to find new principles of a supernational order, which will take existing conditions into account and develop a neutral constitutional system as the crown of the national basic elements. It was up to Germany to find a federative solution of this sort, to recover her past stature by its advocacy, and to maintain her just claim for leadership within the system.

Nothing is more alien to this process than the National Socialist plan of founding a central Power on the basis of the principle of nationality, and forcibly creating a pseudo-State. The National Socialist application of the principle of nationality is fatal to the principle. National Socialism has, therefore, already abandoned it, and is replacing it by the conception of race wherever it is trying to build up instead of destroying. There is nothing scientific about this racial principle; it is simply a political expedient. The principle of nationality was always revolutionary, in opposition to the historic idea of the State. It is a return to natural, indeed biological, considerations, in opposition to the intellectual basis of the historic State. The racial conception has this characteristic in still greater measure. It is therefore as unsuitable as could be as the basis for a constitutional system. Thus it only increases the revolutionary effects of the basis of nationality, instead of overcoming them. The historic State is always an artificial, that is to say a deliberate, creation, an overcoming of Nature. Nothing is more irrational than the charge of artificiality levelled against, for instance, Czechoslovakia. The weakness of that State was not its deliberate creation but its confined territory. For the federative system, a deliberately created and, if you will, an "artificial" system, can in our day be instituted only in the liberating spaciousness of a great territory, an independent economic area.

National Socialism could not attempt to provide a "European" solution for the problems of German foreign policy because, as a revolutionary principle, it is not fitted to do so, and because it does not recognize the inviolability of justice and freedom. The efforts to induce it to seek such a solution are condemned in advance to failure. And their prospect is not improved now that they are being made not by German conservative politicians, but by those of foreign States. These efforts amount to trying to induce the German revolution, which meanwhile has become much more extreme, to abandon its actual principle of existence and transform itself into its opposite. There is only one way of arriving at a "European" conception in German foreign policy—to end the revolution.

It is not surprising if the Western Powers, who had only just emerged from a maze of mistaken political doctrine, and who were five or six years behindhand in recognizing the faulty construction and the fundamental weakness of the League of Nations, prefer to-day to have nothing to do with the dangerous weapon of political ideologies. Whether we like it or not, the European problems are only capable of solution by the use or potential use of force. Perhaps the outbreak of a sanguinary world revolution can be delayed by the creation of a new and elastic equilibrium in Europe. But European problems will not be affected by this; they will continue to live their own life until each finds its particular solution—evolutionary or revolutionary, and, if the latter, certainly at the cost of much bloodshed. Thus the prevention of a vast collapse of Western civilization seems possible only through the rebirth of a constitutional system for Europe.

An appeal for peace would have to be accompanied by a number of concrete proposals. It would have to be dependent on the assumption of fair play and open dealing. All that has so far come before the public on these lines, such as Sir Norman Angell's plan, is inadequate, because it is concerned mainly with the procedure for eliminating the use of force, instead of dealing with the material problems. This peace concerns not only the ordering of Europe itself but that of the colonial territories as a common sphere of European existence. The neo-imperialism of the "dynamic" nations can only be effectively countered by demonstrating that it is a return to nineteenth-century principles, now obsolete, and irrelevant to the new type of solutions demanded by the political and economic conditions of the present time. Just as Great Britain, in the continual evolution of her Empire, has shown by her actual practice that revolution and anarchy can be forestalled by timely change, so the current ideas of colonial systems can be revised on the lines of common exploitation. It may be that ideas of this sort lie at the back of the latest British effort to come to an agreement with Germany. But this effort, however praiseworthy, is bound to fail because of the unreliability of the existing regime as a partner. It would have been better not to make the effort until another partner could be approached. What is wanted is not so much the cession of colonies and raw material sources from the "have" to the "have-not" nations, as a form of unrestricted colonization and unrestricted right of access to economic resources for all European States, which would remove the difference between "haves" and "have-nots" and make an end of revolutionary tension. Similar conservative, anti-revolutionary solutions could be elaborated for the whole field of "dynamic" tendencies, countering the destructive trends of a progressive world revolution.

The elements of a genuine and lasting European order can, however, be brought together only within a new general system of justice and equity. Thus the revolution can only be brought to an end by the united efforts of the nations of Europe, not by those of any one nation. But, certain as it is that the Versailles order is not the general system that can stem world revolution, it is equally certain that Germany's recovery cannot be established by force and violence. Moderation, not the tactical cunning of a revolutionary temperament, is the secret of any practicable European solution. If Hitler were to achieve moderation, to find the great "constructive peace settlement" that was talked about at first, then, indeed, our judgment of National Socialism would be mistaken, and we should gladly recognize that we had been in error and had failed to recognize human greatness. Hitler would then indeed be the great man he is imagined to be by an uncritical nation. But that would logically involve appeasement also within the Reich, with differences resolved no longer by force and domination but by free discussion. It would involve reconciliation with opponents and generosity toward those who in honest conviction stood out against the regime. Such acts of generosity are usual on the part even of dictators and tyrants in the hour of success; this German dictator has shown no sign of generosity even toward the noblest of his opponents. When in all these years has he performed one single act of reconciliation or generosity or good-heartedness towards an opponent? Only generosity can bring healing and reconciliation in the end, and close wounds which, if really great things were at issue, were perhaps inevitable. Then, too, all the things that are of the essence of the present regime would have to go—violence, terrorism, thraldom, and the daily quota of engineered enthusiasm and unison under duress. Then justice and the liberty of the person, freedom of thought and speech and action, the freedom of the immortal spirit of man, would have to be readmitted into Germany.

But how could all this be possible? Would it not mean the abdication of National Socialism? Would it not mean an end of the despicable crime of organized anti-Semitism with its spreading of ruin and its legalized robbery? Would it not mean the readmission of impartial justice and the banning of the very principle of violence? Would it not mean the confession that the "organic-biological" philosophy of the regime is cheap nonsense? That the racial doctrine is an offence against humanity, the fight against Christianity a barbarism?

No! Hitler can no more make peace in Europe, or even accept it, than he can make an end of his own "dynamism." The one depends on the other. Just as National Socialist revolutionism can only work destruction in Germany, so in foreign relations it can only produce war and revolution.

If anything has been gained at all in these years of oppression, it is the recognition they have forced on us of the elementary fact that there is such a thing as impartial justice, and that the doctrine of violence and the exclusive pursuit of power lead inevitably to revolution and destruction. Certainly this recognition is not yet universal. It may be that the nations that in the past regarded themselves as executors of a moral mission, and abandoned this mission at a critical moment, must pass through a period of unprincipled "realism" before they come to this recognition. Nevertheless, there is coming into existence a new Europe of a totally different sort from that of the "realists." It may be that the whole continent must first be shaken by yet another great and universal upheaval, which will leave no country unscathed. And it is not improbable that we shall witness a period of material and moral capitulation, in which States will compete for the favor of the mightiest, as the princes of the Confederation of the Rhine did before Napoleon. The precedents of Austria and Czechoslovakia have legitimized a procedure of which the results are incalculable. Yet, amid this rapid march of anarchy, the nations will bethink themselves sooner or later of their own and Europe's historic forces, the constituent principles of our Western civilization—its past freedoms, national, political, intellectual, spiritual. Then, in spite of all anti-European onslaughts, a rejuvenated Europe will at last arise, and endure.

That is why the political activities of the National Socialist "Third Reich" are so entirely unfruitful. To-day, so long as there are still vestiges of a past order to be destroyed, it is perhaps moving with the stream of political development, and is able to register easy successes. But later it will become evident that everything that it has credited itself with building is weak and rickety, because it runs contrary to nature, contrary to the deepest of men's instincts, contrary to the whole spirit of European civilization.

Never did a Government have a finer chance of serving both the recovery of its own nation and the creation of a common supernational order than the new German Government of January 1933. A powerful Germany, ready to assume leadership in honorable and statesman-like collaboration with the smaller States, instead of dominating them, would have had in its hands the key positions of European advance. This opportunity, which would have given Germany the prospect of initiatives of a very different and far superior sort to the present, was realized at the time. It was realized by some of the German Nationalists and especially the Young Conservatives; by Edgar J. Jung, von Papen's private secretary, by the Herrenklub, and by some influential practical politicians. I directed my own efforts along these lines. It was no utopian effort. But it was the direct opposite of the course pursued by National Socialist nihilism. In 1933 it was by no means inevitable that this doctrineless nihilist revolution should obtain the mastery over the nation and its future. By violent means National Socialism has for the present determined Germany's course both at home and abroad. But its victory need not be final. Even to-day it is possible resolutely to make an end of the revolution, to overcome the drift to anarchy, and to return not only in home but in foreign policy to the ideas which, as is even plainer to-day than six years ago, alone offer the possibility of a permanent restoration of Germany's rank in Europe, and of avoiding the war which would bring world revolution irrevocably into being.

"We, perhaps with the whole of the world to-day," said the Prussian Conservative von Radowitz, friend of the King of Prussia at the time of the first German revolution, "shall not regain healthy political existence or find any sure footing amid the ferment of the times, until the governments frankly and freely disavow the perilous heritage of the revolution, that true shirt of Nessus, modern state absolutism; and until they bear witness by word and deed that it is only the service of the idea of right, and the preservation of peace at home and abroad, that God has imposed on rulers as their duty."